Democratic inclusion

MANCHESTER
1824

Manchester University Press

CRITICAL POWERS

Series Editors:
Bert van den Brink (University of Utrecht),
Antony Simon Laden (University of Illinois, Chicago),
Peter Niesen (University of Hamburg) and
David Owen (University of Southampton).

Critical Powers is dedicated to constructing dialogues around innovative and original work in social and political theory. The ambition of the series is to be pluralist in welcoming work from different philosophical traditions and theoretical orientations, ranging from abstract conceptual argument to concrete policy-relevant engagements, and encouraging dialogue across the diverse approaches that populate the field of social and political theory. All the volumes in the series are structured as dialogues in which a lead essay is greeted with a series of responses before a reply by the lead essayist. Such dialogues spark debate, foster understanding, encourage innovation and perform the drama of thought in a way that engages a wide audience of scholars and students.

Published by Bloomsbury

On Global Citizenship, James Tully
Justice, Democracy and the Right to Justification, Rainer Forst

Published by Manchester University Press

Cinema, democracy and perfectionism: Joshua Foa Dienstag in dialogue, Joshua Foa Dienstag (ed)

Forthcoming from Manchester University Press

Rogue Theodicy – Politics and power in the shadow of justice,
Glen Newey
Law and Violence, Christoph Menke
Autonomy Gaps, Joel Anderson
Toleration, Liberty and the Right to Justification, Rainer Forst

Democratic inclusion

Rainer Bauböck in dialogue

Rainer Bauböck
with responses from:
Joseph H. Carens
Sue Donaldson
Iseult Honohan
Will Kymlicka
David Miller
David Owen
Peter Spiro

Manchester University Press

Published by Manchester University Press
Altrincham Street, Manchester M1 7JA
www.manchesteruniversitypress.co.uk

British Library Cataloguing-in-Publication Data
A catalogue record for this book is available from the British Library

ISBN 978 1 5261 0522 6 hardback
ISBN 978 1 5261 0523 3 paperback
ISBN 978 1 5261 0525 7 open access

First published 2018

The publisher has no responsibility for the persistence or accuracy of URLs for any external or third-party internet websites referred to in this book, and does not guarantee that any content on such websites is, or will remain, accurate or appropriate.

Typeset
by Toppan Best-set Premedia Limited

for Silvia and Anna

Contents

Contributors

Rainer Bauböck has a chair in social and political theory at the Department of Political and Social Sciences of the European University Institute in Florence. His research interests are in normative political theory and comparative democratic citizenship, European integration, migration, nationalism and minority rights. Together with Jo Shaw (University of Edinburgh) and Maarten Vink (University of Maastricht), he coordinates GLOBALCIT, an online observatory on citizenship and voting rights.

Joseph H. Carens, FRSC, is Professor of Political Science at the University of Toronto and Professorial Fellow at the Institute for Social Justice at Australian Catholic University. He is the author or editor of six books, including *The Ethics of Immigration* (Oxford University Press, 2013), which won prizes from the American Political Science Association, the International Studies Association and the Canadian Political Science Association; *Culture, Citizenship, and Community* (Oxford University Press, 2000), which won the C.B. Macpherson prize from the Canadian Political Science Association; and *Equality, Moral Incentives, and the Market* (University of Chicago Press, 1981). He has published over ninety articles and book chapters.

Sue Donaldson is a Canadian writer, and research associate in the Department of Philosophy, Queen's University, Kingston. She is the author, with Will Kymlicka, of *Zoopolis: A Political Theory of Animal Rights* (Oxford University Press, 2011), and of numerous articles concerning group differentiated/citizenship rights for animals appearing in the *Journal of Political Philosophy*, *Oxford Journal of Legal Studies*, *Canadian Journal of Political Science*, *Journal of Social Philosophy*, and elsewhere.

Iseult Honohan is Associate Professor Emeritus, UCD School of Politics and International Relations, and Member of the Royal Irish Academy. Her research interests lie in the foundations of republican political theory and its applications in areas including citizenship, immigration and diversity. Her books include *Civic Republicanism* (Routledge, 2002) and *Domination, Migration and Non-citizens* (Routledge, 2014, co-edited with Marit Hovdal Moan). She has been a research collaborator in EUDO-Citizenship/GLOBALCIT since 2010. Recent work includes: "Civic Integration: The Acceptable Face of Assimilation?" in *Ethics and Politics of Immigration*, ed. A. Sager (Rowman & Littlefield, 2016); and "Liberal and Republican Conceptions of Citizenship" in *The Oxford Handbook of Citizenship*, ed. A. Shachar, R.Bauböck, I. Bloemraad and M. Vink (Oxford University Press, 2017).

Will Kymlicka is the Canada Research Chair in Political Philosophy at Queen's University, and a recurrent Visiting Professor in the Nationalism Studies programme at the Central European University in Budapest. His research interests focus on issues of democracy and diversity, and in particular on models of citizenship and social justice within multicultural societies. His books include *Multicultural Citizenship* (Oxford University Press, 1995), *Multicultural Odysseys* (Oxford University Press, 2007) and *Zoopolis: A Political Theory of Animal Rights* (Oxford University Press, 2011, co-authored with Sue Donaldson).

David Miller is Professor of Political Theory in the University of Oxford, and a Fellow of Nuffield College; he is also a Visiting Professor in Law and Philosophy at Queen's University, Canada. His books include *On Nationality* (Clarendon Press, 1995), *Principles of Social Justice* (Harvard University Press, 1999), *National Responsibility and Global Justice* (Oxford University Press, 2007), *Justice for Earthlings* (Cambridge University Press, 2013) and *Strangers in Our Midst: The Political Philosophy of Immigration* (Harvard University Press, 2016). He continues to work on the issues of immigration, national identity, territorial boundaries and self-determination.

David Owen is Professor of Social and Political Philosophy at the University of Southampton. His most recent books include *Multiculturalism and Political Theory* (Cambridge University Press, 2007, co-edited with Anthony Laden) and *Recognition and Power* (Cambridge University Press, 2007, co-edited with Bert van den Brink). He is currently writing a book on migration and political theory.

Peter Spiro is Charles Weiner Professor of Law, Temple University Law School, and the author most recently of *At Home in Two Countries: The Past and Future of Dual Citizenship* (New York University Press, 2016).

Series editor's foreword

Since the publication of *Immigration and the Boundaries of Citizenship* (1992) and *Transnational Citizenship: Membership and Rights in International Migration* (1994), Rainer Bauböck has been at the forefront of research on the political theory of membership. Bauböck's work is distinctive in at least three respects.

First, his approach to normative theorizing is grounded in empirical research concerning the membership practices of polities and the dynamics that shape these practices. The point of normative theorizing for Bauböck is to guide action by articulating ideals for a *plausible* world. We may think of this project as seeking to reconcile the liberal-republican ideals of constitutional democracy that have emerged within the modern state with the contemporary challenges posed by historical and current migration flows in ways that are sensitive to the varied types of polity and conditions for their stable reproduction as contexts of justice that compose our complex and multi-levelled political order.

Second, whereas the majority of the burgeoning literature on the political theory of migration focuses on the migrant as immigrant and on immigration as a democratic challenge, Bauböck has consistently pioneered a transnational approach to the political theory of migration that focuses on the migrant as both emigrant and immigrant who possesses civic statuses in two (or more) states. This phenomenon of overlapping membership or "transnational" membership is at the centre of Bauböck's reflections on the future of citizenship in an increasingly interconnected world.

Third, while theorizing citizenship is typically directed at reflection on the state, Bauböck's work extends the theory of citizenship across multiple levels of governance to encompass municipal membership and supranational citizenship as well as state membership not only to offer a more comprehensive theory but also, and perhaps more importantly, to draw out the salience of the *type* of polity for normative reflection on the terms of membership that are justifiable for it.

All of these features can easily be discerned in Bauböck's lead essay for this volume which marks the summation and synthesis of his normative inquiries since the publication of *Transnational Citizenship* and the fullest articulation thus far of the *stakeholder* principle which he has proposed as a response to the problems of political membership that characterize our contemporary political reality. At the same time, this principle is situated here within a much fuller discussion of current debates concerning the "demos problem" and Bauböck explores its distinct but complementary relationships to the *all affected interests* and *all subjected persons* principles as well as its differentiated implications for different types of polity.

Bauböck's debates with his interlocutors in this volume range across methodological, conceptual, normative and empirical issues, offering a rich dialogue on the stakes and challenges of theorizing democratic inclusion in our contemporary political landscape.

David Owen

Part I

Lead essay

1

Democratic inclusion: a pluralist theory of citizenship[1]

Rainer Bauböck

1. Introduction

Who has a claim to be included in a democratic polity? This has been a vexing question for political theorists as well as legislators and judges. Philosophers have tried to make the problem go away by adopting one of two contrasting strategies.

The first response is that democratic principles cannot resolve the problem and therefore we have to accept the historical contingency of political boundaries and the powers of nation-states to determine themselves who their citizens are. To be sure, most contemporary political theorists have added some critiques of current state practices or suggestions why some categories of individuals cannot be legitimately excluded from citizenship. Yet they often have done so starting from the premise that the context within which the question needs to be addressed is the international system of states as we know it.[2] The problem is

[1] This essay is an attempt to summarize and condense my thinking on related topics over many years. Several of the arguments I develop here have been explored in earlier publications, most of which are included in the list of references. I have generally not listed each time the publication where a particular idea was first introduced. I have reframed all my older arguments and have not reproduced any part of a previously published text. I presented versions of this text at Universities in Berne, Bonn, Cologne, Rome, Vienna, Victoria, Wellington and Zurich. I am grateful to the participants at these events for critical questions and to Svenja Ahlhaus, Stefano Bartolini, Seyla Benhabib, Joachim Blatter, Peter Dietsch, Joseph Lacy and David Owen for very helpful written comments. Special thanks to Milena Tripkovic for compiling the index.

[2] See Sager (2016) for a critical review of methodological nationalism in normative political theory on migration.

thus reduced to allocating territory and people to states in a way that does not challenge their boundaries and claims to self-determination.

The second response is to stick to a democratic principle and to use it for undermining the legitimacy of existing political boundaries. If boundaries are historically contingent, then they do not have deep moral significance and can also be radically questioned for the sake of democratic inclusion. Some theorists argue that the only democratically legitimate demos is a global one (Goodin 2007); others suggest that the demos ought to change depending on who will be affected by a particular decision (Shapiro 2000); still others regard democratic inclusion principles as norms that allow us to contest exclusion while not necessarily providing positive guidelines on how to construct alternative boundaries (Benhabib 2004, 2006; Näsström 2007).

The theoretical debate thus seems stuck between positions giving priority either to existing democratic boundaries or to principles of democratic inclusion that potentially challenge the legitimacy of all boundaries. But this standoff suggests already that there is something wrong in the way the debate has been framed. Since inclusion conceptually presupposes an external boundary, a theory of legitimate inclusion claims depends on a theory of legitimate boundaries. In other words, there is no point arguing for the right of individuals to be included in a particular demos if the legitimacy of that demos itself is either blindly accepted as a contingent result of historical processes or fundamentally rejected based on inclusion claims that are per se incompatible with drawing legitimate political boundaries.

The other reason for revisiting the democratic boundary problem after forty years of debate[3] is that it simply does not go away in democratic politics even if philosophers try to conjure it away in democratic theory.

---

[3] Frederick Whelan's (1983) and Robert Dahl's (1970, 1989) major contributions can be taken as the starting point. There are of course many earlier references, beginning with Aristotle's discussion of the principles for determining who is a citizen in the polis (Aristotle 1962, iii, 1–2), but it seems that prior to the 1970s the potential circularity of democratic principles for determining membership in the demos had been noticed only by critics of national self-determination, such as Ivor Jenning, who famously remarked that "the people cannot decide unless somebody decides who are the people" (Jenning 1956: 56).

Boundary and inclusion questions are among the most contested practical problems in contemporary democratic states. The rise of these problems on political agendas is arguably a result of democracies becoming more liberal and less self-confident in asserting quasi-natural boundaries of nation, territory and language. If the liberal transformation of democracy has contributed to making the boundary problem politically more salient, then the diagnosis that there is no cure for the problem that democratic theory can provide would be very bad news indeed.

Focusing on recent years in Europe alone, here is a small sample of events in which problems of democratic inclusion and boundaries have come up and had to be addressed by courts, legislators or by citizens in the election booth: the massive global trend of extending voting rights to citizens living abroad and a comparatively weaker European and Latin American pattern of letting non-citizen residents vote in local elections; an ongoing standoff between the European Court of Human Rights and the British government about the exclusion of criminal offenders from voting rights; the introduction of conditional ius soli in Germany in 2000 and Greece in 2010/2015[4] and the abandoning of unconditional ius soli by constitutional referendum in Ireland in 2004; the widespread introduction of language and civic knowledge tests as a naturalization requirement for immigrants in Europe since the late 1990s; the 2010 Rottmann decision of the Court of Justice of the European Union that member states have to take EU law into account when withdrawing nationality and the more recent moves in several EU states to deprive citizens joining a terrorist organization of their nationality; the Scottish referendum on independence in November 2014 and the nearly simultaneous rejection by the Spanish government and Constitutional Court of a similar referendum in Catalonia. All these decisions rely implicitly on contested ideas about democratic boundaries and membership claims. Normative theories of democracy need not be prescriptive in the sense of proposing specific answers for each of these

---

[4] The Greek ius soli legislation of 2010 was struck down by the State Council in 2013. A modified version was adopted by Parliament in July 2015.

issues, but they should at least be able to spell out the principles that ought to guide decisions. Yet many of the contributions to the democratic boundary debate seem keen to avoid this test.

This essay attempts to show that the diagnosis that there is no theoretical answer to the democratic boundary problem that would allow us to address its real-world manifestations is wrong. It takes the practical political manifestations of the boundary problem seriously by proposing that democratic inclusion principles must not only satisfy theoretical criteria, such as compatibility with broader principles of justice and democracy, internal coherence and answers to objections raised by rival theories, but also practical criteria that show how the proposed inclusion principles allow the boundary problems arising within democratic politics to be addressed.

My strategy is to argue that there is not a single principle of democratic inclusion but several principles, and that it is important to distinguish their different roles in relation to democratic boundaries. I also argue that polities into which individuals can claim to be included are of different kinds and it is equally important to distinguish the types of polity addressed by such claims. I do not argue, however, that there is an open-ended variety of inclusion principles or of kinds of polities and that inclusion always depends on context. That would be banal and undermine any effort at theorizing. The basic principles of democratic inclusion are limited and so are the basic types of democratic polities, and in my discussion I will reduce each of them to three. Such ideal-typical generalizations allow for identifying contexts where mixed principles apply or where polities are of mixed types.

The core normative argument of this essay is developed in section 3, where I discuss the principles of including all affected interests (AAI), all subject to coercion (ASC) and all citizenship stakeholders (ACS). I claim that these principles are not rivals but friends. They complement each other because they serve distinct purposes of democratic inclusion. Before this, I consider the general "circumstances of democracy" that consist in normative background assumptions and general empirical conditions under which democratic self-government is both necessary and possible.

Section 4 contextualizes the principle of stakeholder inclusion, which provides the best answer to the question of democratic boundaries of membership, by applying it to polities of different types. I distinguish state, local and regional polities and argue that they differ in their membership character, which I identify as birthright-based, residential and derivative respectively. My conclusion is again that these are not alternative conceptions of political community but complementary ones. Each supports the realization of specific political values (of continuity, mobility and union) and taken together local, state and regional polities form nested democracies with multiple citizenships for all their members.

2. The circumstances and contexts of democracy

2.1 Diversity and boundaries

So how should we think about democratic boundaries? Neither as quasi-naturally given and beyond contestation, nor as features of a non-ideal world that we set aside when discussing what justice requires in an ideal world. Instead, we should think of boundaries as belonging to the circumstances of democracy. In his theory of justice, John Rawls defined the circumstances of justice as "the normal conditions under which human cooperation is both possible and necessary" (Rawls 1999: 109).[5] We can describe political boundaries in the same way as belonging to the normal conditions under which democracy is both empirically possible and normatively necessary. Without claiming that these two conditions exhaust the circumstances of democracy, I suggest that democracy would not be necessary in the absence of a diversity of interests, identities and ideas, and would not be possible in the absence of boundaries.

---

[5] Rawls subdivides these into objective conditions (a territorial concentration of human individuals with roughly similar physical and mental powers, each of whom is vulnerable to attack and to domination by the combined forces of others, and a condition of moderate scarcity of resources) and subjective conditions (a diversity of individual life plans and of moral, religious, social and political doctrines) (Rawls 1999: 110).

In a society where all shared the same interests, a single collective identity as members and the same ideas about the common good, democracy would be pointless, since collectively binding decisions could be adopted unanimously or be taken by each individual on behalf of all others without any need for a procedure that aggregates their political preferences.[6] Democracy is a system of political rule that provides legitimacy for collectively binding decisions and coercive government under conditions of deep and persistent diversity. Political ideologies that consider diversity as a non-ideal condition to be overcome through a transformation of society are therefore always potentially hostile towards democracy. This goes for orthodox Marxism and its ideal of a communist society without religion or economic competition as well as for nationalism and its ideal of matching the boundaries of cultural and political communities (Gellner 1983).

Boundaries are necessary background conditions for democracy for at least three reasons. First, without political and jurisdictional boundaries, democratic decisions would have indeterminate scope. This would be true even if every human being were included in a single global polity, since there would then still be a political boundary between human beings and other animals that could potentially be included.

Second, in the absence of political boundaries there is no distinction between intra- and inter-polity relations. This distinction is, however, constitutive for the political as a distinct sphere of human activity. Carl Schmitt's (1927/2007) friend–enemy dichotomy is just an extreme and implausible version of this distinction. Hannah Arendt expresses the democratic version of this argument:

---

[6] See also Waldron (1999: 101–106), who defines in similar ways "the circumstances of politics", which on his account are disagreement combined with the need for concerted action. Waldron captures well the effects of diversity as a condition of deep and persistent disagreement even about matters of justice and rights, and the need for democracies to adopt laws and take decisions also in the absence of an overlapping consensus on these matters. What I want to add to his account is the condition of political boundaries that make it possible for decisions under conditions of disagreement to be adopted on behalf of a collective of citizens who share an ongoing need for concerted action because they form a distinct political community. This is not a feature of the general circumstances of politics or the law, but of the specific circumstances of democracy.

A citizen is by definition a citizen among citizens of a country among countries. His rights and duties must be defined and limited, not only by those of his fellow citizens, but also by the boundaries of a territory … Politics deals with men, nationals of many countries and heirs to many pasts; its laws are the positively established fences which hedge in, protect, and limit the space in which freedom is not a concept, but a living, political reality. The establishment of one sovereign world state … would be the end of all citizenship. (Arendt 1970: 81–82)

Third, the existence of boundaries is a precondition for the democratic feedback mechanisms of voice and exit (Hirschman 1970). In the absence of any boundary, exit is by definition impossible. While easy exit may weaken the incentives for voice (in Hirschman's original "hydraulic model"), the absence of any possibility of exit fatally undermines the effectiveness of voice. A polity without boundaries is like a spontaneous crowd that has no addressee for voice, since it does not have collective procedures for counting votes and taking decisions.

These three arguments do not imply a defence of any existing boundaries. Instead, they suggest that we should imagine democratic citizenship always in a context where there is a plurality of other polities. The circumstances of diversity and boundaries can thus also be understood as referring to two sides of democratic pluralism: an irreducible internal plurality of interests, identities and political, moral and religious ideas, and an equally irreducible external plurality of political communities.

Although this is not essential for my argument, which focuses on democratic legitimacy, I believe that similar conclusions emerge for theories of justice. A vision of a world without political boundaries is dystopian in the same way as a world in which all human beings share a comprehensive moral perspective or the same way of life. The plurality of bounded political communities is constitutive for justice in the sense of forming a background condition against which questions about justice are raised.[7] I am therefore inclined to think that political

---

[7] Simon Caney makes a similar argument distinguishing a democratic approach to cosmopolitan justice that affirms political borders from a wholly instrumental one that is not so constrained (Caney 2006).

boundaries are also part of the circumstances of justice, which means that they have to be assumed as a background not only for non-ideal, but also for ideal theory. Political boundaries structure theories of justice fundamentally by subdividing them into three distinct sets of questions: justice within political communities (domestic), justice between political communities (inter-polity) and justice across political communities (trans-polity and global).[8]

Of course, theorists of global justice and cosmopolitan democracy generally do not imagine a single undifferentiated polity encompassing all human beings. What they intend to challenge is not so much the existence and utility of political boundaries but their moral status. They conceive of boundaries as instruments that allow for a top-down delegation of responsibility for specific territories and populations to particular governments (Goodin 1988, 2007) or the bottom-up aggregation of democratic votes in a global federation (Archibugi and Held 1995).

Philippe van Parijs summarizes succinctly the attitude of most global justice theorists towards political boundaries: "Nations, politically organized peoples ... are sheer instruments to be created and dismantled, structured and absorbed, empowered and constrained, in the service of justice" (van Parijs 2011: 139). This view regards political boundaries and democracy itself as institutional arrangements whose legitimacy is entirely derived from how well they serve the goal of justice.

Our attitude will be different if we consider democracy as a set of institutions, the goal of which is to realize government of, for and by the people. In this view, popular self-government is a fundamental and intrinsic value, the pursuit of which must be constrained by requirements of justice, but which is at the same time a free-standing value that cannot be entirely derived from what justice requires. The primary purpose of democracy is to provide legitimacy to coercive political rule through popular self-government. While political boundaries should be regarded as a background condition for both justice and democracy, justice is

---

[8]   These three realms of justice were already clearly distinguished by Kant in his essay on "Perpetual Peace" (1795/1991).

not the same value as political legitimacy and may not always strictly require a democratic form of government.

Boundaries will then still be regarded instrumentally, but as a background condition that enables self-government. Particular boundaries remain open to contestation, for example if they are constructed in a way that denies some individuals full membership in a self-governing polity. Yet their democratic purpose is to create spaces of collective self-government of a people, which is incompatible with regarding the people itself as something "to be created or dismantled in the service of justice".

My stance does not commit me to an essentialist conception of democratic peoples as nations. As I will argue in section 4, democratic peoples can be vertically nested within each other and also share horizontally overlapping memberships. At the same time, self-governing peoples must have the capacity to endow governments with comprehensive powers of agenda-setting and decision-making and to hold them also comprehensively accountable. Such peoples cannot be merely functional aggregates of individuals who happen to share an interest in a particular political decision or public good. Some theorists have suggested extending the idea of democratic self-government to "weak" or "functional" demoi whose scope is transnational and global, and varies with the decision at stake (Bohman 2007).[9] While I will argue below that including externally affected interests is indeed a moral imperative for democracy, letting affected interests determine the boundaries of the demos would create indeterminate or ephemeral demoi that are structurally incapable of ruling themselves.[10]

---

[9] See also the discussion in Koenig-Archibugi (2012).

[10] See List and Koenig-Archibugi (2010) for an attempt to identify global issue-specific demoi that are "capable of being organized, in a democratic manner, in such a way as to function as a state-like group agent." (ibid.: 90). For the authors, the condition for the emergence of a global issue-specific demos is that there is sufficient democratic agreement on a specific issue. However, a self-governing demos must have agenda-setting capacities rather than merely the capacity to decide as a group agent on issues emerging from an agenda that it is incapable of controlling. Agenda-setting capacity should not be confused with autonomous regulatory capacity. Global challenges, such as slowing down climate change or regulating financial markets, exceed the power of all individual states, but global regulatory regimes can only be built if particular states put them on the international agenda. There is no global demos that controls this agenda.

To sum up my argument so far: The three reasons for assuming boundaries as background circumstances of democracy point towards a plurality of polities at all levels, including the global one. And asserting the intrinsic value of collective self-government points towards boundaries that demarcate comprehensive jurisdictions rather than issue-specific demoi. Taken together, these ideas are fully compatible with the project of cosmopolitan constitutionalism and the building of a global *legal* community (Habermas 2006), but exclude the vision of a *self-governing* global demos, even if we imagine it as federally or functionally subdivided into a plurality of dependent demoi.

2.2   Territorial jurisdiction and sedentary societies

Following Rawls's terminology, I have tried to identify transhistorical and transcultural circumstances that make democracy both possible and necessary. In a next step, I will now propose that a theory of democratic boundaries and inclusion must also take as given the fact that political boundaries demarcating comprehensive jurisdictions have territorial borders and that contemporary human societies tend to be relatively sedentary within these borders.

Unlike diversity and boundaries, territorial jurisdiction is neither a primary normative requirement for democracy nor a historically invariable condition. What we know about early human societies of nomadic hunters and gatherers suggests that their relation to territory was radically different from that of any political order after the Neolithic agrarian revolution. In our present world we do find non-territorial forms of democracy; some of them are institutionally established and complement a dominant territorial design of political rule,[11] others flourish informally in the new virtual public spaces created by contemporary information and communication technologies. We can also imagine hypothetical future worlds in which territorial borders are much less relevant for

---

[11]   An example is the franchise for non-resident citizens, which is non-territorial as a citizenship right, but territorial with regard to citizens' representation.

democracy than today and individuals are identified as members of political communities based on non-territorial criteria.

Nevertheless, there are pragmatic as well as normative reasons for assuming that the dominant boundary structures of democracy are territorial. The pragmatic reason is that a theory of democratic boundaries would fail the "implications for democratic politics" test that I emphasized in the introduction if it remained at such a general level that it did not even take into account how democratic polities are territorially structured.

The normative reason is that territorial jurisdiction makes it more likely that democracy can emerge and be consolidated under the two circumstances of democracy. In relation to diversity, non-territorial boundary markers, such as shared descent, religion, political ideology, social class or ways of life, necessarily diminish internal diversity within such communities while enhancing differences between them. If comprehensively self-governing polities were primarily demarcated by these criteria rather than by territorial borders, democracy would be less needed since members would be preselected based on an assumed primary interest that they all share. At the same time, non-territorial polities would be so fundamentally dissimilar among each other that it would become very difficult to maintain support for any global legal order based on norms to which they all subscribe, let alone global solidarity and redistributive justice across such boundaries.[12] The circumstances of both democracy and justice might thus be jeopardized in such a world. In relation to boundary stability, territorial jurisdiction has "lock-in effects" that make it more costly for political agents to exit and that strengthen therefore their motivation to exercise political voice (Rokkan and Urwin 1983; Bartolini 2005). If subjects can opt out of a political regime while retaining residence, they have strong incentives to free ride on public goods that can be accessed by all residents. At the same time, political entrepreneurs operating as rival authorities in the same territory will have incentives to rely on coercive extraction of contributions rather than

---

[12] See Bauböck (2004, 2005; Kymlicka 2005) for critiques of non-territorial autonomy arrangements for national minorities on these grounds.

democratic consent. By contrast, consolidated territorial jurisdictions, which need not be united under a single sovereign authority, create conditions under which subjects have reasons for preferring voice over exit and rulers have reasons to be responsive to their subjects.

Although territorial jurisdiction is a weaker and more variable condition for democracy than are diversity and boundaries, these arguments show that it is not a condition for non-ideal theory only. The tragic history of territorial conflicts between city republics, empires and nation-states should not delude us into assuming naively that territorial borders themselves are an obstacle rather than an enabling condition for democracy and peaceful relations between polities.

The territorial nature and borders of comprehensive jurisdictions provide a political-institutional background context for democracy. Yet there is also a closely related *social* condition that we need to spell out before we can address democratic inclusion problems. This is the assumption that territorial borders allow for categorizing human populations into residents and non-residents, with most of the laws that are adopted within a territorial jurisdiction applying to the former but not to the latter.

Human societies have different relations to territory that we can describe as static, nomadic, mobile or sedentary. In territorially static societies (nearly) all members spend (nearly) all of their lives in the territory where they have been born; nomadic societies, by contrast, move collectively through geographic space without ever settling down and taking up permanent residence anywhere; mobile societies share with nomadic ones the feature that (nearly) all members are constantly on the move but in mobile societies individuals move independently from each other, so that there is not even a collective relation to a territory based on the shared experience of joint movement.

The fourth type, which we can call sedentary, is a mixed one. It is a society most of whose members spend most of their lives in a particular territory (not necessarily the one where they were born). Sedentary societies are fundamentally structured around territorial residence. This does not imply that they cannot have members residing outside their territory or that everybody residing inside the territory is automatically a member. Instead, in sedentary societies territorial borders generate distinctions between immigrants, emigrants and natives that do not exist or cannot be distinguished at all in static, nomadic or mobile societies. Human societies since the invention of agriculture have been generally sedentary in this sense. My proposition is that we should accept relative sedentariness as a second background context for democracy.

Let me clarify this a bit further. First, the distinction between the four types of society depends on territorial scale. If we imagine the land mass of Planet Earth as a single territory, then all human societies have been static and will remain so as long as they do not colonize extra-terrestrial space or create swimming island polities in the high seas. If we shrink the territorial units of observation to sufficiently small size, then all societies have been mobile, since human beings are migratory animals who always move their locations of residence when observed over a sufficiently long time period. When examining instead a mid-range geographic and temporal scale, then patterns of human mobility have changed strongly over time, mostly from static and nomadic to sedentary and increasing levels of mobility since the onset of the industrial revolution. Our previous discussion of boundary structures as circumstances of democracy suggests that a normative theory should indeed assume mid-level territorial scales that encompass neither the whole globe nor are so small that comprehensive forms of territorial self-government would become impossible. Within this mid-range we will still find a wide plurality of types of territorial jurisdiction, from large empires and states to small municipalities.

This observation also makes it clear that in a nested multilevel structure of territorial polities, the degree of mobility that we observe depends on which level we use as reference and generally increases strongly as we move down from state to substate-regional to municipal level. This is so because internal borders at a higher level become external borders at the lower one. Municipalities have thus on average much higher percentages of immigrants and emigrants in relation to their sedentary populations than the provinces or states to which they belong because what counts for the state as internal migration is added to what the state classifies as international migration. We can thus describe multilevel polities without contradiction as simultaneously strongly sedentary and relatively mobile. In a multilevel polity, my normative proposition that sedentariness is a background context for democracy must therefore be specified as applying to the highest or strongest level of self-government. In a federal state, this level will be the federal one; in a union of states, it could well be the level of member states rather than that of the union. The condition of sedentariness should thus not be interpreted too strictly. I have suggested elsewhere that democracy would be difficult to sustain in hypermobile societies, which we can define as those in which at any point in time and at the strongest level of self-government a majority of citizens are non-residents and a majority of residents are non-citizens (Bauböck 2011b). This does not imply that a high volume of mobility that is contained as internal movement within a state or a union of states will undermine democracy in such a polity.

Second, I need to clarify why distinctions between immigrants, emigrants and sedentary populations, and the proportions between these, are normatively salient for democracy. One reason is the need to determine the personal scope of territorial jurisdiction. The concept of territory does not refer to land as a physical object, but to a geographically defined space within which political power is exercised over human beings and laws are applied to them (Buchanan 2004; Stilz 2011; Angeli 2015). In a hypermobile society territorial laws would apply mostly to transient populations whose primary political affiliation might be to some non-territorial political community. At the same time, if most citizens reside outside the polity and mobile residents escape legal duties by moving across borders, governments would have strong incentives to compensate for their loss of control over the population in their territory by expanding their extraterritorial jurisdiction and imposing ever more legal obligations (e.g. tax duties) on expatriates,[13] which could

---

[13]   The U.S. is an outlier among contemporary democracies in this regard by exercising global jurisdiction with regard to taxation of American citizens' income.

eventually undermine the salience and stability of territorial political boundaries. A second reason is that democracy also needs a sense of "ownership" and belonging to the polity. It is difficult to imagine how hypermobile populations could be citizens of the territorial polity who authorize the government that issues and implements the laws to which they are subjected. If there is a relatively sedentary core population, then immigrants can integrate into the society while emigrants can remain connected to it across borders. Where there is no such core, it will be difficult to generate among territorial populations a sense of responsibility for the common good of the polity. Their moral obligations towards co-inhabitants will be the same as towards all other human beings outside the borders and the condition of subjection to a territorial government that they share with each other will be insufficient to generate perceived duties of solidarity, political participation or even just voluntary compliance with the laws.

Third, we should once again consider how a condition of relative sedentariness relates to the two circumstances of democracy, as we did with regard to territorial jurisdiction. On the one hand, both static and nomadic societies, by definition, lack substantive exit options and provide therefore inhospitable environments for democratic diversity and the interplay between exit and voice. Hypermobile societies, on the other hand, make it difficult to create comprehensively self-governing territorial jurisdictions, or make it more likely that such jurisdictions will be non-territorial, which diminishes internal diversity. My conclusion is therefore that relatively sedentary societies are a normatively salient condition for democracy, even though this condition has not always been present, may be lacking in particular contemporary societies and could be vanishing in a future hypermobile world.

A final observation is that the relation between the two territorial conditions for democracy is similar to that between the two circumstances of democracy. In both instances I have distinguished political-institutional features (boundaries and territorial jurisdiction) from social ones (diversity and relative sedentariness). And in both instances the two conditions are not independent of each other, but operate in tandem:

boundaries distinguish internal diversity from an external plurality of polities; and territorial jurisdiction distinguishes internal mobility from external migration, while relative sedentariness creates the conditions under which citizens can collectively authorize and hold accountable a territorial government.

I have argued so far that we should address problems of democratic inclusion by assuming that democracies have boundaries of membership as well as territory. I have not argued that either of these boundaries must be sites where entry or exit is controlled and I have not argued that the two kinds of boundaries must match. In fact, I want to challenge both assumptions in section 4 of this essay: at local level, democratic polities have generally open territorial borders and purely residence-based inclusion, which implies that territorial and member-ship boundaries more or less coincide, while at state level migration leads to discrepancies between territorial borders and membership boundaries by generating non-resident citizens abroad and non-citizen residents domestically. The background assumptions I have made are weak. They provide a minimalist description of the world as it is and as we should assume it to remain even for the purposes of ideal theory. We need this background because principles of inclusion can only apply if and where there are boundaries that we consider at least potentially as legitimate. The distinction between the circumstances and the contexts of democracy serves a further purpose: while inclusion principles should only assume the circumstances of democracy, more specific norms of democratic membership depend on contexts that have changed over the course of human history and may still change in the future.

3.   Purposes of democratic inclusion

After sketching the background for a theory of democratic inclusion let me now move to the foreground. Inclusion does not merely refer to the crossing of a boundary; it also implies a relation of correspondence between an individual or collective claim and an associative purpose. We normally do not say that criminal convicts are "included" in a prison, or that conquerors are "included" in the society they colonize because in these cases there is no correspondence between inclusion claims and purposes.

Let me explore this idea a bit further without developing a full conceptual analysis. The term "inclusion" strictly requires only one agent – the subject that includes – whereas the object that is included can be either an agent or a thing. A philosopher can include a particular argument in her analysis, a state can include a territory in its jurisdiction. However, *democratic* inclusion presupposes agency both on the side of those who are included and those who include them. This agency need not be expressed through explicit acts of consent. Families, states and most religious communities include those born into them without asking for their consent. In each of these cases inclusion is based on the notion of birthright. The term "right" makes it clear that there is a reference to a claim. The other agent in the relation is the association or collectivity that includes. A necessary condition for speaking about inclusion is that it serves a purpose pursued by this association. Where there are institutionalized rules for inclusion, they will reflect this purpose in the rules under which individuals or groups are included. A church will admit members based on their adherence to its doctrines and their contributions to the life of the congregation, a sports club based on their skills or their willingness to contribute to its budget and activities.

Neither need agency be expressed in explicit consent on the side of the including agent. We can illustrate the difference between consensual and automatic modes of inclusion by considering the contrast between birthright acquisition of citizenship, which is generally automatic, and naturalization, which requires an application. I will discuss this contrast and the specific purpose it serves in section 4. Here I am concerned with a general purpose of democratic polities, which is to achieve legitimacy for political rule. I propose that democratic inclusion principles specify a relation between an individual or group that has an inclusion claim and a political community that aims to achieve democratic legitimacy for its political decisions and institutions. Inclusion claims and purposes must correspond in such a way that satisfying the former is seen to contribute to the latter.

In the rest of this chapter I will elaborate a normative conception of democracy that relies on three distinct principles of inclusion, each of which serves a specific purpose of legitimation and operates within a specific perimeter. The principles are those of including all affected interests, of including all subject to the law and of including all who have a legitimate stake in membership. In contrast to most political theorists who have analysed the democratic boundary problem,[14] I claim that the three principles differ in scope because they support different inclusion claims. Those whose interests are affected by a decision have a democratic claim that their interests be taken into account in the process of decision-making and implementation. Those who are subjected to the jurisdiction of a polity have a democratic claim to equal protection under the law. And those who have a legitimate stake in participating in the self-government of a particular polity have a democratic claim to be recognized as citizens.

It is tempting to imagine the territorial scopes of these three inclusion principles as concentric circles, with affected interests having the widest and citizenship claims the narrowest perimeter. This seems plausible when one considers that many political decisions have spillover effects across the borders of jurisdictions and that in immigration states there are often significant shares of non-citizens who are subjected to the laws in roughly the same way as citizens. However, this image of concentric circles is also misleading. International migrants are citizens of their states of origin and today they mostly retain rights to political participation and representation there while being only weakly affected by political decisions or subjected to the laws of these countries. Is there any justification for drawing the boundaries of membership wider or narrower than those of impact or subjection?

---

[14]   For an exception see Owen (2012).

This is a puzzle that I will address in section 4. Yet the question is less puzzling if we consider that inside the territorial jurisdiction of representative democracies, too, decisions are taken on behalf of all citizens but often affect the interests of a particular subgroup much more strongly than the rest of the citizenry. Consider, for example, a law that prescribes a certain curriculum in schools. If the law has merely regulatory and no fiscal impact, then elderly childless citizens can hardly claim that their interests are as strongly affected as those of citizens of minor age and their parents, yet the votes of the former and the latter will count equally in a referendum (or in a parliamentary election) that puts this issue on its agenda while children of minor age who are most directly affected will not be directly represented in this decision at all.

In past writings (Bauböck 2007, 2009 a and b, 2015b) I have argued that the AAI and ASC principles are morally attractive but suffer from two flaws. They cannot resolve the democratic boundary problem because the boundaries they suggest are necessarily indeterminate and unstable,[15] and they are polity-indifferent, which means that they generate the same prescriptions for inclusion in local, regional or state polities, although these polities require different membership norms. I have contrasted these and other democratic inclusion principles with an alternative principle of including all citizenship stakeholders that is sufficiently determinate in its practical implications and sufficiently flexible to support different inclusion rules for different types of polities. This argument was to a certain extent lopsided because it focused nearly exclusively on defending ACS as the appropriate principle for determining who should be recognized as citizens. I now want to explore in more depth the virtues of the AAI and ASC principles and why we should regard them as complementing my stakeholder account. But I will also try to show that AAI and ASC fail to meet the mark when they are considered as norms that by themselves cover the whole range of democratic inclusion claims.

---

[15] See also Benhabib (2011: ch. 8).

3.1   Including affected interests

For each of the three principles we have to specify further their scope
(inclusion of whom?) and their domain (inclusion in what?). With
regard to scope, AAI can be interpreted in two contrasting ways: does
it refer to actually affected or potentially affected interests? Robert Goodin
has argued that the former interpretation is incoherent: "[W]hose interests
are 'affected' by any actual decision depends upon what the decision
actually turns out to be" (Goodin 2007: 52). In his view, interests are
affected "not merely by the course of action actually decided upon", but
also by the range of alternative courses of action from which that course
was chosen (ibid.: 54). He concludes that "[m]embership in the demos
ought to extend to every interest that would probably be affected by
any possible decision arising out of any possible agenda" (ibid.: 61–62).

This interpretation of AAI begs the question why an interest in
agenda-setting should count as relevant for purposes of democratic
inclusion. If we regard agenda-setting as the core power of a democratic
legislator, then only those who have a right to authorize this legislator
can be seen as having a legitimate interest in agenda-setting. Goodin's
claim that only a global demos can be legitimate is thus derived from
an implausibly wide conception of AAI that builds the conclusion already
into the premise. A principle of including all potentially affected interests
assumes from the very start the existence of a global demos whose
members have a legitimate interest in participating in or being represented
in setting a global political agenda. A democratically plausible interpretation of AAI must instead refer to interests in the choice between
alternative decisions on an already set agenda (Owen 2012).

Goodin's theory may be implausible in its consequences but it is
certainly coherent: the members of a self-governing demos (or the
representatives they elect) must have agenda-setting powers rather than
merely the power to pick a decision from an already set agenda. If AAI
is the only valid principle for determining membership in a demos, then
all those whose interests are affected by any possible decision arising out
of any possible agenda must be included in the demos. A demos with

agenda-setting powers formed under the AAI principle must therefore be global in scope. In order to refute the conclusion we must either adopt a weaker conception of democracy in which the demos does not have agenda-setting powers and is thus no longer self-governing, or we must reject the claim that AAI is the appropriate inclusion principle for determining membership in a demos. I propose to stick to strong democracy and drop the claim that AAI is the all-encompassing inclusion principle.

If we accept the circumstances of democracy and the plural structure of political boundaries, then the core power of agenda-setting (even for global political agendas) can only belong to particular demoi at the sub-global level. There will then be from the very start a distinction between those who have the power to set the political agenda and those whose interests are affected by political decisions. Persons whose interests are externally affected are those who suffer or benefit from a political decision without belonging to the group whose members have a legitimate interest in agenda-setting in a self-governing demos. Externally affected interests are, by definition, actually affected interests, since otherwise there would be no external boundary whatsoever that distinguishes a self-governing demos from those whom it might affect through its decisions.

The distinction between externally and internally affected interests is rather obvious once we consider that some of the most significant interests that democratic governments have to track emerge only because of the existence of political territories and government institutions. This basic fact explains also why government action normally affects the interests of those who reside permanently within its territory much more comprehensively than those living outside the border. We should thus not imagine political communities as being solely responsible for tracking interests that exist pre-politically, that is, before or independently of the structure of political boundaries and territorial jurisdiction.

While rejecting Goodin's claim that any attempt to limit democratic inclusion to actually affected interests is incoherent, David Owen (2012) has pointed out that a principle of actually affected interests must not be interpreted so narrowly that it refers only to the impact of the decision actually taken. Tracking affected interests requires taking these into account in decision-making, not after that decision has already been taken. Affected interests thus have a claim to be included in the process of deliberation that precedes the decision and not only the process of implementation that follows it. In other words, actually affected interests have a claim to voice. They must be heard and taken into account by those who take the decision. They form the relevant public for political decisions.[16] Those whose interests are affected by democratic decisions, no matter whether they are citizens, subjects or completely outside the jurisdiction, have a right to justification of the decision that respects them as autonomous sources of valid claims (Owen 2011, 2012; Forst 2012).

It is obvious that the current international state system is deeply flawed in this respect. It is designed to reduce the duty of states to justify their decisions towards those on whom they impact outside their territorial borders and boundaries of citizenship. At most, it supports duties of justification towards other states. The representation of externally affected interests depends, then, on these being effectively represented by a government that has the power to confront the authorities of the state that takes a contested decision. Moreover, the mechanisms of intergovernmental representation of externally affected interests operate in most cases only ex post rather than in the run-up to the decision and thus do not satisfy the condition that actually affected interests must be heard before a decision is taken. If inclusion of affected interests is a requirement of *democratic* legitimacy, then the flaws of the international state system, which is not itself democratically structured, are no excuse for a democratic polity to ignore the interests of those who are outside its jurisdiction. Instead of delegating this task to a global demos, it must be regarded as one that each polity is morally

---

[16] Along similar lines, Seyla Benhabib argues that Habermas's discourse principle (that only those norms can claim to be valid that can meet with the approval of all affected in their capacity as participants in a practical discourse) "is a principle of moral and political justification; it is not one for delineating the scope of democratic membership" (Benhabib 2011: 160).

obliged to address whenever the decisions on its agenda are likely to have significant external impact.[17]

The task could be met in different ways, of which intergovernmental consultations and negotiations is only one. A second, and increasingly important, response is government participation in the creation of regional or global governance institutions on issues that systematically spill across jurisdictional boundaries, such as climate change, refugee protection and the persecution of crimes against humanity.[18] The third response is to directly represent externally affected interests in the decision-making process itself.

This might be done, for example, through transborder referendums on issues such as the opening or closure of nuclear power plants close to an international border. Note, however, that transborder referendums presuppose legitimately constituted separate demoi on both sides of the border. A simple majority in a referendum involving two polities in which each vote is counted equally on either side of the border is not a defensible decision rule since the outcome would be determined by the citizens of the larger polity. Creating instead two constituencies of equal size on either side of the border would involve highly arbitrary boundary decisions and would again fail to meet democratic standards of legitimacy since there would be no elected legislators who are accountable to voters for implementing their decision. A reasonable procedure requires thus separate majorities in both polities. The decision rule may vary depending on the nature of the issue at stake, but generally the most plausible one is that a majority in each polity must agree to any

---

[17]   This norm can be seen as an extension of Article 19 of the Universal Declaration of Human Rights, which establishes the right "to seek, receive and impart information and ideas through any media and regardless of frontiers". It extends the right to obtain information into corresponding duties of governments to provide information and also to take into account externally affected interests (Owen 2017). As pointed out by Seyla Benhabib, the practical fulfilment of such duties depends largely on the emergence of discursive publics (often promoted by advocacy groups in civil society) that represent externally affected interests within democratic polities (Benhabib 2004).

[18]   See Kuper (2004), Bohman (2007) and Macdonald (2008) for proposals on how to design global governance institutions democratically so that they are responsive to externally affected interests.

new policy that has significant impact on the other. Granting veto power over a political decision to the citizens of a neighbouring state is obviously a proposal for which it will be hard to get political support. My point here, however, is that doing so does not merge the two demoi into a single issue-specific demos, but retains their identities as separate and self-governing political communities.

The most ambitious idea is to include actually affected interests in the decision-making process through special delegates with voting power in legislative assemblies. Matthias Koenig-Archibugi has suggested a scheme of representing externally affected interests through delegates in each national parliament elected by all non-residents with seats allocated in proportion to the share of world income under the control of that state. In order to take account of the fact that all humans would be equally affected by the rules determining their external representation in every particular demos, he adds to this proposal a globally elected global constitutional assembly that determines these rules (Koenig-Archibugi 2012). By distinguishing coercively subjected individuals with full and equal citizenship claims from externally affected interests with partial citizenship (ibid.: 462), this model tries to combine the notion of a global demos constituted by affected interests with self-government claims of particular demoi. However, it is not obvious how externally affected interests could be involved in the self-government of every demos without undermining the very idea of self-government. Koenig-Archibugi's proposal aims at simultaneously achieving option-inclusiveness and agenda-inclusiveness. Yet if agenda-setting is a reserved power for the members of a self-governing demos, then letting the delegates of externally affected interests participate in determining agendas rather than in influencing decisions through deliberation generates over-inclusiveness with regard to membership.

Distinguishing between the two circles of inclusion could lead to alternative institutional proposals, such as issue-specific mandates for the representatives of externally affected interests to participate in consultative bodies. Even granting them votes in particular legislative decisions would still be compatible with the separation between agenda-setting and option-choosing powers. Extending a model developed for local jurisdictions within states (Frey and Eichberger 1999), such solutions have sometimes been advocated under the label of "functional demoi", but this terminology is misleading if the issues and functions with regard to which a decision can be delegated to such a "demos" are themselves determined by a territorially bounded and agenda-setting demos.

My preliminary conclusion is thus that reasonable versions of AAI that respect the plurality of self-governing polities as a background condition cannot be accepted as comprehensive answers to the democratic boundary problem, since they fail to provide a principle for the legitimate constitution of such polities and claims to inclusion in them.

AAI theorists have replied to this objection that the principles of including all subject to coercion and of including all citizenship stakeholders can be easily restated as particular applications of AAI. In this view, AAI is the broader formula that encompasses the others.[19] In Goodin's words, what really matters for constituting a demos is interlinked interests (Goodin 2007: 49). A reductionist strategy can thus simply include individuals' interests in protection of their rights by a particular government as well as their interests in membership in a particular polity among those interests that governments have to track. While these are logically coherent moves that make ASC and ACS appear to be merely special versions of AAI, they obscure the essentially different normative claims that each of the three principles supports. Maintaining these differences is crucial for democracy and therefore we should consider the three principles as complementary to each other rather than as broader or narrower versions of the same principle. This requires clarifying that, as a democratic inclusion principle, AAI refers specifically to interests in policy *decisions* rather than to interests

---

[19]   Robert Dahl refers to both principles (Dahl 1989), although his account seems more consistent with an emphasis on ASC (López-Guerra 2005; Owen 2012). Beckman believes, however, that "there is an impressive degree of consensus on the 'all affected' principle" (Beckman 2009: 36) and suggests that ASC is essentially a legal interpretation of all affected interests (ibid.: 47).

in rights protection by *government* institutions or to *membership* in a
political community. These last two interests are the domains of the
ASC and ACS principles respectively.

3.2   Including the subjects of coercion

Democratic governments have special responsibility for those whom
they govern. They must treat them with equal respect and concern
(Dworkin 1977) and must secure their basic rights and freedoms. This
is at least true for all liberal versions of democracy under the rule of
law. Government is by its very nature coercive. The ASC principle
captures the idea that the democratic legitimacy of government coercion
depends on securing equal liberties for all whose autonomy it restricts.

This principle differs from AAI in important ways. First, it distinguishes between those who are subject to government coercion and
those who are not, and it attributes special inclusion claims to the
former only. Not everyone whose interests are affected is subjected to
coercion. Governments can legitimately enforce laws only within a
territorially limited jurisdiction and to some extent also over their citizens
outside the territory. Recent developments in human rights have created
universal jurisdiction of national courts for a strictly limited set of
issues, such as crimes against humanity. These are exceptions that confirm
the rule. At least prima facie, the scope of ASC is limited by the scope
of jurisdiction. Second, ASC entails a stronger claim to equality. As
explained above, the impact of democratic decisions on individuals'
interests is notoriously unequal and varies from one decision to the
next. By contrast, ASC refers to subjection to government institutions
rather than exposure to particular legislative outputs. Residents within
a territorial jurisdiction are unequally affected by government decisions
but – with minor exceptions, such as diplomats or tourists – equally
coerced by government institutions. This suggests, third, that the proper
domain of inclusion under ASC is representation of their interests in
protection of their rights within government institutions.

The first of these features, the limited scope of ASC, means that the principle is better adapted than AAI to what I have called the circumstances and territorial contexts of democracy. However, the problem with ASC in this respect is that it is systematically biased towards existing boundaries. If inclusion claims are derived from the scope of current jurisdiction, then ASC may be too conservative in taking for granted borders as they are.

Some decisions taken by governments not only affect external populations' interests but also subject them comprehensively to coercion in a way that fundamentally restricts their autonomy. This is most obviously true for military interventions and explains why these are legitimate only for purposes of self-defence or for humanitarian reasons. In such cases, the ASC principle would support our moral intuitions that states engaging in such forms of extra-jurisdictional coercion have special duties to admit refugees. It would also require that military authorities exercising coercive rule in a foreign territory have to treat the civilian population there with equal respect and concern. But how can ASC account for our intuition that it was legitimate for the U.S. to occupy German territory after World War II, while it would have been illegitimate to annex it (Stilz 2011: 590–591)? The answer must be that the overriding duty of democratic states engaging in military interventions is not one of inclusion; it is a duty of non-interference with the local population's right to self-government.[20] Limiting the protective duties of democratic governments to populations within their jurisdiction is thus necessary to avoid the citizens of independent polities being curtailed in their rights of self-government.

Consider now how this would apply to colonial contexts. Until independence in 1962, Algeria was legally incorporated into the French territory. If ASC is interpreted as a claim for membership inclusion, then the colonial subjects in Algeria had a right to equal citizenship in

---

[20] The duty is a negative one of non-interference rather than a positive one of creating conditions for self-government, since democratic states cannot promote regime change towards democracy as a legitimate goal in military intervention.

France rather than to independence from France. A democratic principle of membership must link individual inclusion claims to collective self-government claims in order to avoid a status quo bias in favour of unjust territorial borders and jurisdictional boundaries.

I share therefore Anna Stilz's conclusion that territorial claims of states must refer to a conceptually prior relation of a people to the territory. Yet Stilz falls back on a statist version of the ASC principle when she defines peoplehood in terms of "a history of political cooperation together by sharing a state (legitimate or otherwise) in the recent past" and the political capacity of the group "to reconstitute and sustain a legitimate state on their territory today" (ibid.: 591). The implication seems to be that colonies without prior statehood would fail the political history test and Algeria would thus have had no claim to independence rather than inclusion in the French polity. Stilz tries to avoid this conclusion by acknowledging that "[e]ven if a group has only shared an illegitimate state in the past, they may qualify as a people if that shared history has been combined with other joint activities that have created the political capacity for them to sustain a legitimate state today" (ibid.: 592). Yet this somewhat ad hoc adjustment remains stuck in the logic of ASC by making self-government claims entirely dependent on prior subjection by a state: "only a history of sharing a state demonstrates the existence of the moral bonds that support political authority" (ibid.: 593). This logic is pernicious for indigenous peoples, who would generally fail both the historical and the capacity tests since their territorial self-determination claims rely neither on a history of, nor a capacity for, independent statehood. Although Stilz is on the right track when insisting that we need an account of peoplehood in order to justify claims to territorial jurisdiction, her view remains too narrowly statist both retrospectively (the political history test) and prospectively (the political capacity test). What we need instead in order to avoid the potentially oppressive over-inclusiveness of ASC is a prior conception of political membership linking individual inclusion claims to collective claims to self-government and a conception of political community that is not limited to sovereign states.

Let us now consider the scope of inclusion under ASC in contexts where current jurisdictional boundaries can be regarded as legitimate. Equal protection must then be offered to all residents but territorial scope ought to be interpreted with some flexibility. The duty of equal protection for all within the jurisdiction needs to track the impact of being subject to coercive legislation on individuals' freedom. While tourists will hardly qualify, temporary migrants may experience significant restrictions of their autonomy, especially if they do not enjoy the same freedom of movement and legal protections as long-term residents. Citizens and residents who are temporarily outside the jurisdiction are clearly covered by ASC and so must be coerced emigrants who have been driven into exile by a non-democratic predecessor regime. In these cases, the situation of individuals is comprehensively marked by subjection to coercion that they have experienced in the past and this creates an ongoing duty of protecting their rights.[21] The situation of emigrant citizens who live permanently abroad is less clear in this regard. In the standard case they will have interests affected by legislation concerning their diplomatic and consular protection, their right to return, and their property rights and tax duties in countries of origin. Yet they are not comprehensively subjected to the legal order of these countries. Claudio López-Guerra insists therefore that voluntary long-term emigrants should lose their citizenship status and voting rights (López-Guerra 2005) while David Owen argues that they remain subjected to those laws that concern their status as citizens abroad as well as to the general constitutional order, and have thus at least a claim to political participation in constitutional referendums (Owen 2010). My own view is that ASC does not provide a solid basis for citizenship status rather than some form of partial membership for long-term emigrants and their offspring born abroad. Their claims can be better understood from a stakeholder perspective applied to the specific context of citizenship in the international state system.

---

[21] See Bauböck (2007) and Owen (2010) for arguments that temporary absentees and coerced emigrants should enjoy also voting rights.

Most ASC theorists invoke the principle in order to determine who has a claim not only to equal protection but also to citizenship status and voting rights. These are two different questions, the answers to which need not be derived from the same inclusion principle. The distinction is clearly drawn in section 1 of the Fourteenth Amendment to the U.S. Constitution:

> All persons born or naturalized in the United States, and subject to the jurisdiction thereof, are citizens of the United States and of the State wherein they reside. No State shall make or enforce any law which shall abridge the privileges or immunities of citizens of the United States; nor shall any State deprive any person of life, liberty, or property, without due process of law; nor deny to any person within its jurisdiction the equal protection of the laws.

The "citizenship clause" of the Fourteenth Amendment specifies a set of rules for determining who are the citizens of the polity. These are territorial birthright, naturalization, and linkage between state and federal citizenship. It also includes a "subject to the jurisdiction" condition that has in the past been invoked restrictively in order to permit citizenship revocation for naturalized U.S. citizens who took up permanent residence abroad. After World War II, the U.S. Supreme Court reinterpreted the Fourteenth Amendment in such a way that today U.S. citizenship can only be lost through relinquishment or voluntary renunciation (Aleinikoff 1986; Weil 2013). While the "privileges and immunities" clause still refers specifically to citizens, the two subsequent clauses speak about persons rather than citizens. The distinction is intended and important: due process of law and equal protection of the laws are owed to any person within U.S. jurisdiction, not only to those whom the first clause identifies as U.S. citizens. Conversely, not all who have a claim to due process and equal protection have thereby also a valid claim to citizenship.

This is not yet a conclusive normative argument. First, there is no reason for privileging the U.S. Constitution as an authoritative source for interpreting democratic inclusion over other constitutions or international legal documents. Second, the rules listed in the citizenship clause are legal mechanisms rather than normative principles. So we still need to find normative reasons why those who have a claim to equal protection should not also have a claim to citizenship status. This will be the task of the following section on stakeholder citizenship.

Before embarking on this task, we need to consider further the domain of inclusion under ASC and which institutional arrangements can track the interests of those subject to coercion. The potential problem with the equal protection claim is that it does not explain why democratic governments can be trusted to secure the freedom of those whom they coerce. The democratic answer to the old question: "who will watch the watchmen?" must be: "those who are watched by the watchmen". In order to qualify as democratic, the protection of rights through government institutions must include rights to contest government authority and decisions. In other words, democratic institutions must not only provide equal protection to those subjected to them, but must also open up channels for contestation.

The contemporary version of republicanism that has been called "neo-Roman" and is best represented by intellectual historian Quentin Skinner and political theorist Phillip Pettit provides a solid normative grounding for this interpretation of the ASC principle. Pettit has put special emphasis on contestability as a condition for non-domination. He distinguishes between "authorial" and "editorial" control of govern-ments and tends to privilege the latter: "Government will be authorially controlled by the collective people under electoral arrangements whereby issues are decided by plebiscite or representatives are chosen to decide them. And government will be editorially controlled by the people under arrangements of a broadly contestatory kind" (Pettit 2006: 3). Both types of control are relevant for democratic legitimacy but the collective people that exercises them is not necessarily the same. The normative claim to be able to contest government institutions and their decisions follows directly from being coercively subjected to them, whereas the claim to be included in the demos that exercises "authorial control" does not. The very term "control" is also somewhat misleading in the latter context, since governments have to be authorized through popular vote before they can exercise power that is then controlled by the people.

Pettit's theory is in this respect at odds with other republican traditions, such as Rousseau's, Kant's, Arendt's and Habermas's, that have emphasized the link between individual and collective self-government. Pettit's exclusive focus on domination defined as vulnerability to arbitrary interference that fails to track one's interests (Pettit 1997, 2012) risks losing sight of the regulatory ideal of popular sovereignty and its – always imperfect – realization through democratic procedures for electing – rather than only controlling – governments. This shortcoming makes neo-Roman republicanism a somewhat limited perspective for a comprehensive theory of democratic inclusion, but one that has elective affinity with the ASC principle and is well suited to provide normative support for it. Although Pettit's general description of domination seems to be compatible with AAI, vulnerability to arbitrary interference is a condition in which individuals find themselves as the result of exposure to coercive government institutions rather than to negative externalities of particular decisions.

In contrast with the representation of externally affected interests in political deliberations and decisions, the institutional devices for securing equal protection of the law and opportunities for contestation are conventional and do not have to be newly invented. They include constitutional protection of fundamental rights and judicial review of ordinary legislation by constitutional courts as well as institutionalized complaints and contestation procedures for individuals in courts and ombudsman bodies and, finally, the rights to protest against governments and their decisions through political speech and activities.

From an inclusion perspective the important question is who should be protected and have access to contestation opportunities. If the answer is: all subjected to government jurisdiction, then citizens and non-citizen residents must enjoy these rights equally. This is not only implied by the U.S. Fourteenth Amendment. In Europe a principle of non-discrimination on grounds of nationality with regard to protection of fundamental rights is enshrined both in the European Human Rights

Convention and in EU law.[22] Yet the scope of such protection is continuously under dispute. Concerning contestation rights, restrictions on aliens' rights of political association and activity were very common throughout the twentieth century and linger on in a number of contemporary European states with regard to rights to membership in political parties.[23]

On some interpretations, however, the scope of ASC is even wider than this. Arash Abizadeh has argued that immigration control is coercive towards non-citizen non-residents in a way that gives them a claim to be included in the demos for the purpose of making legitimate immigration law (Abizadeh 2008, 2010). The idea that outsiders have a right to participate in the making of the very laws that exclude them is a good example of how standard versions of the democratic boundary problem can generate rather perplexing paradoxes.[24] David Miller's reply to Abizadeh is that would-be immigrants are not coerced if immigration control merely removes one option from their choice set of potential destinations (Miller 2010). If one accepts Miller's response, one may still hold on to ASC while avoiding the consequence that immigration control subjects the rest of the world to coercion and generates thus a global issue-specific demos for purposes of regulating immigration.

Yet even under Miller's interpretation, very significant numbers of actual rather than potential migrants could claim to be coerced because they do not have sufficiently robust opportunities to choose alternative destinations. This argument would apply to refugees as well as to dependent family members of immigrants and possibly also to large numbers of poverty- or environmentally driven migrants. Abizadeh's argument has the merit of drawing our attention to the fact that coercive jurisdiction is not only exercised *within* territorial borders, but also

---

[22] ECHR Article 14, Charter of Fundamental Rights of the European Union, Article 21.
[23] According to the 2015 edition of the Migrant Integration Policy Index, "[a]ll 11 EU countries in Central Europe and [Turkey] deny non-EU foreigners some of their basic political liberties, such as joining a political party or founding a political association" (http://www.mipex.eu/political-participation, accessed 22 July 2015).
[24] See also my brief discussion in Bauböck (2015b).

that borders themselves are potentially coercive instruments if they are not only used for demarcating jurisdictions but also for controlling migration flows. No matter whether this happens at the border or coast, inside the territory, at the high seas or through "remote control", points of departure in other countries, it is hard to see how state responsibility for the protection of migrants whom they turn away – and who have stronger claims to admission to this country than anywhere else – could be denied under any plausible version of ASC.[25] This suggests a somewhat more expansive scope of the ASC principle but does not yet support Abizadeh's conclusion that immigrants have to be included in the demos already before entry. This latter conclusion relies on interpreting ASC as a membership principle, which is what I intend to question.

I close this section by pointing to another problem with such an interpretation of ASC: it is likely to support not merely voluntary but also mandatory inclusion in the demos. Since the end of the nineteenth century, states have generally refrained from naturalizing first generation immigrants against their will. Yet if a legitimate demos has to include all who are subject to political coercion, then foreign nationals belong to it already by virtue of residing within the jurisdiction. So it is not clear why they should have a freedom to opt out while staying in the territory. At the same time, democracies may have relevant interests in naturalizing foreign residents. They may lack legitimacy if they rule over large numbers of foreign residents who cannot participate in elections. A persistent internal boundary between foreigners and citizens may also undermine social cohesion and a sense of joint responsibility for the common good. Finally, foreigners who refuse to naturalize may do so in order to free ride on public goods to which only citizens contribute (such as military defence where citizens are drafted). All

---

[25] Thomas Nagel argues that "[i]mmigration policies are simply enforced against the nationals of other states; the laws are not imposed in their name, nor are they asked to accept and uphold these laws" (Nagel 2005: 129–130). This presupposes that states' relation with foreigners at their borders is a Hobbesian state of nature. Yet contemporary democracies generally recognize their human rights obligations towards foreigners and consider their immigration laws as legally binding for those who wish to be admitted.

these are serious concerns and the idea of mandatory citizenship for immigrants has therefore found a few defenders among political theorists (Rubio-Marín 2000; Carens 2005; López-Guerra 2005; de Schutter and Ypi 2015).

As I will argue in section 4 of this essay, the problem is not with the idea as such, but with its application to the specific context of citizenship in the international state system under conditions of relative sedentariness. It is in this context that mandatory citizenship for immigrants clashes with their right to choose between alternative citizenship statuses as well as with mutual obligations between independent states. The problem with ASC is not that it supports automatic acquisition of citizenship based on residence within a jurisdiction, which is entirely appropriate for citizenship at the local level, but that it does not allow for distinguishing between national and local contexts.

3.3   Including citizenship stakeholders

The versions of AAI and ASC that I have outlined and supported above cannot be accepted as sufficient for democratic inclusion because they could potentially be fulfilled also by non-democratic regimes. Imagine an enlightened and benevolent autocratic government that does not have any democratic mandate to rule but whose sole aim is to govern well according to liberal standards of justice. Such a government would fully take into account all interests that are actually affected by policies that it has put on its agenda and would invite representatives of groups whose interests could be impacted to its deliberations. Its decision would then be based on a careful calculation in which these voices are weighted by the strength of preferences and potential impact. The government would also make sure that it protects the full panoply of civil and social rights for anybody in its jurisdiction while refraining from interfering in this regard with the jurisdiction of neighbouring governments. It would expose its policies to strong forms of judicial review by independent courts, would provide multiple opportunities for complaints and would not curtail freedom of political speech, association and activity. But this liberal government would be appointed by an enlightened monarch. In the absence of a popular mandate we would not call such a government democratic.

Proponents of AAI and ASC will of course protest that their versions of the two inclusion principles are democratic because – in contrast to my account – they are not limited to giving voice to affected interests and protection to the subjects of coercion, but identify also the members of the demos who elect the government and to whom it must be accountable. Yet if we stick to a strong version of democracy as popular self-government, then we end up in circular reasoning: the demos is constituted through the impact of a government that can itself only be constituted through the very same demos.[26] In order to avoid this circle, we would have to accept that governments create democratic peoples rather than the other way round.[27] Elections would then be just another device for "editorial control" over governments rather than an original source of their legitimacy. And when constitutions invoke the "people" as the ultimate constitutional law-giver this would be little more than empty political rhetoric. So it seems AAI and ASC can maintain their democratic credentials only at the price of accepting weak versions of democracy that abandon the normative ideal of self-government and replace it with a supposedly more realist conception according to which democracy is about controlling government power rather than authorizing it. Since such control comes ex post, the role of the demos is then effectively similar to that of an independent judiciary.

---

[26]   See Goodin (2007: 43). In private correspondence, David Owen has raised the objection that there is no contradiction in saying: "I am entitled to choose whether and what to promise because I am the one who will be bound by my promise" and by analogy: "We are entitled to choose whether and what laws to have because we are the ones who will be bound by these laws." Yet in the former case, my identity as an individual that has the capacity to make promises does not depend on the fact that I will be bound by the promises I make; it is given prior to me making any promises. In the same way, the identity and composition of a collective "we" as law-makers must be given independently of and prior to us being bound by the laws we have given to ourselves.

[27]   As David Owen has pointed out to me, this would mean accepting Hobbes's argument against republicans that it is subjection to a sovereign that transforms the multitude into a people. See also Chwaszcza (2009).

If we understand citizenship instead not merely as a bundle of rights and duties but as a status of membership in a self-governing polity, then a democratic inclusion principle that determines who has a claim to citizenship must focus on the relations of individuals to a particular political community rather than to a government and its decisions. The stakeholder principle that I have defended is only one among several inclusion principles that satisfy this formal condition. Elsewhere I have distinguished pre-political and political principles (Bauböck 2015b). Democratic and liberal nationalists propose that the political community should be understood as a nation with a historically stable cultural and territorial identity. The nation is a pre-political community not because of its origins, since national consciousness is often the result of nation-building policies pursued by states. It is pre-political because of the cultural content of shared identity and the corresponding criteria for membership. Constitutional patriotism is not enough (Kymlicka 1995, 2001b). In order to be included in the imagined community of the nation, individuals must either be born into it or adopt cultural repertoires shared by its members. By contrast, social contract theories that imagine the political community as a voluntary association of individuals are political in the sense that they ground the identity and legitimacy of a polity in a shared political purpose. The problem with both ideas is that they are difficult to square with liberal conceptions of democracy.

From a nationalist perspective, admitting new members to the political community must serve the purpose of nation-building. In some historical contexts, this meant inviting immigrants from diverse origins; in others it meant selecting them on the basis of presumptive cultural fit or prior national membership; in still others it meant closing the borders and denying access to citizenship for the sake of preserving national identity. If political community can only be achieved through nation-building, then the inclusiveness of the polity for minorities and newcomers is not a matter of democratic principle but of historically contingent circumstances. A nationality principle may be compatible with liberal democratic standards in some contexts but will conflict with them in others. It can thus not serve as a general guideline for democratic inclusion.

The idea that a democratic polity should be imagined as a voluntary association of citizens leads to similar problems. A voluntary association is self-governing if its members are not only free to exit, but also to admit or exclude outsiders who are willing to join. This is a political and at first glance also democratic conception if it leaves decisions about membership to democratic procedures that track the collective will of current members. As pointed out by Robert Dahl when rejecting Schumpeter's claim that "we must leave it to every *populus* to define himself" (Schumpeter 1942/1976: 245), this would entail that any polity is democratic as long as it is governed by a body that is internally democratic even if it excludes the vast majority of those subject to its laws (Dahl 1989: 121–122). Christopher Wellman's conclusion that states deriving their legitimacy from a principle of voluntary association and dissociation are free to select immigrants on grounds of race and "entitled to reject all potential immigrants, even those desperately seeking asylum from corrupt governments" (Wellman 2008: 141) must be equally disturbing for liberal democrats.

The stakeholder principle starts from a different conception of political community that consists of both empirical and normative assumptions. I have already spelled out the empirical assumption when introducing the circumstances of democracy: a plurality of bounded political communities is part of the human condition. Humans are social animals. They have strong stakes in being recognized as members of particular political communities because being an outsider who does not belong to any such community is a condition of extreme precariousness. To put it positively: membership in a polity is a necessary condition for human autonomy and well-being. It is not, however, a sufficient condition because political rule can also destroy freedom and deprive people of their subsistence, as it has done in most of its manifestations over the course of human history. A person's stake in being a member of a particular polity depends thus on that polity being governed in a way that protects its members' autonomy and well-being. So far, this seems like another version of the ASC principle. The democratic twist comes with the further assumption that those who have an interest in protection of their individual freedom and well-being by a particular polity thereby share with each other an interest in the collective freedom and flourishing of that polity. Citizens are stakeholders in a democratic political community insofar as their autonomy and well-being depend not only on being recognized as a member in a particular polity, but also on that polity being governed democratically. Political legitimacy in a democratic polity is not derived from nationhood or voluntary association but from popular self-government, that is, citizens' participation and representation in democratic institutions that track their collective will and common good.

Unlike AAI and ASC, ACS derives inclusion claims from a correspondence between individuals' interests in autonomy and well-being and the collective interests of all citizens in their polity's self-government and flourishing. The term "stakeholder" can be easily misunderstood as referring to a stake in particular democratic decisions or in the protection of one's rights by a particular government (see for example Beckman 2009: 41). It should instead be understood as having a stake in *membership*, which is why I refer to "citizenship stakeholders".

Assuming that individuals have a general interest in membership in a self-governing polity is much less demanding than those versions of republicanism that attribute intrinsic value to political participation. As pointed out by Will Kymlicka, this ideal is unattainable in contemporary liberal states. It conflicts with liberal toleration of a plurality of conceptions of the good and can serve to justify citizenship exclusion based on lack of civic virtue (Kymlicka 2001a: ch. 7). The idea that membership in a self-governing political community is a universal and intrinsic value is, instead, fundamentally inclusive and compatible also with ways of life that are inherently apolitical. Even the members of reclusive monastic orders will be better off as citizens of a democratic polity than as stateless persons or as subjects of autocratic rule.

At the same time, and unlike AAI, ACS provides normative reasons against over-inclusiveness. The relation between individual and collective self-government is bidirectional. Individuals have a claim to inclusion if their autonomy depends on the collective freedom of the polity. But the polity can also reject the inclusion of non-stakeholders on grounds that it would undermine the capacity of citizens to govern themselves. One illustration for over-inclusiveness is provided by current laws in many European states that allow for unlimited descent-based transmission of citizenship status across generations born abroad. Such perpetual ius sanguinis generates selective openness based on national origin for immigrants who have no stronger stake in the polity than others that are denied entry. Moreover, since in a majority of democratic states citizenship status is today sufficient for exercising the franchise, under such a rule the votes of outsiders are counted together with those of citizenship stakeholders, which infringes the self-governing rights of the latter.[28]

The reference to collective claims to self-government means that, unlike ASC, ACS is not inherently conservative with regard to existing borders. If these borders prevent a particular political community from governing itself, they infringe thereby also on the claims of individuals to citizenship in that community. The question of how conflicting claims to self-government can be sorted out is too complex to be fully addressed here. Accepting a plurality of polities as part of the circumstances of democracy entails that collective self-government claims are legitimate only insofar as they accept territorial and membership arrangements that allow for simultaneous fulfilment of all legitimate claims by other polities. Such a "compossibility principle" will in many cases lead to territorially nested forms of self-government, in which the legitimacy of national majority claims to self-government within a territory that includes national and indigenous minorities will depend on accepting a constitutional identity of the state as a plurinational polity and territorial autonomy for these minorities (Kymlicka 2001b: ch. 5; Tully 2001, 2008: vol. I, ch. 6). Conversely, under these conditions territorial

---

[28] I will explore more fully in section 4 how the boundaries of stakeholder citizenship should be drawn for independent states, for local and for regional polities.

minorities can be morally and legally obliged to respect the territorial integrity of a state that grants them sufficient autonomy and accepts them as constitutive communities in a plurinational polity (Bauböck 2000, 2002). Nested self-government is not always possible, however. Where territorial populations are oppressed as external colonies or where internal minorities are excluded from majority nation-building projects, they have remedial rights to self-determination that may result in the formation of autonomous territories or new independent states.[29]

Compossibility is a side-constraint on legitimate self-government claims, but it is not sufficient to sort out spurious from genuine claims. The condition in this regard is that genuine claims must be representative of either an existing citizenry in a legitimately established polity or of a potential citizenry that has manifested a desire for collective self-government for some time and has experienced the absence of self-government institutions as a form of oppression. In the former case, self-government claims may be directed against attempts to curb or dismantle current powers of territorial autonomy; in the latter they may support devolution or – in the extreme case – independence. Testing the representativeness of claims is potentially as difficult as assessing compossibility.[30] My point here is, however, a theoretical one. A representativeness condition provides us with a political and democratic account of the legitimacy of peoplehood as an alternative to nationalist and associative explanations. From this perspective, a democratic people is created through representation of its claims to self-government. Democratic representation is not merely a procedural device through which citizens can control a government that rules over them; the democratic people itself is constituted through representation of its claims to self-government.

---

[29] I thus agree broadly with Buchanan's remedial-only theory of secession (Buchanan 1991, 1997, 2004), but propose that unilateral self-determination rights with regard to territorial borders are in all cases derived from violations of prior claims to self-government. A primary right to self-determination is incompatible with the compossibility principle.

[30] See Rehfeld (2006), Saward (2010), Lacey (2017: ch. 2).

The legitimacy of jurisdictional boundaries is a question that must be solved before individual inclusion claims can be addressed. This makes the question of who ought to be enfranchised in plebiscites about territorial independence or border changes, such as the 2014 Scottish referendum, a particularly perplexing one (Ziegler, Shaw and Bauböck 2014). Once territorial borders can be regarded as democratically legitimate because they are uncontested, because they enable simultaneous nested self-government or because they are the just outcome of remedial exercises of self-determination rights, then the claims of individuals to inclusion in a particular polity can be decided on the basis of a "genuine link" principle.

"Genuine link" is a doctrine in public and private international law that is invoked to establish or dispute the right of states to award their nationality and to grant diplomatic protection to or impose duties on individuals whom other states also claim as their nationals.[31] For purposes of democratic theory, genuine link can serve instead as a critical standard for assessing the strength of ties between an individual and a particular polity. Keeping in mind that the substantive purpose for citizenship attribution is to secure, on the one hand, political conditions for individual autonomy and well-being and, on the other hand, collective self-rule, this strength cannot be measured in a uniform way either as a subjective sense of belonging or through objective indicators such as duration of residence or family ties in the territory. What counts as genuine link depends also on the nature of the polity itself and will be different for citizenship in states, municipalities and regions. Having been born and raised in the jurisdiction will generally be irrelevant for claims to local citizenship, whereas it may be sufficient for claims of first generation emigrants to retain their nationality of origin and the right to return.

Let me conclude this section by considering a major challenge for a stakeholder perspective. Even if the link between individual autonomy and collective self-government need not imply that citizens have a *duty*

---

[31]   The doctrine was first established in the 1955 Nottebohm judgment of the International Court of Justice. For a critical discussion of the scope of the doctrine see Sloane (2009).

to participate actively in the political life of the polity, it does imply that they must have the *opportunity* to do so. But this opportunity in turn depends on their *capacity* to participate. The citizenship status of minor children or cognitively disabled persons might then be in jeopardy under this conception, whereas AAI and ASC would have no difficulty in arguing for their inclusion. For AAI, individuals must be capable of having interests, which presupposes sentience, a sense of selfhood and capacity for purposive action. As Donaldson and Kymlicka point out, not only minor children and most cognitively disabled persons but also many animal species meet these criteria (Donaldson and Kymlicka 2011). Policies could then be regarded as democratically inclusive for these human and non-human individuals if they track their interests through mechanisms of indirect representation. ASC may be somewhat more demanding if we distinguish coercion from harm by presupposing an individual will (in the sense of a capacity for forming and pursuing projects) that can be coerced. Still, even this condition does not plausibly draw a line between intelligent human and non-human beings, nor between minor children and mentally disabled humans, on the one side, and adults, on the other side. Does a view of citizens as stakeholders in a self-governing polity exclude any or all of these categories?

The case of minor children seems easiest, since they are expected to develop the cognitive capacities that will allow them to participate politically. Children's rights activists have, however, rejected a view according to which children are merely in need of protection and without capacity to participate. Instead, they see them as having a right to participate according to their capacities in shaping the conditions under which they live and grow up (Donaldson and Kymlicka 2015). This cannot mean that minor children have a claim to voting or standing as candidates in legislative elections. And giving parents proxy votes that they can cast on behalf of their minor children looks more like a violation of the one-person-one-vote principle in favour of a particular category of adults than a vehicle for children's participation in the polity. If there is no democratic way of providing children below a certain age with opportunities for participating in electoral politics, does this mean that from a stakeholder perspective they are just partial citizens? And what about newborn children? How can they be considered *citizens* rather than merely as persons whose interests and well-being democratic states have a duty to protect?

I think the answer lies in the conditions for continuity of a self-governing polity over time. Newborn babies are attributed citizenship not just because we regard them as *future* citizens. If this were the case, one might as well wait until they have reached the age of majority and consider them until then subjects within the jurisdiction who have a claim to equal protection.[32] The reason why we recognize them as citizens is that political communities are transgenerational human societies. The status of membership in such communities is acquired at birth and does not depend on age-related cognitive or other capacities. In democracies, it is the larger transgenerational society that collectively governs itself and not the subcategory of adults who have the capacity and opportunity to vote or hold public office. Minor children are citizenship stakeholders because of their belonging to a transgenerational political community.

This does not mean that voting rights are irrelevant to democratic inclusion. They are the most important power that citizens hold equally and restrictions of access to this power must be justified. The benign liberal autocracy that I introduced at the beginning of this section treats adult citizens as if they were minor children and this is deeply degrading no matter how wise and benevolent the decisions taken by the government. By contrast, there is nothing degrading about treating children as children, which includes responsibilities to allow them to participate in all decisions concerning them. For adults this is not enough. In democracies, governments do not allow citizens to participate politically insofar as they are fit to do so. It is the other way round: citizens allow governments to govern them insofar as governments are fit to do so.

A stakeholder conception does therefore suggest a distinction between the *demos*, consisting of all those who have the franchise, and the *citizenry*, composed of all who have a stake in being members of a transgenerational political community. This distinction does not exclude either minor

---

[32] For a defence of this view see Dumbrava (2014: ch. 8).

children or mentally handicapped persons from citizenship on grounds of cognitive incapacity. What it does, however, is cast some doubt on the idea promoted by Donaldson and Kymlicka that domesticated animals should also be considered citizens (Donaldson and Kymlicka 2011: ch. 5). It is hard to reject this idea on the basis of AAI and ASC and it is difficult to accept it from a stakeholder perspective. As Donaldson and Kymlicka explain convincingly, domesticated animals can and should be treated with respect and concern as members of the *oikos*. Duties of care towards such animals should also be backed by public policies and laws. But the plurality of bounded and transgenerational political communities is part of the *human* and not of the animal condition. Membership in such communities is therefore species-specific. Challenging this political boundary will do little to improve the conditions of domesticated or other animals and might do great harm to the idea of *equality* of membership that is fundamental for democracy.

3.4   *Synthesis and tensions*

I have examined three different types of democratic boundaries: those marking the impact of political decisions, boundaries of government jurisdiction and boundaries of membership in a self-governing polity. For each of these there is a corresponding principle that identifies individuals who have claims of inclusion: those whose interests are affected, those who are subject to government coercion and those who have a stake in citizenship. Finally, each of these principles includes individuals in different democratic activities: in the deliberation and decision of policies, in the protection by and the contestation of political authority, and in the authorization of governments and of specific policy decisions through democratic elections and referendums. Since democratic inclusion serves different normative purposes, there is no compelling reason why the three boundaries ought to be congruent. Their incongruence ought to be accepted as a permanent feature of democracy in a world with strong interdependence and migration flows between autonomous polities. Trying to bring about congruence would be harmful for democracy. Expanding the boundaries of jurisdiction and membership to the widest circle of all affected interests would unjustly invade the self-government rights of the plurality of political communities that has always populated the political map of the world. Conversely, shrinking the scope of inclusion of affected interests to the internal ones of resident citizens would unjustly ignore the pervasive interconnectedness of human affairs across political boundaries in the present world.

The three inclusion principles have mostly been considered rivals because they tend to be linked to different conceptions of democracy. AAI is rooted in utilitarian and public choice views of democracy according to which its legitimacy and advantage over alternative forms of political rule lie in its capacity to maximize the satisfaction of political preferences and to resolve collective action dilemmas in the production of public goods. ASC is rooted in a liberal conception of democracy as the system of political rule that is most likely to guarantee fundamental rights. And the stakeholder conception is rooted in a liberal-republican conception of democracy that regards it as the always imperfect but closest possible approximation of collective self-rule.[33] While there are clearly tensions between these views of democracy, they are not irreconcilable. On the contrary, it is plausible that – as in the story about the blind men describing an elephant based on the parts that they touch – from each of these perspectives an important aspect of democracy can be perceived, but not the whole.

Synthesis requires abandoning holistic claims raised in defence of each of the three inclusion principles. The elephant is not a snake, a spear or a pillar; it does not even consist of any of these parts. The three inclusion principles can be reconciled with each other only if they are stated in such a way that the claims they support can be analytically separated. The crucial step is to drop the idea that AAI and ASC serve

---

[33] As I explained in section 3, Pettit's theory (Pettit 1997, 2012) leans in this respect towards a liberal view of democracy as instrumental for securing individual non-domination more than towards a republican one that puts equal emphasis on collective non-domination and self-government.

the purpose of determining membership in a demos. The following versions of the three principles can be endorsed simultaneously and without contradiction:

> AAI: All whose interests are actually affected by a decision on the agenda of a democratic legislator have a claim to representation of their interests in the decision-making process.

> ASC: All who are subject to the jurisdiction of a government have a claim to equal protection of their rights and freedoms by that government and a right to contest its decisions.

> ACS: All whose individual autonomy and well-being depend on the collective self-government and flourishing of a polity have a claim to citizenship in that polity.

The fact that these versions of AAI, ASC and ACS are compatible with each other does not mean that there are no conflicts between them. I will conclude section 3 by demonstrating how democratic inclusion norms generate tensions that cannot be resolved through theoretical reflection alone.

The first step follows from the solution of the democratic boundary paradox that I have proposed: in order to provide democratic legitimacy for policies, governments and polities, democratic inclusion must be sequenced. Policies cannot be democratically legitimate if they have not been adopted or supported by a democratically legitimate government. And a democratically legitimate government must in turn have been authorized by an inclusive demos.

In a second step we realize that the combination of the three principles as stated above does not yet provide a full account of the democratic process. The sequence from polity to government to policies reveals significant gaps that have to be filled with partially conflicting interpretations of the three principles. A political community must first constitute itself as a legitimate polity through including all citizenship stakeholders and adopting a constitution under which it can authorize a government through democratic elections before this government can provide equal protection to all subjected to its laws. A government authorized by citizens through democratic elections must also be accountable to those citizens. Moving from ACS to ASC requires, however, constraints on the popular mandate of democratic governments through constitutional and judicial protection of the rights of all subjected to the laws and not only of those citizens who can hold it electorally accountable.

A similar gap emerges in the transition from ASC to AAI. The democratic legitimacy of policy decisions depends on a prior process of debates in a wider public sphere and deliberation in decision-making bodies that track the interests of all who would be affected by the policy options on a political agenda. The institutions of parliamentary democracy and independent courts are generally not sufficient for this task. Yet there is a tension between giving voice to special interests and securing equal protection to all individuals within the jurisdiction. The tension becomes even stronger when the interests of non-citizen non-residents are included who normally do not have either a vote in democratic elections or access to the national courts.

Table 1 presents a more systematic account of the complementarity and tensions between the three inclusion principles. The diagonal in this table shows the specific domains of inclusion to which each of the three principles applies. If we just focus on these cells, then there do not seem to be any conflicts.

When reading the table horizontally, that is, row after row, we see that the three principles not only have different scope but also different capacity to provide legitimacy. Three cells in the upper left corner remain empty. The underlying proposition is that AAI is a single purpose principle, whereas ASC and ACS serve dual and triple purposes respectively. In my view, AAI is uniquely suited to provide legitimacy for policy responses on issues with dispersed and border-crossing impact. For this reason, it has been invoked mostly by theories of global or transnational governance. Yet governance is not the same thing as government. The latter needs stable and bounded jurisdiction, mostly of a territorial kind, and AAI is therefore not capable of providing legitimacy for government. Even

Table 1:   Conditions for democratic legitimacy

Domain / Inclusion	Political communities	Governments	Policies
Affected interests	-----	-----	track and give voice to all affected interests
Subjected to coercion	-----	provide equal protection and opportunities for contestation	track the common good of all subjected to the laws
Citizenship stakeholders	include all citizenship stakeholders	are authorized by and accountable to citizens	track the will of the people

less is it a useful principle for specifying the legitimate boundaries of self-governing political communities.

By contrast, ASC does convey legitimacy to governments if they provide equal protection and opportunities for contestation for all within their jurisdiction. Yet such legitimacy would be rather meaningless if it could not be connected to norms for policy-making. Democratic governments must take decisions that go beyond the task of securing fundamental rights. To gain the kind of legitimacy that I have suggested would also be available to an enlightened autocratic government that is guided by equal concern and respect for all those included in their jurisdiction, and this means pursuing their common good. An ASC conception of democracy can therefore account for the tension between securing rights and promoting the common good that is inherent to liberal democracy and is institutionally articulated through divisions of power and mutual checks and balances between government institutions.

Stakeholder citizenship is the only principle among the three that addresses the membership question independently of a prior account of policy and government legitimacy, which is in my view the condition for resolving the democratic boundary problem. The table suggests also that ACS is the only principle that applies across all three domains by yielding specific conditions for legitimacy of governments and policies: governments are authorized by citizens and therefore accountable to them. Citizens and only citizens have the power to elect and change democratic governments. This implies also a standard for democratic policies: they must not only serve the common good of all who are subjected to the law, but they must also track the will of the people with regard to the law. There is thus again a potential for tension between the interpretations of ACS when applied to the three domains. As discussed in section 3.3, the citizenry and the demos cannot be co-extensive, but exclusions are inherently problematic. After overcoming formal exclusions on grounds of gender, race, religion and class, those remaining focus on cognitive capacity and desert (when criminal offenders are disenfranchised) and they remain problematic, even regarding age, for which thresholds and alternative modes of participation continue to be contested. Another potential tension exists between tracking the will of the people, which is required under the collective self-government aspect of ACS, and the inclusion of all citizenship stakeholders, which is required under the individual autonomy and well-being aspect. Inclusion of all stakeholders and exclusion of non-stakeholders must be translated into admission policies that are among the most hotly contested political issues in contemporary democracies.

Reading the table horizontally, the incompleteness of AAI and ASC and the inherent tensions within ASC and ACS suggest that we indeed cannot accept any of the three principles as a free-standing and full account of democratic legitimacy. Instead, we must try to combine them, which means reading the table vertically, that is, column after column. Yet doing so reveals even more tensions.

Since ACS is the only relevant principle for determining membership, interpretations of AAI that call for including as citizens all whose interests are affected by policy decisions should be firmly rejected. The case of membership inclusion on the basis of ASC is stronger, but subjection to the laws is neither a necessary nor a sufficient condition for citizenship claims in contexts such as colonial and minority oppression. And whenever it is sufficient, as it is in the case of long-term resident immigrants, the normative case for inclusion as an individual option rather than a duty can be stated better on grounds of stakeholdership.

While the absence of plausible alternative answers to the membership question means that there are no tensions in the first row of the table, there are significant ones in rows 2 and 3. A democratic government must show equal respect and concern for all within its jurisdiction, but its democratic mandate is derived from those who are citizens of the polity. Under which conditions is there no discrepancy between the answers to the two corresponding questions: Whose fundamental rights must a democratic government protect? To whom must democratic governments be accountable? First, if there is no migration between societies and, second, if citizenship is residence-based, as I claim it ought to be in municipalities. Under either of these two conditions, the answer to both questions will be: all persons residing in the jurisdiction. If in static societies all residents and only residents are citizens, this cannot determine the citizenship status and claims of immigrants and emigrants in relatively sedentary societies exposed to significant migration flows. The second condition needs some broader normative reflection that I will present in section 4 of this essay. Why should voting rights and thus membership in the demos not be derived from residence in all polities that experience significant migration across their borders? My answer will be that principles for determining citizenship and the franchise vary with the nature of the political community and that the conditions that make it appropriate for local citizenship to be based on residence are absent in the international state system.

Table 1 indicates the greatest potential for tensions in the domain of democratic policy decisions. Tracking all affected interests will often conflict with giving priority to the common good of all included in the jurisdiction. And the common good of all may conflict in turn with the will of the people as expressed through democratic procedures. These tensions cannot be simply resolved through theoretical fiat by giving priority to one or the other inclusion principle. They must instead be worked through in democratic processes of contestation and deliberation within each polity and "democratic iterations" (Benhabib 2004) across the plurality of polities. With regard to policies that aim at securing fundamental rights and protecting interests of those inside or outside the jurisdiction, the will of the people must sometimes be bound through constitutional guarantees that cannot be overruled by popular mandate (i.e. through referendum or ordinary parliamentary legislation). Yet constitutional constraints on the popular will must ultimately be accepted by the people as expressing its constitutional identity and thus its higher order will to protect such rights and include such interests (Tully 2002). In other words, resolving the tensions will only be possible if a democratic people is capable of integrating the interests of externally affected outsiders and of non-citizens subjected to its laws into its own political will.

The outcome of these reflections is not a simple and elegant theory of democratic legitimacy and inclusion. My attempted synthesis has not revealed a meta-principle from which all three inclusion principles could be derived. But this does not mean that the attempt has failed. We can read the result of this analysis in a different way: a normatively attractive conception of democracy must be pluralistic not only in the two senses that I have initially suggested but in a third sense as well. In section 2 I proposed that democracy presupposes an internal diversity of interests, ideas and identities as well as an environment populated by a plurality of bounded democratic polities. We can now add that democracies ought to accept also a plurality of inclusion principles that apply in different ways to their policies, governments and political communities. The task of political theory is to articulate the tensions between these principles rather than to resolve them. The task of coping with them in real-world contexts is a practical one. It needs to be addressed through intelligent institutional design and prudent political action.

4. Constellations and membership character of polities

Normative theories of political boundaries often lead to prescriptions that jar with our well-considered moral and political intuitions. In some cases, such as Goodin's argument that only a global demos can be legitimate (Goodin 2007), these conclusions follow from applying the wrong inclusion principles to the membership domain. In other cases, such as de Schutter's and Ypi's defence of mandatory naturalization of immigrants (de Schutter and Ypi 2015), they follow also from considering democratic polities in isolation from each other and paying insufficient attention to specific contexts.

Our discussion of democratic inclusion principles has so far been rather abstract in the sense of being decontextualized. The circumstances and territorial contexts of democracy that I outlined in section 2 apply to all contemporary democracies. None of the current politically contested boundary issues I listed in the introduction can be properly addressed as long as we stay at this level of generality and do not pay closer attention to contexts.

In this essay, I refrain from discussing particular cases, except by way of illustrating more general problems. What I try instead is to theorize contexts by proposing a general typology of political communities and relations between them. The basic intuition behind this move is that norms of inclusion across political boundaries must be specified for *constellations* of polities (Bauböck 2010) rather than for a single polity considered in isolation. This follows from my initial assumption that the coexistence of a plurality of bounded polities forms the background that makes democratic inclusion both possible and necessary. In other words, a theory of democratic inclusion must always account for the presence of other polities, in which those whose inclusion claims are considered may have been previously members, may become future members or may have simultaneous membership claims.

A second consideration is that the constellation that we call the international state system is a historically very peculiar context and even today not the only relevant one for democratic inclusion claims. As a normative background structure for membership claims, the contemporary international state system is characterized by non-overlapping territorial jurisdictions, the absence of any inhabitable terra nullius and legal equality between independent states. There are other constellations characterized by vertically nested polities that are neither independent of each other nor necessarily equal among each other in their legal status and powers of self-government (Bauböck 2006). I will briefly discuss the general properties of such constellations in the next section before considering how inclusion norms apply in such contexts.

My discussion will from now on focus on membership inclusion, setting aside the important task of further specifying contexts of application for the AAI and ASC principles.[34] The two aspects of my general definition of stakeholder citizenship give rise to two questions that can guide us when considering how to apply it to laws and policies in real-world contexts:

1. Why and how do the autonomy and well-being of an individual or group depend on collective self-government and flourishing of a particular political community, given the way the latter is embedded in a larger constellation of polities?
2. What are the conditions under which a particular polity embedded in a constellation can become or remain self-governing without encroaching on equally legitimate self-government claims of other political communities, and what norms of membership inclusion correspond to the purpose of self-government under these conditions?

---

[34] Among others, this would involve considering how those affected by decisions taken by non-state polities (such as municipalities, regional governments, territorial autonomies, supranational polities like the EU or global governance institutions) can be included in the relevant discursive publics and what protection and contestation rights such governments have to grant those whom they subject to their authority.

4.1   Multilevel democracy

In contemporary democratic states there is a strong tendency to introduce or to strengthen the powers of existing levels of government below the national one and a weak tendency to create new institutions for joint government at a supranational level. These historical trends add vertical depth to the dominant global structure of the international state system described above. Instead of a two-dimensional political map of the world, the global constellation of democratic polities can be visualized as a three-dimensional image with a dominant flat horizon formed by sovereign states, a few hills where supranational polities are erected on a terrain encompassing several member states, and a deep structure of territorial subdivisions of states in the foreground.

Normative theories of democratic inclusion have been mostly written from a single-polity perspective. They consider how individuals relate to a political community or authority that is the addressee of an inclusion claim and they treat polities as if they were all separate from each other and similar to each other. This approach reflects a methodological statism that assumes the international state system as a quasi-natural background. Even for an analysis of inclusion claims in democratic states, a single-polity perspective is flawed because it fails to consider how such claims emerge only once individuals are involved in relations with several states (e.g. through migration or a history of shifting borders). A normative theory of citizenship in the international state system must therefore distribute inclusion responsibilities between states and appropriate norms will generally depend both on the relation of individuals to states and of states to each other.

The flaws of a single-polity perspective become even more obvious once we consider inclusion claims in substate polities (self-governing regions or municipalities) and suprastate polities (unions of states) (Maas 2013). Insofar as these substate and suprastate polities are governed democratically, they must determine who their citizens are just as states have to do. Yet they clearly cannot do so without regard for the membership norms of the states in which they are embedded or of which they are composed. I cannot make sense of claims to inclusion in the city of Florence, the region of Tuscany or the European Union without describing first the different nature of these polities and their relations with the Italian state.

The relations that I will consider are those of states to other states, and those of municipalities, substate regions and unions of states to their "parent states". There are other constellations that could be added, such as those connecting transborder regions or global cities. These are more complex since they involve several states as well as several substate polities. I will leave them aside in this short general discussion.

Those who support democracy because of its unique ability to legitimize political authority should not merely welcome its horizontal spread through democratic transition and consolidation in previously non-democratic states, but also its vertical deepening through democratization of substate and suprastate polities. The traditional argument in favour of multilevel government is subsidiarity, a principle that has its origin in nineteenth-century Catholic social doctrine but has now been enshrined also in the European Union Treaties (TEU Article 5). Subsidiarity is generally interpreted as requiring that in a system of multilevel government decisions should be taken by the lowest level authority that has the competence to take them and can implement them efficiently. Subsidiarity defined in this way is of limited use for deepening democracy vertically. First, the principle applies to government output rather than to democratic input. Second, it applies within an already established system of multiple tiers of government but does not require that new layers should be created where they are absent. Third, the principle favours decentralization of competences within any hierarchy of government levels independently of the specificity of polities at different levels and of relations between them. Finally, subsidiarity is a rule of priority rather than complementarity, which makes it unfit as a principle for comprehensive inclusion in multilevel democracy. It does not make sense to say that individuals should be included as citizens primarily at the local rather than at the national or European level; they must be included simultaneously in all of these polities, albeit in different ways.

The republican principle of non-domination provides better normative support for the vertical deepening of democracy.[35] This argument relies, first, on the empirical premise that executive government and public administrations are structured territorially so that certain decisions are taken or implemented by local or regional level authorities. The reason for this is that in modern states government tasks are so comprehensive and government control over the population is so pervasive that a completely centralized machinery would be extremely inefficient and would soon crash under its own weight. To put it the other way round: in a libertarian night-watchmen state that only provides internal and external security and that can do so efficiently through centrally organized police and army forces, there would be no strong demand for multilevel democracy.

The next step consists in identifying the risks of domination in a single-layered system of democracy in states with a comprehensive and territorially structured public administration. The first risk is that at substate level local and regional populations would be dominated by national majorities. Since the national regime is democratic, all citizens have equal control over the institutions of national government that are in charge of administrating substate territories. But the populations living there would have just a fraction of that control that is proportional to their share in the national demos. The government of each of these territories would thus be accountable to a much larger demos in which each substate population forms a permanent minority. Substate territorial populations would thus be exposed to arbitrary exercises of power

---

[35] Joseph Lacey (2017: ch. 1) has proposed a "principle of maximum voting opportunities" that goes some way in justifying a demand for multilevel democracy. His idea is that in large scale democratic polities citizens should have multiple opportunities to vote on many different levels in referendums and elections – subject to constraints such as avoiding overburdening citizens or disempowering representative government. While this principle provides stronger support for multilevel democracy than subsidiarity, it does not yet address the specificity of self-government claims at different levels of democratic polities.

on behalf of national majorities, which is exactly what domination means according to neo-Roman republican theory. In order to avoid such domination, territorially devolved executive power and public administration must be put under the control of democratic institutions representing the citizens of these territories. This argument provides not only a reason for preserving local or regional self-government, which often pre-dates the emergence of the modern state, but also for introducing it in unitary and highly centralized states.

My non-domination argument for substate democracy seems to correspond to historical trends. By and large, democratic self-government has become stronger at substate levels. While the strength of regional level self-government varies greatly between federal and unitary states, regional elections and parliaments have become more common even in historically very centralized states, such as France and the Scandinavian countries.[36] There is less variation with regard to local democracy: locally elected mayors and/or assemblies with policy-making powers are a nearly universal feature of consolidated democratic states.

The second risk of domination is much more contextual. Where states have been formed by uniting historically self-governing territories, such as provinces or colonies of empires, or where they include territorially concentrated national and indigenous minorities, substate self-government becomes a constitutive feature of the larger polity. In these contexts, the legitimacy of democratic government at the level of the wider state depends on preserving or introducing territorial autonomy at substate levels, with the consequence that these substate territories have potential claims to independence if their self-government rights are severely and persistently violated (Bauböck 2000; Patten 2014: ch. 7).

---

[36] See Hooghe, Marks and Schakel (2010) for the trend towards strengthening substate regional authorities. Although the European Union is currently still a singular case of a politically integrated union of states with strong legislative powers and a common citizenship, there are directly elected regional parliaments (the Central American Parliament and the Andean Parliament) and supranational free movement agreements in Latin America and other parts of the world (Closa and Vintila 2015).

This risk of domination by national majorities is quite obvious in the case of distinct territorial minorities that lack powers of self-government. In mono-national federations such as Germany or the United States, where regional identities are not in tension with a shared national identity, the risk of domination may be less apparent. Yet a federal demos consists in any case of the citizens of the federation as well as of the citizens of the constitutive territories. The fact that these are identical sets of individuals does not mean that citizens of the federation cannot dominate those of the constitutive territories. If all political decisions were determined exclusively by majorities among citizens of the federation, then the citizens of each constitutive territory (assuming that no single territory has more than 50 per cent of the total citizen population) would be vulnerable to arbitrary exercises of power that fail to respect their constitutional right to self-government. Since federal democracy conceptually implies multilevel government, such a scenario is impossible while upholding a federal constitution. However, we can still consider it relevant for a hypothetical change that would merge constitutive territories, weaken their powers or abolish regional level self-government altogether.[37] Such a decision could not be legitimately taken by a majority of the federal demos or its representatives in a popular chamber of parliament without counting separately the votes of the affected substate territories.

Risks of domination through single level democracy emerge also at the suprastate level. Today's international state system is not a Hobbesian state of nature, but thickly populated with intergovernmental organizations and regulatory regimes. Political decisions taken within these suprastate institutions and legal norms adopted by them are seen to be democratically legitimate if they are non-coercively endorsed by governments that are themselves representative of their citizens. This assumption can be challenged from two sides. One objection is that a

---

[37] This scenario is not entirely fictional. In Austria, reducing the number of federal provinces or abolishing provincial governments altogether has been occasionally advocated for the sake of enhancing government efficiency and reducing the costs of public administration.

strict condition of unanimous consent backed by democratic support for government policies in each participating state turns the demos of each state into a veto player in international governance and prevents thus any effective policy responses to problems affecting large numbers of states. The domination is in this case exercised by individual states blocking intergovernmental policy solutions that are democratically endorsed in most other states. The converse risk is that international regulatory regimes are imposed by individual states or private actors, such as global corporations, wielding superior military or economic power, in such a way that non-compliance or opt-outs are no longer feasible options for states whose citizens prefer alternative policies. Wider forums for democratic participation and deliberation of stakeholders in intergovernmental decision-making (Bohman 2007; Macdonald 2008) provide a plausible response to either risk.

Yet, as I argued in section 3.1, this response should not be confused with the creation of a self-governing demos. A supranational demos can only emerge within a permanent union of states that pool their sovereignty to a significant degree by creating legislative institutions with independent agenda-setting powers and mechanisms for enforcing collectively binding decisions that do not rely exclusively on voluntary compliance by member state governments. Although the EU is still perceived by many observers as an intergovernmental organization, the presence of such powers makes it plausible to characterize it as a supranational polity. Within such a union of states, the risk of domination through intergovernmental unanimity requirements blocking decisions that are democratically widely endorsed and the risk of domination by powers that are able to impose decisions that are democratically not endorsed are similar to those arising in intergovernmental institutions. The response to these risks must be, however, different. It is not sufficient that the supranational government gains its legitimacy from joint legislative powers of democratically legitimate governments and provides other policy stakeholders with access to deliberative arenas and contestation opportunities. It must also derive its own legitimacy directly from the citizens of the union who exercise their powers of self-government not only at state and substate, but also at a suprastate level. There is thus an additional risk of domination within a union of states that is the converse of central governments subverting substate autonomy. If democratic citizenship remains confined to the member states' separate demoi, the citizens of the union will be dominated by the citizens of the member states through the exercise of supranational power that escapes the control of the wider demos of which they are jointly equal members. Consider as an example the abysmal failure of the EU to adopt and implement an appropriate burden-sharing and relocation scheme for refugees during the 2015/16 crisis. This failure was due to the decision of individual member states, with ample support from their voters, to block any such scheme. As a result, most refugees ended up in those states that had kept their borders initially open in 2015 or remained stuck in those countries that were the first points of entry on the refugee migration routes. In other words, the governments and citizens of those states that were not willing to take in refugees imposed on the citizens of the Union a morally arbitrary supranational distribution of responsibilities and burdens.

This argument for the need for democracy in a politically integrated union can be defended on grounds of both the ASC and ACS principles. From the perspective of the former, the difference between intergovernmental organizations and supranational unions is not so obvious and depends merely on the degree of executive or judicial powers to which individuals are collectively subjected. A stakeholder perspective draws a sharper line in requiring that the citizens of the union must be able to see themselves and each other as members of a transgenerational political community whose government institutions have to track the collective will of the citizenry. This more demanding republican conception of democratic community cannot apply to international organizations and many would also contest that it applies to the European Union in its present shape. Yet the Union has already grounded its political legitimacy to a large extent on equal treatment and democratic representation of the citizens of the Union, which is why at least in Europe citizenship above the nation-state is no longer a chimera.

4.2   Birthright citizenship

The principle of including all citizenship stakeholders, which I have defended as the best solution to the democratic boundary problem, assumes a correspondence between individual and collective interests in self-government. It implies therefore the need to consider the conditions under which a polity can be self-governing over time and in relation to other polities. Since polities are of different kinds and involved in different types of relations with other polities, ACS must be further specified when applying it to distinct types of polities. For example, the principle itself does not tell us whether residence in a territorial jurisdiction is a necessary or sufficient condition for holding a stake in its self-government and having therefore a claim to citizenship. I will argue in this and the next two sections that the answer to this question depends on the "membership character" of the polity. We can define the membership character of a democratic polity empirically as a basic rule that determines who holds its citizenship. For independent states this rule is that citizenship is acquired automatically at birth and is presumptively held for the rest of one's life.

I use the expression "membership character" rather than "membership rule" for two reasons. First, membership rules operate at different levels of generality, while the character of a polity refers to its most basic features. Birthright citizenship is the membership character of all independent states, but they differ from each other in their specific mixes of the two birthright rules – by descent (ius sanguinis) or by birth in the territory (ius soli). Moving down the ladder of abstraction, we can next distinguish specific "modes of acquisition" of birthright citizenship, such as ius soli at birth and after birth, or ius sanguinis ex matre and ex patre.[38] Nationality laws contain even more specific rules determining conditions for the application of these modes, such as prior

---

[38]   "Modes of acquisition and loss" is the terminology used by the EUDO CITIZENSHIP observatory for a comparative typology of citizenship law provisions. See http://eudo-citizenship.eu/databases/modes-of-acquisition, accessed 22 May 2017.

legal residence of parents as a condition for ius soli in most European states that apply it to second generation immigrants. Finally, there are rules of implementation that are often spelled out in ministerial decrees or that emerge from observing informal administrative practices. The comparative study of citizenship status is concerned with examining all these types of rules and explaining their variation. A normative theory of democratic inclusion should instead provide a critical standard for assessing such rules against a principle for democratic inclusion, while not being overly prescriptive since democratic legislators must have some leeway to adopt citizenship laws that differ from those of other democracies.

Second, "membership character" suggests that we are concerned here with a constitutive feature of the polity rather than with a rule that it could adopt, abandon or modify. If a state turned automatically all its residents into citizens and deprived all non-residents of their membership, or if it derived its own citizenship from that of a supranational union, it would cease to be recognizable as an independent state. Conversely, if a substate region started to restrict local membership and voting rights to those born in its territory or to descendants of its current citizens and treated the citizens of the larger state as foreigners who have to apply for naturalization, it would in important ways act like a state and signal its desire for independence.

Automatic acquisition linked to circumstances of birth and lifelong retention by default are the core features of birthright citizenship. This does not mean that all birthright modes of acquisition are fully automatic and determine citizenship at birth. For example, children of the second generation born to two foreign parents in France acquire French citizenship through ius soli as an entitlement around the age of majority rather than at birth and they have the right to decline the offer. What it means instead is that, while their rules differ significantly for those born to non-citizen residents or non-resident citizens, all independent states have rules that lead to automatic acquisition at birth for those born to citizen parents residing in their territory. This suggests that the basic function of birthright citizenship is to secure the transgenerational reproduction of a citizenry in a way that involves neither individual nor collective political choice.

Birthright membership also does not mean that citizenship cannot be acquired in other ways. All democratic states have provisions for the naturalization of immigrants. There is a lot of variation with regard to conditions and procedures. A stakeholder criterion provides a clear normative standard for accepting some state practices while rejecting others. From this perspective, long-term resident foreigners are obviously citizenship stakeholders, which makes all criteria apart from residence suspect.[39] Moreover, naturalization should be an entitlement for those who meet the residence condition rather than a discretionary decision by the authorities. Yet the crucial point here is that naturalization is never automatic or mandatory and requires an application by the individual concerned.[40] Ius domicilii is no independent ground for acquiring state citizenship of the same kind as birth in the territory or descent from citizen parents; residence is only sufficient when combined with an expression of will to join the political community.[41] Naturalization therefore does not challenge the membership character of states but affirms it instead: by applying for naturalization, immigrants declare their

---

[39]   See Carens (1989, 2013: ch. 2) for convincing arguments why even language or criminal record tests are suspect.

[40]   Automatic naturalization based on ius domicilii was not uncommon in empires. In the Austrian monarchy, foreigners were automatically naturalized without their consent after ten years of residence until 1833, when this practice was abandoned because of diplomatic protests by countries of origin (Bauböck and Çınar 2001).

[41]   There are two exceptions that confirm this rule. The first is the determination of citizenship in state succession. Ius domicilii is the dominant rule for attribution of citizenship in newly formed states, accompanied by option rights for individuals who have strong links to several states emerging from secession or break-up. Automatic attribution occurs thus at the birth of individuals as well as at the birth of states, and residence at the time of independence is the default criterion of attribution in the latter case. The second exception is individual statelessness, which is a condition of profound vulnerability that justifies not only the condition that voluntary renunciation is not permitted if the person does not hold or get immediate access to another nationality but could, in my view, also justify an automatic rather than optional naturalization of stateless persons in their country of long-term residence. Automatic ius domicilii substitutes thus for birthright only where the transgenerational continuity of citizenries is interrupted through shifting borders or the exclusion of individuals from membership in the international state system.

intention to join a political community based on birthright. Whether this application requirement can be justified depends on the legitimacy of birthright from a stakeholder perspective, which I will defend below. Finally, presumptively lifelong citizenship does not mean that birthright citizenship cannot be lost. All democratic states have rules for voluntary renunciation of their citizenship and most also have rules for involuntary deprivation. Renunciation is in a way the converse of a naturalization entitlement: the right to change one's citizenship status is in both cases held by the individual and exercised through an application or declaration. While those who naturalize normally reside in the territory, those who may renounce normally have to reside abroad. Both naturalization and renunciation also involve a relation of the individual to another state; in the former case a foreign national becomes a citizen, in the latter a citizen becomes a foreign national.

Unlike voluntary naturalization and renunciation, involuntary deprivation is hard to reconcile with a birthright conception of citizenship under which the citizenry reproduces itself automatically across generations and under which naturalization attributes to new citizens the same lifelong membership as to those who acquired the status at birth. Why should states have the power to take away what they do not have the power to grant or withhold? The grounds of deprivation that can be found in nationality laws are many and they rely on distinct reasons. We may group them into five: (1) reasons related to public security concerns (e.g. treason and other forms of disloyalty or crimes against the state, military or other service for a foreign state); (2) non-compliance with conditions for retention of citizenship (e.g. a requirement to renounce a foreign citizenship); (3) flawed acquisition of citizenship (through individual fraud or administrative error or abuse); (4) derivative loss (e.g. in case of loss of citizenship by a spouse or parent); and (5) loss of genuine link (e.g. long-term residence abroad or acquisition of a foreign citizenship). Bauböck and Paskalev (2015) claim that only revocation in case of fraudulent acquisition is clearly compatible with the integrity of the birthright citizenship regime and even this ground of loss must be qualified by the avoidance of statelessness and a statute of limitation that takes into account the time of residence and of holding citizenship status. It may seem paradoxical to claim that from a citizenship stakeholder perspective even deprivation on grounds of loss of genuine link is highly suspect, but this follows from the assumption that the genuine link is one to a birthright-based polity. Long-term residence abroad or acquisition of a foreign nationality is not a sufficient indicator for a loss of genuine link if there is a presumption of lifelong membership and the individual has not herself declared the intention to renounce her status.

At the beginning of this section, I stated that birthright is the empirical core of the membership character of independent states. I have now suggested a normative argument that the integrity of birthright citizenship should also be defended against states' powers of deprivation. This leap from empirical to normative reasoning still needs to be backed by an ethical defence of birthright that I will outline below. Yet first I need to make clear that birthright is not itself a normative principle whose application guarantees that citizenship is allocated fairly. Depending on the specific modes of acquisition, birthright can be either severely exclusionary or over-inclusive. In other words, I am suggesting that birthright is generally compatible with a citizenship stakeholder principle and without alternative for state-based polities, but that specific birthright regimes and rules must always be assessed by using this principle as a critical yardstick.

The exclusionary nature of purely ius sanguinis-based regimes, which are still prevalent in continental Europe, has been highlighted in the critical and normative literature on immigrant integration (see Dumbrava 2014). It is indeed unjustifiable that the children of immigrants who are born and raised in the territory are treated as newcomers who have to apply for naturalization in order to become full citizens. This birthright deficit can be overcome by combining ius sanguinis with ius soli. What is less commonly pointed out is that pure ius soli regimes, which are prevalent in the Americas, are similarly exclusionary with regard to the so-called generation 1.5, that is, those who immigrate after birth as minor children.[42] There is no justification for asking residents who have spent their childhood and school years in the country to wait until the age of majority before they can become citizens. The solution is in this case an inclusive naturalization regime that drops age and other requirements that cannot be defended from a stakeholder perspective. Sweden, for example, applies ius soli only to foundlings and otherwise stateless children, but the parents or guardians of minor children who have spent three years in the country can get them Swedish citizenship by a simple declaration.

Ius sanguinis is also rightly criticized for being over-inclusive if it is stretched beyond the second generation born abroad. It is obvious that third generation emigrants will generally not have a sufficiently strong stake in a grandparent's country of origin to claim citizenship, unless their parents have themselves renewed their links to this country through taking up residence there. In the case of second generation return (King and Olsson 2014), the next generation of children born abroad are again second generation emigrants and qualify for citizenship based on their ties to parents who are themselves strongly linked to the country awarding the status. It is more consistent with the birthright character of national citizenship to let it expire for the distant descendants of emigrants through non-acquisition at birth instead of depriving first or second generation holders of this status on grounds of long-term residence abroad and acquisition of a foreign citizenship. It seems, however, reasonable to exclude second generation emigrants who have never resided in the country from voting rights, even if they retain a lifelong citizenship status. Since voting rights are anyhow not acquired at birth but only around the age of majority, the concern about over-inclusiveness of an external franchise can be easily taken

---

[42] Pure ius soli regimes would also exclude the children of first generation emigrants born abroad. This is, however, rarely the case because practically all states apply some version of ius sanguinis to this group. Some American ius soli countries do, however, treat them as a separate category of citizens with fewer rights and a more insecure status compared with those born in the territory.

into account by tying the external franchise to a condition of prior long-term residence in the country;[43] this would include not only first generation emigrants but also second generation returnees, while the children of emigrants who have never resided in the country would never acquire the franchise instead of being deprived of a birthright status.

The potential over-inclusiveness of ius soli is more often articulated by critics who worry about "birthright tourism" and "anchor babies" in countries with unconditional territorial birthright. The anti-immigration slant of this critique, which focuses on the potential for individual abuse, should not detract from its substantively sound core. In a society exposed to significant transborder mobility, the mere fact of territorial birth alone should not be sufficient for the acquisition of lifelong membership, since this would generate a distribution of the privileges and burdens of citizenship that cannot be justified from a stakeholder perspective. Why should children who were born accidentally or intentionally in a country where their parents have no claim to membership be awarded with unconditional immigration rights denied to others who grow up under otherwise comparable circumstances? Unconditional ius soli can also be over-inclusive with regard to citizenship duties, such as a military draft, imposed on individuals who have no genuine link to the country they are supposed to defend at the risk of their lives.

Many authors have used the prevalence of ius sanguinis or ius soli in a citizenship law as an indicator for the ethnic or civic character of a nation (e.g. Brubaker 1990; Koopmans et al. 2005). This is historically dubious (Panagiotidis 2015) and empirically implausible. As demonstrated by countries like Sweden, ius sanguinis regimes are compatible with inclusive naturalization, which means that the next generation of Swedish citizens by descent will be as ethnically diverse as its general population.

---

[43] Swedish practice again provides a good example: citizens residing permanently abroad are automatically registered for European and national elections if they have ever been domiciled in Sweden. Registration needs to be renewed every ten years (Bernitz 2013).

It is true that ethno-nationalist governments have abused the idea of descent-based membership as a pretext for claiming influence over foreign territories inhabited by their ethnic kin minorities. But it is equally true that strong ius soli conceptions have provided pretexts for denying internal self-government rights of ethnic minorities or relegating naturalized immigrants to a second class citizenship status that denies them full political rights or provides them with less protection against deprivation.[44]

Finally, an especially problematic form of over-inclusion emerges in regimes that do not allow for voluntary renunciation of citizenship. This is the case in most Arab states, whose nationality laws are based on ius sanguinis (Parolin 2009), but also in a significant number of Latin American states where ius soli is especially strong. The old notion of a duty of "perpetual allegiance" is an illiberal perversion of presumptively lifelong citizenship that denies that individuals' citizenship stakes can change over the course of their lives when they develop new ties to other polities.

The upshot of this brief discussion is that unjust exclusion and over-inclusiveness are not inherent features of birthright citizenship, but the result of lopsided laws that do not combine ius soli and ius sanguinis in a balanced way or fail to provide fair opportunities for naturalization and renunciation.

Having defended the compatibility of birthright citizenship with stakeholder inclusion, I shall now consider why independent states rely predominantly on birthright for determining their citizens and whether they are ethically justified in doing so.

Birthright citizenship serves ethical purposes that alternative rules for determining membership would either be unable to meet or not fulfil equally well. In the international state system, it minimizes stateless-ness and assigns to states stable responsibilities for particular individuals.

---

[44] This is still the case in many Latin American states. Article 2 of the U.S. Constitution, requiring that candidates for the office of president or vice-president must be "natural born citizens", is a residue of this tradition and emerged from a concern to prevent foreign influence over the highest executive offices.

Birthright contributes, first, to the prevention of statelessness through the relative administrative ease of determining birthplace or descent and the automaticity of awarding citizenship when these criteria are met. Second, states have a duty under international law to readmit their own nationals, and birthright citizenship makes it more difficult for them to shun this duty. If state citizenship were instead grounded on residence or consent, states could much more easily dump their unwanted citizens on other states by forcing them into exile and depriving them of their membership status.

From a domestic political perspective, birthright citizenship serves to promote a sense of transgenerational continuity of the polity among its citizens and reduces the risk of political conflicts over membership boundaries. First, if citizens see each other as members in a transgenerational political community they are more likely to adopt a long-term orientation towards the common good and to include the interests of future generations of citizens in their policy preferences. Second, birthright citizenship depoliticizes the determination of membership and turns it into a quasi-natural social fact. It constrains opportunities for rulers to manipulate citizenship by excluding adversaries and handing out membership as a special favour to loyal supporters. Birthright citizenship prevents also that the basic composition of the citizenry is exposed to the preferences of democratic majorities. Full and equal membership of territorial or ethnic minorities is not open to question if their members are citizens by birth.

From an individual perspective, finally, birthright provides minor children with guaranteed access to a secure legal status. Ius sanguinis ensures, moreover, that they share their parents' citizenship, which prevents families being torn apart should parents and children have different migration and residence entitlements. Lifelong citizenship status acquired at birth also ensures that children's citizenship is not affected by the death or divorce of their parents.

These arguments strengthen the ethical case for birthright citizenship given the nature of states and the basic structure of the international state system. But they do not yet address the more fundamental moral question of whether a person's circumstances of birth should determine her membership in a political community and the specific benefits and burdens that result from such membership.[45]

Liberals often point out that circumstances of birth are contingent facts that should not impact on a person's opportunities and rights. The first thing to note about this critique is that, from a first person perspective, where and to whom one is born are not at all contingent facts. They are instead unchosen and fundamental features of a person's identity. The normative question is whether it is morally arbitrary to use these facts as criteria for determining membership in a political community. The charge of moral arbitrariness relies on two claims: (1) newborn babies are not responsible for the circumstances of their birth and thus cannot have deserved to be born as citizens of one state rather than another; and (2) citizenship in different states entails unequal opportunities and rights.

The first of these claims relies on the premise that desert is a relevant criterion for the allocation of citizenship. This premise is not only incompatible with the citizenship stakeholder principle that I have defended, but it would also fatally undermine any conception of citizenship as an equal status in a territorially inclusive political community. The second claim is empirically undisputable and morally indeed troubling. However, once it is separated from the first claim, it becomes clear that the target of critique cannot be the automatic attribution of citizenship based on circumstances of birth. The target must instead be the inequality of opportunities and rights that different states offer to their citizens.

Inequality between states can originate from political decisions taken by legitimate governments authorized by their citizens, in which case

---

[45] See Shachar (2009) and my review of her critique of birthright citizenship in Bauböck (2011a).

it is unobjectionable from a pluralist democratic perspective. Or it can emerge from unequal natural and social resources (including historical conditions) for which current citizens and governments cannot be held responsible. Finally, it can result from inter-state or global forms of domination for which other states can be held responsible. Liberal theories of global justice will differ in their attitudes towards the second source of inequality, but ought to agree that the first source is normatively unproblematic while the third gives rise to claims for redistribution or redress. I do not have to enter here the vast literature on global social justice, since the conclusion for our present concern is straightforward: inequalities of rights and opportunities for the citizens of different states have to be addressed independently of whether or not citizenship is determined by birthright.

Joseph Carens's famous argument that, from a global perspective, birthright citizenship is like a feudal status (Carens 1987, 2013) relies on an additional empirical premise: states control immigration and preserve global inequality by preventing the citizens of poor countries from seeking better opportunities in wealthy ones. This argument raises several new questions:[46] Is immigration control an inherent feature of states or can we imagine a world of states with open borders and birthright citizenship? As I will argue below, this is not a fanciful idea if we consider freedom of movement and open borders in the current European Union, whose member states are also full members of the international state system and whose citizenship is still based on birthright. Would open borders between states be an adequate remedy for inter-state inequalities of the second and third kind? While dismantling migration restrictions is likely to contribute to reducing global inequality indirectly it is probably a very ineffective remedy for the misery of the globally worst off populations who lack the social and economic resources needed for migration to wealthy destinations.

I will further explore the link between citizenship and free movement in the following sections. For now, my conclusion is that birthright is

---

[46] See my review of Carens (2013) in Bauböck (2015a).

an implausible culprit for those injustices that liberal egalitarians rightly worry about.

4.3 Residential citizenship

The birthright regime that characterizes contemporary states has its historical origin in the city. A democratic conception of citizenship as membership in a self-governing political community originated in the Greek and Roman city republics and was later revived in the late medieval and early modern free cities of northern Italy, Germany and the Netherlands. These cities' membership regimes resembled in many ways those of modern states: they had fortified borders and gates for controlling immigration, and the status of a citizen or free burgher was generally acquired through birthright or naturalization. By contrast, the borders of the empires within which most of these city states flourished were loosely controlled and frequently shifting frontiers rather than stable demarcations of jurisdiction. Empires did not have citizens but turned everyone inside their territory into subjects, while they had little leverage over those who had left and were thus often more concerned about controlling emigration than immigration.

Of course this description of boundary structures does not do justice to the endless historical varieties of city polities and empires. I use it here only to provide a contrast that helps to sharpen our perception of the historically contingent and quite exceptional nature of membership boundaries in our current world. My point is that the boundary constellation that once related free cities to empires has been turned inside out in creating the contemporary boundary constellation of democratic states and their self-governing municipalities. Today birthright citizenship is a universal and nearly unique characteristic of independent states, while open borders and residence-based membership form the boundary conditions for local self-government.

This historic reversal has come about through what the British sociologist T.H. Marshall described as the "geographic fusion" and "functional differentiation" of citizenship (Marshall 1949/1965: 79). As long as citizenship was primarily local, cities were in control of settlement in their jurisdiction, and the institutions providing for justice, political representation and social welfare of urban citizens were hardly differentiated. The economic and political transformations that gave birth to the modern capitalist economy and nation-state tore down the city walls, dismantled the local welfare regimes and established uniform civil, political and social citizenship rights at the national level provided through the separate institutions of courts, parliaments and public administrations.

Yet local citizenship did not vanish completely. As I pointed out in section 4.1, local democracy is a universal feature of democratic states. Where local councils or mayors are elected and where referendums on local policies are held, there must be a corresponding demos of citizens eligible to participate in these elections. Using this empirical test, we would arrive at the conclusion that the local citizenry is determined differently across contemporary democratic states. In most, the franchise in local elections combines the conditions of residence in the municipality with that of nationality of the encompassing state. However, this rule is not applied consistently. Under EU law, local voting rights (but not the franchise in regional or national elections) are also awarded to the nationals of other member states residing in the municipality. Portugal and Spain grant local voting rights to specific other countries on the basis of reciprocity. In the UK, these are extended to Irish and Commonwealth citizens (with no reciprocity in the latter case). Most significantly, twelve EU countries, as well as Norway, Iceland and several Swiss cantons, plus a significant number of Latin American states, disconnect the local franchise from nationality altogether.[47] While these empirical observations are not conclusive for a residence-based normative conception of local citizenship, they demonstrate its empirical compatibility with a birthright-based conception of national citizenship.

---

[47] There are only very few democratic states that grant also national voting rights to all non-citizens meeting certain residence requirements. The most inclusive franchise of this kind exists in New Zealand.

The normative argument can rely on three features of local self-government in democratic states that are relevant to its membership character. First, the competences of municipalities are limited to providing public goods and services for local residents, whereas independent states perform the additional task of representing their citizens towards other states. Unlike states, municipalities do not have extraterritorial personal jurisdiction. Local voting rights are therefore very rarely extended to former residents.[48] Generally, only residents thus form the local citizenry. This does not mean that local policies are necessarily territorially confined. Towns engage frequently in twinning projects across borders, and the governments of global cities are important players in transnational issues such as trade and finance, migration and environmental policies. City governments often borrow policies from cities in other countries and deliberative bodies of city legislators and executives could work out solutions to some global problems upon which states are unable to agree (Barber 2013). Unlike federal provinces striving to enhance their autonomy, cities disconnect from the international state system when propelling their soft power across borders. In Warren Magnusson's (2011) words "seeing like a city" means considering public policy issues from a non-sovereignty perspective.

Second, the right of free movement inside a state territory is not a privilege of national citizens, but has been codified as an international human right.[49] Not only national citizens have an unconditional right to establish residence in a municipality, but also non-citizens who have been admitted to legal residence in the state territory. From the perspective of

---

[48] In Europe only Norway grants extraterritorial local voting rights to citizens residing abroad. Italy and Ireland allow non-residents to participate in local elections but only through in-country voting. See http://eudo-citizenship.eu/electoral-rights/comparing-electoral-rights, accessed 22 May 2017.

[49] Universal Declaration of Human Rights, Article 13 (1); International Covenant on Civil and Political Rights, Article 12 (1). In Joseph Carens's view, the establishment of free movement inside a state territory provides a "cantilever argument" for international free movement. Carens claims that "treating the freedom of movement across state borders as a human right is a logical extension of the well-established democratic practice of treating freedom of movement within state borders as a human right" (2013: 237). The extension is, however, not a logical one once we consider municipalities and states as polities of different kinds with distinct membership characteristics.

municipalities that provide public services to their resident population, distinctions between those born in the city, newcomers who are nationals of the state and others who are foreign nationals are arbitrary since they cannot be grounded in any democratically legitimate purpose of municipal self-government. If this is true for policy output legitimacy, there is a prima facie case that all residents ought to be treated equally also with regard to democratic input. The local citizenry should therefore exclude non-residents and include all residents.

Third, the case for shifting from a birthright-based to a residence-based conception becomes stronger the more mobile and the less sedentary is the society within the territorial jurisdiction. By creating open internal borders inside their territorial jurisdiction, states expose local municipalities to much more mobility than they are themselves exposed to. As I explained in section 2.2, cross-border migration increases as the scale of territory shrinks. Paradoxically, it is thus the dominance of birthright-based polities over other self-governing polities inside their territory that leads to the emergence of a space for an alternative residence-based citizenship at the local level.

These three reasons are supportive but not yet decisive for my normative claim, since similar arguments could be made about counties, provinces, regions and other kinds of substate territories. The fourth reason is that citizenship should be based on residence in all substate territories that are self-governing and not involved in a constitutive relationship with the encompassing state polity. I will examine citizenship in constitutive territories in section 4.3. My argument there is that in constitutive relations between polities (such as between a federal province and the federal state or between a member state and a supranational union of states), citizenship ought to be derivative, so that all citizens of the constitutive territory are also citizens of the encompassing polity. By contrast, where substate territories are not involved in a federal relation with the state, there is no plausible reason for linking citizenships between the two levels. Doing so imposes a state-based conception of citizenship on polities that are neither states nor involved in constitutive relations with states that secure their political autonomy. In current democratic countries, municipalities are too often regarded as "creatures" of the state (or – as in the U.S. – of the several states of the federation). This constitutional doctrine allows higher level polities not only to dictate the laws for the local franchise, but also to change the borders of local jurisdictions or to dismantle them altogether. As I suggested in section 4.1, the absence of local levels of self-government amounts to a structural domination of local by state citizens. This is also true if local self-government is a dependent creature of the state.

The constitutional doctrine of the "homogenous people" invoked by the German and Austrian Constitutional Courts when striking down local voting rights for non-citizens ought to be rejected for the same reason.[50] The German court claimed that the German people must be identical across all levels of the German polity and therefore cannot include foreign nationals at the local level who are excluded from the franchise in national elections. The Austrian court referred to Article 1 of the Federal Constitution that proclaims that the law emanates from the people and concluded that the people must be defined as all those possessing Austrian nationality. This notion of a homogenous franchise in all elections is anyhow incompatible with membership in the European Union, which implies voting rights for non-national EU citizens in local and European Parliament elections.

While the fourth reason provides a decisive argument for rejecting a state-imposed condition of national citizenship for local voting rights, the three other reasons explain why the normative conception of local citizenship should be based on residence rather than local birthright or local self-determination. The former option would undo the geographic fusion from which national citizenship had emerged. But why should municipalities not be able to decide for themselves whether they include only resident national citizens or also non-national residents? The reason is the same as that which led us to reject democratic self-determination with regard to inclusion at the national level. Each type of polity has

---

[50] For Germany: BVerfG 83, 37, 30 October 1990, BVerfG 83, 60, 30 October 1990; for Austria: VfGH G 218/03–16, 30 June 2004.

to rely on a basic membership rule that must not be exposed to the political will of its demos because the rule is what constitutes its legitimate demos in the first place.[51]

I conclude that for non-constitutive but self-governing substate polities, the only normatively defensible rule is to consider all residents and only residents as citizenship stakeholders. This argument does not apply specifically to cities. There are, after all, independent city states, such as Singapore, and federal city provinces, such as Berlin, Hamburg, Bremen and Vienna.[52] And it does not apply to any administrative substate territory where there are no local governments accountable to local citizens. The argument is therefore not so much about cities and municipalities as a specific type of polity, but about the need for spaces of residence-based citizenship inside the territory of democratic states. In democratic states, citizenship should not be based on birthright or derived from birthright citizenship all the way down. Residence-based citizenship creates an alternative space for democratic self-government in which all those who live together in a territory at a certain point in time can see each other as political equals.

4.4 Derivative citizenship

I have so far discussed two polity constellations – states in relation to other states and states in relation to substate non-constitutive polities, such as municipalities, – and I have defended birthright citizenship for the former and residence-based citizenship for the latter. There is a third polity constellation that puts states in constitutive relations to

---

[51] Local self-determination should not be constrained in order to secure state dominance over local self-government but only for the sake of realizing a normatively attractive conception of local citizenship. This goal can be achieved either by national legislation prescribing a residence-based franchise in local elections (as is the case in twelve EU states) or by a national constitution that permits municipalities or regions to introduce such a franchise (as is the case in Switzerland).

[52] In Berlin, Hamburg, Bremen and Vienna EU citizens are excluded from voting for local legislative assemblies since these function simultaneously as provincial legislatures.

regional polities at substate or suprastate levels. Citizenship in such regional polities is derivative of state citizenship. This is their basic membership character.

What I mean by derivation is a linkage between two polities through which those who are citizens of one are automatically also recognized as citizens of the other. In nested two-level polities derivation can be either downwards or upwards. In the former case, the citizenship of the encompassing polity determines that of the constituent entities; in the latter case, it is the other way round. Contemporary federal states are nearly universally characterized by downward derivation. The regional polities have no autonomous rule for determining their citizenship. The Fourteenth Amendment of the U.S. Constitution provides the general formula: "All persons born or naturalized in the United States, and subject to the jurisdiction thereof, are citizens of the United States and of the State wherein they reside."

In confederations or unions of states, derivation is instead upwards. As already mentioned, Switzerland seems to be the only contemporary state where federal citizenship is formally derived from that of the cantons. Upward derivation is, however, the basic membership characteristic of the European Union (as well as of more rudimentary forms of supranational citizenship in Latin America): "Every national of a Member State shall be a citizen of the Union. Citizenship of the Union shall be additional to and not replace national citizenship" (TEU, Article 9).

Since the polities involved in a federal relation are not identical, derivation must be complemented with an activation rule that ensures a smooth uptake of citizenship by those who move across internal borders. This rule can only be based on residence, no matter whether derivation is downwards or upwards. Imagine that the Fourteenth Amendment had declared persons born in the U.S. to be citizens of the United States and of the State wherein they *have been born*. A citizen born in New Jersey who resides now in California would then remain subject to the laws of New Jersey where she could also vote in State elections, whereas in California she would be eligible only for federal citizenship protection and benefits. New Jersey and California would then relate to each other as foreign countries that have signed an international agreement providing for a common floor of rights enforced by a government in Washington, D.C.

In the EU, the situation is different since the citizenship that is activated through taking up residence in another member state is not the national one of that state, but the European one itself. All nationals of member states are formally citizens of the EU, no matter where they reside, but most of the specific rights and protections provided by EU citizenship kick in when EU nationals are involved in "cross-border situations", which include internal migration to another member state or just having family members or conducting business there. We can again imagine a counterfactual scenario in which member state nationals would automatically acquire the citizenship of another member state where they take up residence. This would reverse the direction of derivation and transform the EU from a union of states into a federal state.

Federal states and supranational unions are thus structurally similar, since in both cases the "source citizenship" is that of an independent state and the derivative citizenship is activated through internal mobility, while the source citizenship remains unaffected (Jackson 2001). This similarity is also suggested by the very term "region" that applies both to substate political territories and to unions of states. Although in the European polity there are four levels of citizenship (local, substate regional, state and supranational), there are only three distinct polity constellations and corresponding membership rules (birthright, residence-based and derivative). In section 4.3 I described how the modern relation between states and self-governing local polities has emerged from turning the previous constellation of free cities in empires inside out. We can now add to this the further observation that supranational regional citizenship also looks like substate regional citizenship turned inside out, with the important difference that there is no historical transition from one to the other, but their simultaneous presence in the same European polity.

The term "region" is, however, unspecific insofar as it does not entail a self-governing polity with its own citizenship. Most unions of states, such as the African Union or the Association of Southeast Asian Nations, are better described as regional international organizations rather than as supranational regional polities. Some regions group together territories on either side of international borders that share cultural similarities or economic resources. In a few cases, such cross-border regions have established consultative political bodies in which delegates of provincial governments or parliaments deliberate about cooperation. Yet such cross-border regions cannot become polities in their own right without challenging the territorial integrity of states in which they are embedded. A third type of region that is not a polity is exemplified by administrative subdivisions somewhere between the local and the national level, such as the French *départements* or the British counties. Regional self-government at substate as well as suprastate level is a matter of degree. It exists without doubt in all genuinely federal constitutions as well as in the European Union. In unitary states, such as France or the Scandinavian countries, there are often elected regional assemblies and thus also a form of regional citizenship. Yet in these constitutions regional self-government is not qualitatively different from local self-government. As I have already suggested in the previous section, the determination of membership should then be based on residence rather than derivation. This is what we find indeed in Denmark, Sweden and Slovakia, where third country nationals can vote in both local and regional elections (Arrighi et al. 2013).

What I am concerned with here is not a typology of regional self-government (see Hooghe, Marks and Schakel 2010), but the scope of application for derivative citizenship. For this, there must be a second condition apart from institutions of regional self-government, and this is a constitutive relation with other polities through which sovereignty is dispersed and shared. Such a relation is inherent in federal constitutions, but exists also in others that are not formally federal and need not involve all parts of a state territory. Britain and Spain are not federal states, but devolution has turned Scotland, Catalonia and the Basque Country into polities whose degree of autonomy is now a matter of negotiation between regional and central governments. The same can be said about special autonomy arrangements, as in the Finnish Åland islands or the north Italian province of South Tyrol, that set certain regions apart from the rest of the state territory. A constitutive relation is one in which there is not only multilevel self-government, but also in which the encompassing polity is composed of distinct polities with whom it shares sovereignty, no matter whether this constellation has come about through "coming together" federation or "holding together" devolution (Stepan 2001). In such a relation, the territorial integrity and political legitimacy of the encompassing polity depend on constitutional safeguards for the autonomy of the polities of which it is composed. Governments involved in these relations have reciprocal duties to respect each other's spheres of autonomy and to cooperate in areas of joint government.

Derivative citizenship is an essential ingredient of this constellation because it turns all citizens of constitutive polities into citizens of the encompassing one. Each individual citizen has thus a double stake in the self-government of both polities. Such dual citizenship is different from multiple citizenship for migrants that reflects their individual ties to independent states. It is also unlike dual citizenship at local and state levels that differentiates between resident population and national citizenry. In a constitutive relation, dual citizenship serves instead to connect polities that could potentially be separate.

The isomorphism between substate and suprastate regional citizenship is certainly not perfect. For example, just like local citizenship, substate regional citizenship generally does not have an extraterritorial dimension. A few largely symbolic exceptions, such as the embassy-like representation of German provinces in Brussels or the Foreign Ministry of Quebec and its presence in Canadian embassies and consulates around the world, confirm this rule. By contrast, EU citizenship has an explicit external dimension that includes the right to diplomatic and consular protection in third countries through the representations of other member states and EU delegations (TFEU, Article 20(2)c). Whether EU citizens residing in third countries enjoy also external voting rights for European Parliament elections depends, however, somewhat incoherently, still on national legislation of their country of nationality (Arrighi et al. 2013).

Such differences between regional citizenship within states, on the one hand, and EU citizenship, on the other hand, emerge quite naturally from the fact that the latter shares the global stage of international relations with independent states, including those of which it is composed. This raises the larger question about the transformative potential of supranational citizenship for the global political order. Cosmopolitan optimists have sometimes regarded the EU as an approximation of, or vehicle for, a Kantian world federation of democracies, while realists tend to see it as a singular European experiment that is essentially still an intergovernmental organization and inherently limited in geographic scope. I want to sketch a position between these two extremes that does not rely on geopolitical considerations but considers instead the internal constitutional dynamics of a regional union of democratic states.

The European Union differs from federal and confederal polities because of a combination of four constitutive principles: (1) a common citizenship with direct elections and representation at union level; (2) the dominance of member states in constitutional law, entrenched through a unanimity requirement for EU treaty change; (3) partial opt-out opportunities from union policies and full exit options for member states, spelled out in the Lisbon Treaty (TEU, Article 50); and (4) deeper political integration as a goal, expressed in the ever-closer-union commitment in the preamble of the Treaty of Rome.[53] These are not merely principles that characterize the current constitutional arrangements of the EU; they articulate a general model of political community between the state and the global level.

In stark contrast with federal or confederal constitutions, the four principles do not aim for a stable equilibrium. While the unanimity requirement for constitutional change risks blocking reform, the exit opportunity and ever-closer-union principles introduce a dynamic vision

---

[53] In Joseph Lacey's analysis (2017), the first three of these principles characterize the European Union as a "demoicracy". He borrows this term from Nicolaïdis (2004) and Cheneval and Schimmelfennig (2013), giving it a more precise meaning. I have added the fourth feature of ever-closer union, which further enhances the contrast with federal and confederal constitutions.

of a polity whose composition and degree of integration change over time. The tensions between these static and dynamic elements keep the historic possibilities of disintegration or transformation into a federal state alive, but neither of these possible outcomes can be a legitimate goal pursued by member states under the current constitution.

Although the EU has grown continuously from 1957 to the 2013 accession of Croatia, I have deliberately not included enlargement among its constitutive features. The political reunification of Europe after the Cold War was the second great historical mission of the EU after securing permanent peace between the adversaries of two world wars. Yet a goal of continuous enlargement is particularly hard to square with a unanimity requirement in treaty legislation and a commitment to ever-closer union. The reason why, until the Brexit vote, the EU has been capable of simultaneously deepening its political integration and expanding to twenty-eight member states is that each new accession was conditional upon accepting the acquis that entrenched the current state of integration. Had the Union started from an initial number of twenty-eight states, it would have probably remained an international organization focused on common markets. Supranational citizenship and democracy would have been a very unlikely achievement under this condition (Lacey and Bauböck 2017). The tradeoff between enlargement and political integration is ineluctable and increasingly obvious in current attempts to overcome the divisions between debtor and creditor states.

The upshot of these considerations is that supranational democratic polities such as the EU can be successful in terms of their declared goals only if they remain limited to regional unions. If the historic experiment of the EU succeeds, it will neither result in a new regional superstate nor in an ever-expanding union with claims to global hegemony. Instead, it will be imitated in other parts of the world, thus reinforcing the pluralistic circumstances of democracy by populating the world with a novel type of polity – democratic regional unions of states.

The ethical purposes of derivative citizenship are not universal ones, unlike those of birthright and residence-based citizenship. Not all democracies need to adopt federal constitutions or introduce autonomy arrangements for some parts of their territory. And not all democracies need to join democratic regional unions. The imperatives for such solutions arise in specific historical and geographic contexts. But where they arise, they do have considerable normative force. Moreover, from a global perspective we can also see how the dispersal and pooling of sovereignty at substate and suprastate levels reduces the risk of political domination within states and enhances opportunities for democratic self-government beyond the state.

5. Conclusions: maintaining self-government under conditions of polity plurality

In section 2 of this essay, I claimed that a plurality of polities of different kinds should be accepted as a basic feature of the circumstances of democracy. I suggested that the three democratic principles of including all affected interests, all subjected to coercion and all citizenship stakeholders are equally valid but address three different questions: Whose interests should be represented in policy decisions? Who should be protected by government power and have the right to contest it? Who should be a citizen of a self-governing political community? At the end of section 3, I acknowledged that this correspondence between inclusion principles and democratic domains is not perfect, but insisted that the membership question can only be resolved within a democratic stakeholder conception of citizenship.

In section 4, I examined how a principle of stakeholder inclusion applies to polities of different types. I suggested that this question cannot be answered by considering polities in isolation from each other. Stakeholder claims to inclusion refer to a relation between the conditions for individual and collective self-government. The conditions for collective self-government depend in turn on the relation of a polity with other polities. I examined three different types of such polity constellations – relations between independent states in the international state system, between states and local self-government, and between constitutive polities and unions of polities – and identified birthright, residential and derivative citizenship as the corresponding basic rules for determining individual membership.

I will conclude in a similar way as I ended section 3, with an attempt to synthesize and to point out some of the complexities that emerge from combining the three membership regimes. This attempt is guided by an old republican question. Republicanism is a political philosophy that gives equal weight to individual and collective freedom and connects the two. Under the influence of modern liberalism, contemporary republican theorists have shifted the emphasis towards individual freedom from domination and have tended to neglect collective freedom, while the classic republicanism of Machiavelli or Rousseau was biased in the opposite direction and primarily concerned with the conditions for collective freedom. Machiavelli, in particular, was obsessed with "mantenere lo stato" – preserving the conditions under which republican government would be able to endure. In his view, this required permanent vigilance against internal enemies of the republic (the nobles) as well as external enemies (rival polities). The threats of internal corruption and external domination have not of course vanished. But the great transformations that have created the modern state and the international system have raised new challenges for maintaining self-government that are not reflected in the classic texts. The membership regimes that I have outlined in the previous sections can be best understood and defended when we read them as partial answers to three such challenges.

The first is the challenge of how to maintain the continuity of a self-governing polity across generations. This is not itself a modern question, but it has acquired a new urgency for several reasons. One is the vanishing of quasi-natural boundaries of political community based on religion, race or ethnicity that made it easy to distinguish natives from foreigners. These markers have lost both empirical salience and normative legitimacy. Another reason is the increasing awareness that policies have long-term effects and need to factor in the interests of future generations in sustainable environments or welfare regimes. Birthright citizenship is certainly not a sufficient answer to this challenge, but it may be a necessary one once we consider the alternative of grounding all political memberships on residence. In a diverse society, both ius soli and ius sanguinis remove the divisive question of who has a claim to full citizenship from the political agenda and make citizens aware that they form part of a long chain of generations who are all unconditionally included in the political community.

The second challenge is how to maintain territorial self-government in contexts of territorial mobility and migration. I have initially assumed relative sedentariness as a context for democratic inclusion and it is important to emphasize the qualifier "relative". Freedom of movement is an essential aspect of individual freedom that liberals and republicans care about. Yet how can there be stable democratic self-government if large numbers of native-born live abroad and large numbers of foreign-born join the resident population? In such contexts membership must be determined also on the basis of residence. In contemporary democracies this happens in two different ways. The initial allocation of citizenship through birthright is corrected through residence-based naturalization opportunities and absence-based renunciation opportunities. And inside the territory of democratic states, municipalities have open borders for mobility and accept all residents as local citizens. The difference between national level naturalization and local level ius domicilii can only be maintained as long as national societies are generally sedentary, in the sense that most mobility remains contained within state borders and a majority of birthright citizens have permanent residence in the territory. If this condition changed – and not just in a single polity but as a general feature of the international state system –, then birthright regimes would lose their legitimacy, with the problematic consequence that citizens would have a much weaker sense of transgenerational continuity.

The third challenge is how to maintain self-government in contexts where political communities are bound together – by history or choice – into larger unions. Federal democracy with multilevel citizenship was invented by the American Revolution, which has provided a template for many other federal states around the world. In our time, the European Union has developed a model for a democratic union of independent member states that has so far triggered only timid imitations. Maintaining multilevel self-government within nested polities each of which could potentially be independent requires an automatic link between their memberships through downwards or upwards derivation. Such federal and union citizenship turns individuals into multiple stakeholders that do not only have individual inclusion claims but also an interest in the maintenance of the union itself. The link between constitutive and federal or union citizenship is certainly not sufficient for resisting centripetal as well as centrifugal forces. But it should contribute to stabilizing such arrangements by articulating the ideas that the self-government of each level depends on that of the other and that every citizen has a stake in democracy at both levels.

Although there is a strong correspondence between the three membership norms and the three challenges for self-government, this is not a set of unique pairs. In other words, each of the three challenges can be seen through the prism of each of the three membership norms. Table 2 illustrates this idea. What emerges from considering all these combinations is that the three membership norms ought to be seen as complementing each other, just as I suggested in section 3.4 with regard to the three democratic inclusion principles.

Table 2: Membership norms and political challenges for democratic polities

Challenge ⟋ Membership	Continuity	Mobility	Union
Birthright-based	transgenerational people	reciprocity-based free movement	-----
Residence-based	territorial institutions	open borders and free movement	-----
Derivative	constitution	union citizenship	constitutive self-government

Consider first the second cell in the first column. How can a sense of transgenerational continuity be maintained also in polities with residence-based citizenship and very high levels of mobility? In superdiverse cities (Vertovec 2007), where being native is a minority identity and large numbers are only temporarily present, people will still be aware that there are government institutions whose laws apply to them and that these institutions have been there before their arrival and will continue to rule the city after their departure. If they can also participate politically in the making of these laws, this will strengthen their sense of being stakeholders in the self-government of the city. The political time horizon of mobile urban citizens is still likely to be much shorter compared with the horizons of those who take a decision to naturalize. This could pose a major problem for political integration if cities were like independent states. It is the local polity's embeddedness in national birthright regimes that secures stability and legitimacy for the institutions of self-government also in superdiverse and hypermobile cities.

Moving down to the last cell in the first column, continuity is generally more fragile in federations and unions with derivative citizenship than in unitary states. The threat of breakup might linger on as a historical memory of past conflicts or be a present fear that undermines trust and the willingness to collaborate. Under such conditions, secession or partition into independent states, as well as merger into a unitary democratic polity, imply the discontinuity of self-government of either the encompassing or the constitutive polities. Continuity can be achieved through a constitution that entrenches self-government rights at both levels and divides powers between them in a way that minimizes permanent conflict.

Let us now look at the second column of the table and consider how birthright-based and derivative membership can cope with migration in the sense of border-crossing mobility. Although all independent states claim the right to control immigration, their birthright citizenship creates significant spaces for free movement. Birthright citizenship entails a right to unconditional residence and readmission. Since it is not lost through emigration and can be passed on to at least the second generation born abroad it creates a potential for "return migration". Moreover, gender neutral ius sanguinis and the combined effects of ius soli and ius sanguinis have led to a proliferation of multiple nationality, which has been further enhanced through a global trend in both sending and receiving states towards accepting that a previous citizenship can be retained in case of naturalization. Multiple citizenship, however acquired, creates unconditional free movement rights between several states. Finally, international freedom of movement could be extended much further on the basis of a birthright conception, if states accepted a duty to promote their own citizens' opportunities for migration by concluding free movement agreements with other states on a basis of reciprocity (Bauböck 2009a).

In federal states, derivative citizenship in constitutive polities does not add much to the general right of free internal movement in state territories that has become a universal human right. If anything, the autonomy of constitutive polities may sometimes justify restrictions of free movement rights for the sake of protecting vulnerable linguistic or indigenous minorities or provincial welfare regimes. By contrast, in unions of independent states derivative citizenship at the union level is a major source of free movement. In the EU it has not only led to very extensive mobility rights attached to Union citizenship, but also to a general abolishing of border controls within the Schengen zone. Moreover, EU enlargement has transformed millions from third country nationals subjected to tight immigration control into potential free movers protected by strong non-discrimination rights. Precisely because of its focus on free movement, EU citizenship may however have indirectly contributed to creating new political cleavages between mobile Europeans and sedentary nationals who do not see themselves as European stakeholders.

The third column of the table considers, finally, the capacity of birthright- and residence-based membership regimes to promote or preserve structural union between polities. The answer is generally negative. Birthright citizenship cannot be replicated across levels. If both levels have it, they are de facto independent states; if one level has it without a derivative citizenship for the other, then the latter polity is not self-governing and there is thus no union. By contrast, citizenship can be coherently residence-based at all levels, but then nested polities will be merely *similarly* exposed to inflows and outflows of their temporary citizens, without being *linked* to each other in a citizenship union.

The need for a robust derivative citizenship is especially strong in territorially divided societies. As I explained in section 4.2, the quasi-natural equality among birthright citizens protects racial, religious and indigenous minorities that had historically been excluded from full citizenship. At the same time, birthright inclusion in a supposedly homogenous political community can undermine minority self-government unless the latter is secured through constitutional autonomy arrangements and derivative citizenship. For fair inclusion of minorities that do not have a history and claim to territorial self-government the challenge is to re-imagine the larger polity as a multicultural, multiracial and multireligious one in which birthright does not need the support of thicker conceptions of national identity.

Residence-based citizenship combined with free movement is often perceived as a threat rather than a benefit by national and indigenous minorities that fear being overwhelmed by majority citizens and immigrants settling in their territory. Replacing derivation with ius domicilii is therefore not conducive to maintaining union in multinational democracies. However, there are also cases where national minorities (such as the Catalans, Basques or Scots) have strategically adopted an implicitly residence-based conception of regional citizenship as a device for stemming demographic decline and opposing restrictive immigration and immigrant integration policies pursued by central governments.

If these considerations seem rather inconclusive, this is for two reasons. The first is that they reflect on a messy reality in which polities of different types do not always respect each other's legitimate self-government claims, enjoy very unequal powers and are often locked in conflict with each other. This is a reality that we already know very well from the contrast between the norm of equal sovereignty of states and de facto dominance and inequality of power in the international state system. Just as the norm of equal sovereignty remains valid and operative for purposes of international law, despite a contrasting reality, we should think of the norms of democratic inclusion and self-government in the more complex environment populated by multiple types of polities as having validity independently of the distortions that we find in the contemporary world.

The second reason is that the commitment to pluralism that has guided my analysis in this essay is not limited to the arguments that an internal diversity of interests, ideas and identities and an external plurality of different types of polities form the circumstances of democracy in the political world. At the end of section 3, I added a third pluralism of democratic inclusion principles. Going one step further, I am also inclined to accept Isaiah Berlin's view that there is an irreducible plurality of values in the moral world (Berlin 1991). The values of individual freedom and collective self-government cannot always be fully and simultaneously realized because there is tension between them that occasionally results in deep democratic dilemmas. This is no reason to favour one at the expense of the other. The principles of democratic inclusion guide us when we try to resolve this tension.

References

Abizadeh, Arash. 2008. "Democratic Theory and Border Coercion: No Right to Unilaterally Control Your Own Borders." *Political Theory* 36 (1): 37–65.

Abizadeh, Arash. 2010. "Democratic Legitimacy and State Coercion: A Reply to David Miller." *Political Theory* 38 (1): 121–130.

Aleinikoff, Alexander. 1986. "Theories of Loss of Citizenship." *Michigan Law Review* 84 (7): 1471–1503.

Angeli, Oliviero. 2015. *Cosmopolitanism, Self-determination and Territory: Justice with Borders.* Houndsmills, Basingstoke: Palgrave Macmillan.

Archibugi, Daniele and David Held, eds. 1995. *Cosmopolitan Democracy: An Agenda for a New World Order.* Cambridge: Polity Press.

Arendt, Hannah. 1970. *Men in Dark Times*. San Diego: Harvest Books.

Aristotle. 1962. *The Politics*. Transl.: T.A. Sinclair, revised, and commentary: J. Saunders ed. London: Penguin.

Arrighi, Jean-Thomas, Rainer Bauböck, Michael Collyer, Derek Hutcheson, Lamin Khadar, Madalina Moraru and Jo Shaw. 2013. *Franchise and Electoral Participation of Third Country Citizens Residing in EU and of EU Citizens Residing in Third Countries*. Brussels: European Parliament, Committee on Constitutional Affairs.

Barber, Benjamin. 2013. *If Mayors Ruled the World: Dysfunctional Nations, Rising Cities*. New Haven: Yale University Press.

Bartolini, Stefano. 2005. *Restructuring Europe: Centre Formation, System Building, and Political Structuring between the Nation State and the European Union*. Oxford: Oxford University Press.

Bauböck, Rainer. 2000. "Why Stay Together? A Pluralist Approach to Secession and Federation." In *Citizenship in Diverse Societies*, edited by Will Kymlicka and Wayne Norman. Oxford: Oxford University Press: 366–394.

Bauböck, Rainer. 2002. "United in Misunderstanding? Asymmetry in Multinational Federations." *IWE Working Paper 26*. Vienna: Austrian Academy of Sciences.

Bauböck, Rainer. 2004. "Territorial or Cultural Autonomy for National Minorities?" In *The Politics of Belonging: Nationalism, Liberalism and Pluralism*, edited by Alain Dieckhoff. Lanham: Lexington Books: 221–258.

Bauböck, Rainer. 2005. "Political Autonomy or Cultural Minority Rights? A Conceptual Critique of Renner's Model." In *National Cultural Autonomy and its Contemporary Critics*, edited by Ephraim Nimni. London and New York: Routledge: 97–111.

Bauböck, Rainer. 2006. "Political Boundaries in a Multilevel Democracy." In *Identities, Affiliations and Allegiances*, edited by Seyla Benhabib and Ian Shapiro. Cambridge University Press: 85–112.

Bauböck, Rainer. 2007. "Stakeholder Citizenship and Transnational Political Participation: A Normative Evaluation of External Voting." *Fordham Law Review* 75 (5): 2393–2447.

Bauböck, Rainer. 2009a. "Global Justice, Freedom of Movement and Democratic Citizenship." *European Journal of Sociology/Archives européennes de sociologie* 50 (1): 1–31.

Bauböck, Rainer. 2009b. "The Rights and Duties of External Citizenship." *Citizenship Studies* 13 (5): 475–499.

Bauböck, Rainer. 2010. "Studying Citizenship Constellations." *Journal of Ethnic and Migration Studies* 36 (5): 847–859.

Bauböck, Rainer. 2011a. "Boundaries and Birthright: Bosniak's and Shachar's Critiques of Liberal Citizenship." *Issues in Legal Scholarship* 9 (1): 1–19. doi: https://doi.org/10.2202/1539-8323.1123.

Bauböck, Rainer. 2011b. "Temporary Migrants, Partial Citizenship and Hypermigration." *Critical Review of International Social and Political Philosophy* 14 (5): 665–693.

Bauböck, Rainer. 2015a. "From Moral Intuition to Political Change: On Joseph Carens' Theory of Social Membership and Open Borders." *Political Theory* 43 (3): 393–401.

Bauböck, Rainer. 2015b. "Morphing the Demos into the Right Shape: Normative Principles for Enfranchising Resident Aliens and Expatriate Citizens." *Democratization* 22 (5): 820–839.

Bauböck, Rainer and Dilek Çınar. 2001. "Nationality Law and Naturalisation in Austria." In *Towards a European Nationality: Citizenship, Immigration and Nationality Law in the European Union*, edited by Randall Hansen and Patrick Weil. London: Macmillan: 255–272.

Bauböck, R. and Vesco Paskalev. 2015. "Cutting Genuine Links: A Normative Analysis of Citizenship Deprivation." *Georgetown Journal of Immigration Law* 30 (1): 47–104.

Beckman, Ludvig. 2009. *The Frontiers of Democracy: The Right to Vote and Its Limits*. Houndmills, Basingstoke: Palgrave Macmillan.

Benhabib, Seyla. 2004. *The Rights of Others*. Cambridge: Cambridge University Press.

Benhabib, Seyla. 2006. *Another Comopolitanism: With Jeremy Waldron, Bonnie Honig and Will Kymlicka, edited by Robert Post*. Oxford: Oxford University Press.

Benhabib, Seyla. 2011. *Dignity in Adversity: Human Rights in Troubled Times*. Cambridge: Polity Press.

Berlin, Isaiah. 1991. *The Crooked Timber of Humanity*. London: Fontana Press.

Bernitz, Hedvig. 2013. "Access to Electoral Rights. Sweden." In *EUDO Citizenship Observatory: Electoral Rights Reports*. 2013/22. Florence: EUI.

Bohman, James. 2007. *Democracy Across Borders: From Dêmos to Dêmoi*. Cambridge: Cambridge University Press.

Brubaker, Rogers W. 1990. "Citizenship, and the Nation-State in France and Germany: A Comparative Historical Analysis." *International Sociology* 5: 379–407.

Buchanan, Allen. 1991. *Secession: The Morality of Political Divorce from Fort Sumter to Lithuania and Quebec*. Boulder: Westview Press.

Buchanan, Allen. 1997. "Theories of Secession." *Philosophy and Public Affairs* 26 (1): 31–61.

Buchanan, Allen. 2004. *Justice, Legitimacy, and Self-determination: Moral Foundations for International Law*. Oxford: Oxford University Press.

Caney, Simon. 2006. "Cosmopolitan Justice and Institutional Design." *Social Theory and Practice* 32 (4): 725–756.

Carens, Joseph H. 1987. "Aliens and Citizens: The Case for Open Borders." *Review of Politics* 49 (2): 251–273.

Carens, Joseph H. 1989. "Membership and Morality: Admission to Citizenship in Liberal Democratic States." In *Immigration and the Politics of Citizenship in Europe and North America*, edited by Rogers W. Brubaker. Lanham and London: University Press of America: 31–49.

Carens, Joseph H. 2005. "The Integration of Immigrants." *Journal of Moral Philosophy* 2 (1): 29–46.

Carens, Joseph H. 2013. *The Ethics of Immigration*. Oxford: Oxford University Press.

Cheneval, Francis and Frank Schimmelfennig. 2013. "The Case for Demoicracy in the European Union." *Journal of Common Market Studies* 51 (2): 334–350.

Chwaszcza, Christine. 2009. "The Unity of the People, and Immigration in Liberal Theory." *Citizenship Studies* 13 (5): 451–473.

Closa, Carlos and Daniela Vintila. 2015. "Supranational Citizenship: Rights in Regional Integration Organizations." Draft paper. Florence: European University Institute.

Dahl, Robert. 1970. *After the Revolution? Authority in a Good Society*. New Haven: Yale University Press.

Dahl, Robert. 1989. *Democracy and Its Critics*. New Haven: Yale University Press.

de Schutter, Helder and Lea Ypi. 2015. "Mandatory Citizenship for Immigrants." *British Journal of Political Science* 45 (2): 235–251.

Donaldson, Sue and Will Kymlicka. 2011. *Zoopolis: A Political Theory of Animal Rights*. Oxford: Oxford University Press.

Donaldson, Sue and Will Kymlicka. 2015. "Rethinking Membership and Participation in an Inclusive Democracy: Cognitive Disability, Children, Animals." Draft paper. Kingston: Queens University.

Dumbrava, Costica. 2014. *Nationality, Citizenship and Ethno-cultural Belonging: Preferential Membership Policies in Europe.* Houndmills, Basingstoke: Palgrave Macmillan.

Dworkin, Ronald. 1977. *Taking Rights Seriously.* Cambridge: Harvard University Press.

Forst, Rainer. 2012. *The Right to Justification: Elements of a Constructivist Theory of Justice.* New York: Columbia University Press.

Frey, Bruno and Reiner Eichberger. 1999. *The New Democratic Federalism for Europe: Functional, Overlapping, and Competing Jurisdictions.* Cheltenham: Edward Elgar.

Gellner, Ernest. 1983. *Nations and Nationalism.* Oxford: Blackwell.

Goodin, Robert. 1988. "'What is So Special about Our Fellow Countrymen?'" *Ethics* 98: 663–686.

Goodin, Robert. 2007. "Enfranchising All Affected Interests, and Its Alternatives." *Philosophy and Public Affairs* 35 (1): 40–68.

Habermas, Jürgen. 2006. *The Divided West.* London: Polity Press.

Hirschman, Albert O. 1970. *Exit, Voice, and Loyalty.* Cambridge: Harvard University Press.

Hooghe, Lisbeth, Gary Marks and Arjan H. Schakel. 2010. *The Rise of Regional Authority: A Comparative Study of 42 Democracies.* London: Routledge.

Jackson, Vicky. 2001. "Citizenship and Federalism." In *Citizenship Today: Global Perspectives and Practices,* edited by Alex Aleinikoff and Doug Klusmeyer. Washington, D.C.: Carnegie Endowment for International Peace: 127–182.

Jenning, Ivor. 1956. *The Approach to Self-government.* Cambridge: Cambridge University Press.

Kant, Immanuel. 1795/1991. "Perpetual Peace: A Philosophical Sketch." In *Kant: Political Writings,* edited by H.S. Reiss. Cambridge: Cambridge University Press: 93–130.

King, Russel and Erik Olsson. 2014. "Introduction: Diasporic Return." *Diaspora* 17 (3): 255–261.

Koenig-Archibugi, Mathias. 2012. "Fuzzy Citizenship in Global Society." *Journal of Political Philosophy* 20 (4): 456–480.

Koopmans, Ruud, Paul Statham, Marco Giugni and Florence Passy. 2005. *Contested Citizenship: Immigration and Cultural Diversity in Europe*. Minneapolis: University of Minnesota Press.

Kuper, Andrew. 2004. *Democracy Beyond Borders: Justice and Representation in Global Institutions*. Oxford: Oxford University Press.

Kymlicka, Will. 1995. *Multicultural Citizenship: A Liberal Theory of Minority Rights*. Oxford: Oxford University Press.

Kymlicka, Will. 2001a. *Contemporary Political Philosophy*. 2nd ed. Oxford: Oxford University Press.

Kymlicka, Will. 2001b. *Politics in the Vernacular: Nationalism, Multiculturalism and Citizenship*. Oxford: Oxford University Press.

Kymlicka, Will. 2005. "Renner and the Accommodation of Sub-state Nationalism." In *National Cultural Autonomy and Its Critics*, edited by Ephraim Nimni. London: Routledge: 117–127.

Lacey, Joseph. 2017. *Centripetal Democracy: Democratic Legitimacy and Political Identity in Belgium, Switzerland and the European Union*. Oxford: Oxford University Press.

Lacey, Joseph and Rainer Bauböck. 2017. "Enlargement, Association, Accession – a Normative Account of Membership in a Union of States." *Journal of European Integration*, online first at http://dx.doi.org/10.1080/07036337.2017.1327523.

List, Christian, and Mathias Koenig-Archibugi. 2010. "Can There Be a Global Demos? An Agency-Based Approach." *Philosophy and Public Affairs* 38 (1): 76–110.

López-Guerra, Claudio. 2005. "Should Expatriates Vote?" *Journal of Political Philosophy* 13 (2): 216–234.

Maas, Willem, ed. 2013. *Multilevel Citizenship*. Philadelphia: University of Pennsylvania Press.

Macdonald, Terry. 2008. *Global Stakeholder Democracy: Power and Representation Beyond Liberal States*. Oxford: Oxford University Press.

Magnusson, Warren. 2011. *Politics of Urbanism: Seeing Like a City*. London: Routledge.

Marshall, Thomas H. 1949/1965. "Citizenship and Social Class." In *Class, Citizenship, and Social Development: Essays by T.H. Marshall*, edited by Thomas H. Marshall. New York: Anchor Books: 71–134.

Miller, David. 2010. "Why Immigration Controls are not Coercive: A Reply to Arash Abizadeh." *Political Theory* 38 (1): 111–120.

Nagel, Thomas. 2005. "The Problem of Global Justice." *Philosophy and Public Affairs* 33 (2): 113–147.

Näsström, Sofia. 2007. "The Legitimacy of the People." *Political Theory* 35 (5): 624–658.

Nicolaïdis, Kalypso. 2004. "We, the Peoples of Europe." *Foreign Affairs* 83 (6): 97–110.

Owen, David. 2010. "Resident Aliens, Non-resident Citizens and Voting Rights." In *Citizenship Acquisition and National Belonging*, edited by Gideon Calder, Philip Cole and Jonathan Seglow. London: Palgrave: 52–73.

Owen, David. 2011. "Transnational Citizenship and the Democratic State." *Critical Review of International Social and Political Philosophy* 14 (5): 641–663.

Owen, David. 2012. "Constituting the Polity, Constituting the Demos: On the Place of the All Affected Interests Principle in Democratic Theory and in Resolving the Democratic Boundary Problem." *Ethics and Global Affairs* 5 (3): 129–152.

Owen, David. 2017. "Citizenship and Human Rights." In *Oxford Handbook of Citizenship*, edited by Ayelet Shachar, Rainer Bauböck, Irene Bloemraad and Maarten Vink. Oxford: Oxford University Press: 247–267.

Panagiotidis, Jannis. 2015. "Tainted Law? Why History Cannot Provide the Justification for Abandoning Ius Sanguinis." *EUI Working Papers*. RSCAS 2015/80. Florence: European University Institute.

Parolin, Gianluca. 2009. *Citizenship in the Arab World: Kin, Religion and Nation-State*. Amsterdam: Amsterdam University Press.

Patten, Alan. 2014. *Equal Recognition: The Moral Foundations of Minority Rights*. Princeton: Princeton University Press.

Pettit, Philip. 1997. *Republicanism: A Theory of Freedom and Government*. Oxford: Oxford University Press.

Pettit, Philip. 2006. "Democracy, National and International." *The Monist* 89 (2): 301–324.

Pettit, Philip. 2012. *On the People's Terms: A Republican Theory and Model of Democracy*. Cambridge: Cambridge University Press.

Rawls, John. 1999. *A Theory of Justice*: Revised Edition. Oxford: Oxford University Press.

Rehfeld, Andrew. 2006. "Towards a General Theory of Political Representation." *Journal of Politics* 68 (1): 1–22.

Rokkan, Stein and Derek W. Urwin. 1983. *Economy, Territory, Identity: Politics of West European Peripheries*. London: Sage.

Rubio-Marín, Ruth. 2000. *Immigration as a Democratic Challenge: Citizenship and Inclusion in Germany and the United States*. Cambridge: Cambridge University Press.

Sager, Alex. 2016. "Methodological Nationalism, Migration and Political Theory." *Political Studies* 64 (1): 42–59.

Saward, Michael. 2010. *The Representative Claim*. Oxford: Oxford University Press.

Schmitt, Carl. 1927/2007. *The Concept of the Political: Expanded Edition (1932), translated by G. Schwab*. Chicago: University of Chicago Press.

Schumpeter, Joseph. 1942/1976. *Capitalism, Socialism, and Democracy*. London: Allen and Unwin.

Shachar, Ayelet. 2009. *The Birthright Lottery: Citizenship and Global Inequality*. Cambridge: Harvard University Press.

Shapiro, Ian. 2000. *Democratic Justice*. New Haven: Yale University Press.

Sloane, Robert. 2009. "Breaking the Genuine Link: The Contemporary International Legal Regulation of Nationality." *Harvard International Law Journal* 50 (1): 1–60.

Stepan, Alfred. 2001. "Towards a New Comparative Politics of Federalism (Multi) Nationalism, and Democracy: Beyond Rikerian Federalism." In *Arguing Comparative Politics*, edited by Alfred Stepan. Oxford: Oxford University Press: 315–361.

Stilz, Anna. 2011. "Nations, States, and Territory." *Ethics* 121 (3): 572–601.

Tully, James. 2001. "Introduction." In *Multinational Democracies*, edited by Alain-G. Gagnon and James Tully. Cambridge: Cambridge University Press: 1–33.

Tully, James. 2002. "The Unfreedom of the Moderns in Comparison to Their Ideals of Constitutional Democracy." *Modern Law Review* 65 (2): 204–228.

Tully, James. 2008. *Public Philosophy in a New Key*. Cambridge: Cambridge University Press.

van Parijs, Philippe. 2011. *Linguistic Justice for Europe and for the World*. Oxford: Oxford University Press.

Vertovec, Steven. 2007. "Super-diversity and Its Implications." *Ethnic and Racial Studies* 29 (6): 1024–1054.

Waldron, Jeremy. 1999. *Law and Disagreement.* Oxford: Oxford University Press.

Weil, Patrick. 2013. *The Sovereign Citizen: Denaturalization and the Origins of the American Republic.* Philadelphia: University of Pennsylvania Press.

Wellman, Christopher H. 2008. "Immigration and Freedom of Association." *Ethics* 119 (1): 109–141 .

Whelan, Frederick G. 1983. "Prologue: Democratic Theory and the Boundary Problem." In *NOMOS 25: Liberal Democracy,* edited by J.R. Pennock and J.W. Chapman. New York: New York University: 13–47.

Ziegler, Ruvi, Jo Shaw and Rainer Bauböck. 2014. "Independence Referendums: Who Should Vote and Who Should be Offered Citizenship?" *EUI Working Papers.* RSCAS 2014/90. Florence: European University Institute.

Part II

Responses

2

The boundaries of "democratic inclusion": some questions for Rainer Bauböck

Joseph H. Carens

I have been exchanging ideas with Rainer Bauböck for over twenty years, and I have always gained a great deal from these exchanges. Reading this essay is no exception. Bauböck has a rare gift for constructing illuminating typologies and analytical frameworks. He is able to map out the logical structure of the relationships between different conceptions, principles and practices in ways that are useful to philosophers, empirical researchers and policy-makers alike. Those gifts are clearly on display here as Bauböck explores the virtues and limitations of three different principles of democratic inclusion: all affected interests (AAI), all subject to coercion (ASC) and all citizenship stakeholders (ACS). Bauböck argues that the three principles complement one another, with each providing legitimation for a different set of democratic institutions and practices.

Bauböck has many illuminating things to say about these three principles, including the ways in which they are derived from different but compatible conceptions of democracy. I agree with him that it is important for many of the purposes of collective democratic decision-making to have stable political units with clear jurisdictional authority over a wide range of issues within a specific territorial space; and that for this reason AAI, at least in a stark and singular form, does not provide suitable guidance for organizing human political affairs demo-cratically, although, as Bauböck himself says, AAI does draw our attention to morally relevant concerns that we should take into account in whatever democratic institutional arrangements we adopt. I also agree with

Bauböck that questions about who ought to have legal rights within a jurisdiction and what rights they ought to have should be distinguished from questions about membership, so that ASC cannot be used *tout court* as a guide to the allocation of citizenship. Finally, I share many of Bauböck's views about who ought to be granted citizenship in a democratic political community and why. He prefers the language of stakeholdership (ACS) and I prefer the language of social membership in exploring these issues, but in substantive terms our views of what democratic principles entail with respect to who is entitled to citizenship and why are very close. Let me add that I applaud the fact that, unlike many political theorists, Bauböck does not view the political world solely through the lens of the modern state. He explicitly regards municipalities and other entities exercising extensive jurisdictional authority over a territorial space as "polities" or "political communities" whose members should be seen as citizens engaged in the important task of collective self-government.

Despite its many virtues, this essay also leaves me puzzled in some important respects. In my response to Bauböck, I propose to ask a series of questions about what he is trying to accomplish and about how the different parts of his discussion fit together. I recognize that he will not be able to answer all of these questions in his reply, but my hope is that he will be able to take up a few of them and that the questions themselves will help to advance the conversation. One central theme of Bauböck's essay is that questions about boundaries are central to any discussion of democratic inclusion. One way to capture the central theme of my response is to say that I would like Bauböck to say more about the boundaries of his project. What is included and what is excluded in the way that he discusses democratic inclusion?

As I see it, Bauböck is offering an interpretive and critical account of democratic inclusion. On the one hand, it is interpretive because Bauböck is starting from a commitment to democratic principles and trying to understand what they entail or how they are best understood. In that respect, it differs from an approach that would seek to justify democracy itself on the basis of some other foundation. On the other hand, Bauböck's discussion is also critical. He does not simply accept existing democratic practices or existing understandings of democratic principles but subjects both the practices and the principles to critical scrutiny.

So far, so good. Still, there are many different ways to develop this sort of interpretive and critical analysis. Every inquiry has to bracket some questions in order to pursue others. It is important for the reader to know when a line of investigation has been excluded simply as a way of limiting the discussion and keeping it within manageable bounds and when it has been excluded on the grounds that it is irrelevant or has been found wanting. What limits has Bauböck imposed on his inquiry and why has he imposed these limits? For example, does a concern for feasibility or practical relevance play an important role in limiting what questions he asks or in how he answers these questions?

Some passages in the text suggest that the answer to this question is "no". Bauböck is sometimes at pains not to restrict the potential critical range of his inquiry in advance. See, for example, the second paragraph of his essay or his critical remarks on "methodological statism" on p. 57. On the other hand, he says on p. 6 that he wants to identify normative principles that could guide public policies with respect to actual problems of inclusion as they arise in contemporary democratic states. For example, he says that the discussion of principles should help us to address practical questions about access to legal citizenship, voting rights, and so on.

This generates a first set of questions for Bauböck. Might not these two tasks stand in deep tension? Is it not possible that democratic principles, if understood correctly and taken seriously, would require such fundamental changes in current policies and institutions that they cannot provide much guidance for how we should respond to practical problems that arise from contexts shaped by the morally problematic institutions and policies that exist now? Indeed, might there not be some policies or practices that seem morally desirable now only because of background features of current arrangements that are morally problematic? Does Bauböck's commitment to a single account that both illuminates basic principles and provides practical guidance permit him to consider with an open mind all of the fundamental questions that can emerge from a concern for democratic inclusion?

Global democracy

Consider now something that Bauböck wants to exclude in the name of democratic inclusion: global democracy. He says explicitly at the end of section 2.1 that the ideas advanced in that section "exclude the vision of a *self-governing* global demos" (p. 12). I must say that I am somewhat perplexed as to the nature of the argument against global democracy. Is Bauböck making a conceptual claim, a normative claim, an empirical claim or perhaps some combination of all three? Does he think that the idea of a self-governing global demos is conceptually incoherent? Or is he saying instead that a self-governing global demos would be a bad political arrangement in principle from a democratic perspective? Or is he arguing on empirical grounds that a self-governing global demos would work less well from a democratic perspective than a global political order that divided power among multiple polities? I am inclined to think that his main focus is on conceptual arguments against the idea of a global demos, although, as we shall see, there are countervailing indicators.

Early on Bauböck says, "Since inclusion conceptually presupposes an external boundary, a theory of legitimate inclusion claims depends on a theory of legitimate boundaries" (p. 4). One sometimes hears the claim that the very idea of global democracy is intrinsically flawed because inclusion implies exclusion, and a global demos does not exclude anyone. So, it might seem as though Bauböck is going to construct that sort of argument against the idea of global democracy. But then in his discussion of the first reason why boundaries are necessary for democracy, Bauböck says, "even if every human being were included in a single global polity … there would then still be a political boundary between human beings and other animals that could potentially be included"

(p. 8). That observation seems to provide a basis for rejecting the inclusion/exclusion conceptual argument against global democracy. So, is Bauböck therefore intending to reject the inclusion/exclusion conceptual argument against global democracy?

If he is, I am with him. I am not persuaded by the claim that inclusion always implies exclusion (as distinct from the conceptual possibility of exclusion), but even if one does accept that claim, I doubt that it can ever do much substantive work. As Bauböck's comment shows, it is usually possible to find some category of beings that is excluded no matter how the polity is identified.

We could elaborate Bauböck's point further. A global demos that includes animals as well as humans would still exclude other life forms (both in the world and potentially outside it) as well as inanimate beings like mountains and lakes that some think ought to have moral and legal standing. Later in his essay Bauböck introduces a distinction between the citizenry and the demos in which the demos is that subset of the citizenry who are able to participate and entitled to do so. Given this distinction, we could say that it would be wrong to describe a global demos as including all humans, since the demos excludes those humans who are incapable of participation. A global demos may or may not be a good idea, but Bauböck's discussion shows that it is a mistake to imagine that one can rule it out on the conceptual grounds that inclusion implies exclusion and a global demos excludes no one.

While this conclusion seems to be an implication of Bauböck's analysis, it is less clear to me that it was the goal of his discussion of boundaries in section 2.1, since he does ultimately seek to exclude the vision of a self-governing global demos. What is the purpose of his discussion of the first reason why boundaries should be seen as one of the circumstances of democracy? How is that discussion related to his exclusion of the idea of a global demos?

Although Bauböck rejects the inclusion/exclusion conceptual argument, in his subsequent discussion in section 2.1 it seems as though he is advancing other, somewhat different conceptual arguments against global democracy. In presenting his second reason for seeing boundaries as one of the circumstances of democracy, Bauböck says that "in the absence of political boundaries there is no distinction between intra- and inter-polity relations" (p. 8). This distinction, he says, is "constitutive for the political as a distinct sphere of human activity" (p. 8). What does this mean? Is Bauböck trying to say that the idea of global democracy makes no sense because there could be no inter-polity relations between a global polity and other polities? Because of the abstract character of the argument, I find it hard to know precisely what Bauböck has in mind here. Taken at face value, it seems like an implausible claim. Even if there were no inter-polity relations, why would that imply the absence of the political? For example, suppose we were to learn about some human community, past or present, that had no contact with any other human community but did have internal conflicts and mechanisms for resolving those conflicts. (In fact, we could probably come up with some actual examples of such communities.) Would we be obliged to say that such a community's decision-making and dispute-resolving activities were not "political"? Why should we accept the claim that inter-polity relations are "constitutive for the political"? Isn't that a rather arbitrary definition of what should count as "political"?

Even if we did accept the claim that inter-polity relations are constitutive for the political, why would that rule out global democracy? After all, as Bauböck himself acknowledges, advocates of global democracy "generally do not imagine a single undifferentiated polity encompassing all human beings" (p. 10). No one (or almost no one) favours a global political order in which one polity exercises exclusive jurisdiction over everything, sets all agendas and makes all policy decisions. So, even if there were some sort of global democracy, would there not still be inter-polity relations between the global polity and other polities, as Bauböck himself understands the term "polities"?

Another quasi-conceptual argument against global democracy comes in Bauböck's positive citation of this passage from Arendt: "A citizen is by definition a citizen among citizens of a country among countries … The establishment of one sovereign world state… would be the end of all citizenship"(p. 9). While it is true that if one defines citizenship in the way that Arendt does, it can be used to exclude global democracy on conceptual grounds, the passage itself gives no reason why we should accept that definition. More to the point here, this definition of citizenship seems incompatible with the way Bauböck himself uses the terms "citizen" and "citizenship". He is at pains to deny that the term "citizen" is appropriately restricted to membership in a sovereign state. He talks explicitly about the varieties of democratic polities and the different ways in which citizenship is and ought to be constructed in each: municipalities, provinces, regional organizations, and so on. So, aren't Arendt's definition and the conceptual argument it supports problematic from Bauböck's own perspective?

Another variant of what seems to be a conceptual argument against global democracy can be found in Bauböck's third reason for seeing boundaries as one of the circumstances of democracy. He contends that "the existence of boundaries is a precondition for the democratic feedback mechanisms of voice and exit (Hirschman 1970)" (p. 9). I worry that here, as elsewhere in this section, conceptual stipulations are being substituted for arguments that ought to be both substantive and qualified. Bauböck says, "In the absence of any boundary, exit is by definition impossible" (p. 9). What are the implications of this conceptual claim? Is there some concrete political arrangement that it is designed to challenge? If exit is impossible by definition where there are no boundaries, does it follow that democracy is also (by definition?) impossible where exit is impossible? Why?

Perhaps Bauböck is not trying to make a conceptual argument about the impossibility of global democracy but rather an empirically informed argument about why it would be a bad idea in practice. The statement that boundaries are a precondition for democratic feedback through voice and exit sounds like an empirical claim, not a conceptual one. Hirschman's work, which Bauböck cites, is indeed based on empirical research but I don't think that it supports the kind of sweeping claim that Bauböck makes.

Bauböck acknowledges (following Hirschman) that easy exit may actually reduce voice, but then he insists, "the absence of any possibility of exit fatally undermines the effectiveness of voice" (p. 9). To me, this sounds like an empirical claim that cries out for specificity and evidence. What are the factors that enhance or reduce the effectiveness of voice in democratic polities? How important is the possibility of exit compared with other factors in enhancing democratic feedback mechanisms? Does the absence of exit possibilities render democratic voice entirely ineffective, and, if so, why? Or does it only reduce the effectiveness of democratic voice, and, if so, by how much? Or does it only create a risk that democratic voice will be stifled, and, if so, how great is that risk and how does that risk compare with the risks of other arrangements?

It seems to me that if one wanted to argue against global democracy on the basis of an empirical claim that the absence of exit is harmful to democracy, one would have to ask "harmful compared to what alternative?" For example, is it worse from a democratic perspective to have a democratic polity in which one can participate but from which one cannot exit or to have no access at all to collective democratic decision-making about important issues that affect one's life? If a global polity can be portrayed as the former, the absence of a global polity can be pictured as the latter. Which is worse from a democratic perspective?

I do not doubt that the possibility of exit is one important factor under some circumstances in enhancing democratic voice, but on any plausible account it is only one factor, and, for that matter, the effectiveness of feedback is only one consideration in assessing the democratic character of a polity. Perhaps there will turn out to be tradeoffs between the availability of exit and other factors that enhance democracy, and on balance it would make sense to accept the absence of exit for the sake of these other factors. Or perhaps not. The point is that an empirically unsupported claim that the absence of exit fatally undermines the possibility of democratic feedback does not seem to me to be a good argument for the claim that global democracy is intrinsically impossible.

Perhaps these comments reflect a misunderstanding of Bauböck's project. What is the nature and purpose of this discussion in section 2.1?

Let's approach this from another perspective. Why might people think that some sort of global democracy would be a good idea, perhaps even something required as a matter of justice from an ideal perspective? Climate change is one obvious reason. Here is a global phenomenon that is affecting everyone on the planet and will affect everyone in the future even more profoundly. So, some might say, everyone ought to be able to participate in decisions about how to deal with this problem. Of course, as Bauböck rightly argues, democracy requires more than issue-specific participatory decision-making. It requires stable jurisdictional authority over a wide range of issues and some relatively stable understanding of who is a member and entitled to participate in decision-making. But climate change is not the only global problem. It is merely an example of the type of problem that seems to require a global polity if it is to be addressed democratically.

Is it conceptually impossible to imagine the existence of global democratic institutions for dealing with a wide range of global problems (including the relationships among these problems)? For example, could we not imagine a global political assembly with powers (including agenda-setting powers) specified by a constitution, representatives elected by universal suffrage on a global basis, and so on?

Let me be clear. I am not recommending global democracy as just outlined as an ideal or arguing that it is a necessary feature of a just global order. One can certainly raise challenges to such an idea from many different perspectives, even as an ideal. And from a practical perspective, the challenges are much stronger. Global democracy seems to me to be a non-starter as a way to address most urgent global problems (like climate change) in the near term. If climate change and other global problems are to be addressed now, it will have to be done primarily through the cooperation of states, as in the recent Paris Treaty (though I do not mean to understate the important role of global civil society actors in pushing for global solutions). By the way, this is an illustration of the potential tension between ideals and practical problems that I identified above. One might think that global democracy is the ideal institutional arrangement and required as part of a just global order but also that this does not help much in deciding how best to deal with current global problems. It does not seem to me, however, that these reasons for challenging global democracy – its normative flaws as an ideal or its practical limitations in the world as it is – are Bauböck's reasons for excluding it from his discussion of democratic principles after section 2. Again, perhaps I have misunderstood. If Bauböck does intend to exclude global democracy on conceptual grounds, I encourage him to clarify that argument in light of the questions I have raised in this section. If his arguments against global democracy have some other basis, I encourage him to be more explicit about what that is.

AAI and the global political order

We turn now to Bauböck's discussion of the principle of all affected interests. In section 3.1 when discussing AAI, Bauböck says that the "current international state system is deeply flawed" because "it is designed to reduce the duty of states to justify their decisions towards those on whom they impact outside their territorial borders" (p. 24). Notice how this formulation implicitly accepts many of the features of the current international system, even while criticizing others. If we take the interests of all human beings seriously, we might think that the biggest flaw in the current state system is not that it fails to require states to take external interests into account in policy decisions but rather that the way the entire system is constructed favours the interests of the few – mainly those living in rich states – over the interests of the many – most of those living elsewhere in the world. In any event, that is my own view. Is Bauböck willing to entertain this sort of fundamental challenge to the current global order or is that something that he seeks to exclude, at least in this essay?

I am not sure of the answer to this question. At a number of points, starting with the second paragraph of the book, Bauböck explicitly criticizes the idea of accepting the moral legitimacy of the current international order as a starting point. He offers occasional sharp criticisms of that order in the course of his essay, and he seems to want to subject the entire global political order to critical scrutiny from the perspective of a commitment to democratic inclusion as reflected in the three principles of AAI, ASC and ACS. And yet, so far as I can tell, Bauböck does not seem to think that these three principles raise any fundamental questions about the justice or legitimacy of the current global political order.

I find that puzzling. Let's set aside the question of global democracy and assume here what I previously challenged, namely that Bauböck's discussion of the circumstances of democracy establishes the case against the idea of a single political community exercising some form of territorial jurisdiction over the entire world. So, following Bauböck, we take the plurality of polities as a fundamental requirement of a global political order based on democratic principles. What does this tell us about how the world should be organized politically? Very little, actually.

It does not follow from the fact that democracy requires plurality that these plural polities have to be like modern states in the powers and privileges they possess or in their relationships with one another and with the members of other polities. Bauböck's own discussion of municipalities and regional associations shows that it is a mistake to think of the modern state as the only possible way to organize political life democratically, even if one accepts the need for distinct polities with territorial jurisdictions and agenda-setting powers. And the concept of a self-governing people is not self-explanatory, especially if one rejects, as Bauböck does, an essentialist account of nations. To say that self-governing peoples "cannot be merely functional aggregates of individuals who happen to share an interest in a particular political decision or public good" (p. 11) does not tell us very much about what powers and privileges are necessary for a people to be self-governing or about the extent to which individuals should be free to change their membership in one self-governing people for membership in another. Bauböck wants to argue, I think, that hypermigration is incompatible with a polity functioning as a self-governing people, but that still leaves open a very wide range of alternative arrangements regarding movement into and out of polities and peoples.

Let's return to the principle of AAI and ask what that entails in a context where we are not starting with any presupposition about the existing global political order except the need for a plurality of polities and perhaps the desirability of self-governing peoples. Doesn't this abstract principle require us to ask what ways of constructing polities and their relationships with one another and with individuals inside and outside their jurisdictions are most likely to serve the interests of all most effectively over time and thus to satisfy the requirements of democratic inclusion?[1]

There are, of course, many different ways to answer such a question. Here is mine. Even if we accept that a just global order will include distinct polities and self-governing peoples, we should try to bind these different polities and peoples together in various ways. One desirable form of mutual binding would be the acceptance of procedures for the peaceful resolution of conflicts. Another would be a commitment to mutual economic support that would prevent the emergence of large economic differences between polities and peoples. A third would be a commitment to permit individuals to move freely from one polity to another, leaving their people of origin and joining a new one, at least so long as the overall level of movement into a polity was not so high that it undermined a people's capacity for self-government. I would add that if individuals do want to move at rates that would interfere *to some extent* with a people's capacity for self-government, a just global order from an AAI perspective would have to weigh the negative effects of such interference on the interests of those within

---

[1]   I deliberately used the term "all" rather than "all humans" in this sentence to leave open the possibility that a concern with democratic inclusion obliges us to ask how alternative arrangements serve the interests of animals as well as humans. For the sake of simplicity, however, and because I am confident that Will Kymlicka and Susan Donaldson will explore that issue more effectively than I could, I will hereafter refer only to humans in my discussion.

the polity against the negative effects of exclusion on those outside a polity trying to get in. There are few normative absolutes. Degrees matter morally.

I recognize, of course, that not everyone would share my view of what a morally desirable global political order would be, and I am not trying to develop a positive case for that view here. I present this just to illustrate the possibility that someone might think that a commitment to taking the interests of all seriously would require a fundamental transformation of existing arrangements, even if one accepts a plurality of polities as a starting point. What is Bauböck's stance towards this sort of view? Does he think that the principle of AAI does *not* have these sorts of far-reaching implications? If so, does he think that his analysis explains why it does not? Or is he intending to bracket this sort of fundamental question in order to concentrate on questions with more immediate practical relevance?

There are some indications in the essay that Bauböck is indeed interested in exploring fundamental questions about what a just global political order would require from a democratic perspective. For example, early on in the essay he says that the ideas he has developed about the circumstances of democracy "are fully compatible with the project of cosmopolitan constitutionalism and the building of a global *legal* community" (p. 12). That seems close to the first form of mutual binding of polities that I suggested we should see as part of a just global political order, and far from the current state of affairs. It suggests that Bauböck is open in principle to a fundamental examination of the requirements of a just global order. Moreover, in section 4 of the essay Bauböck does touch briefly on questions about global justice in connection with his discussion of birthright citizenship, and there he makes some assertions about the kinds of inequalities between polities that are and are not justifiable.

On the other hand, Bauböck's discussion of these sorts of fundamental questions is limited, taking the essay as a whole. His mention of the possibility of a global legal community is made in passing, not offered as the conclusion of his own arguments. The discussion of global justice in section 4 is very brief and is somewhat peripheral to his primary focus in that section. Moreover, at many points in section 3, including his discussion of AAI, Bauböck seems to assume that it makes sense to proceed without addressing questions about the ways in which distinct polities are or should be related to one another. In his discussion of AAI, he seems to presuppose that he is exploring the implications of that principle for a world organized politically much like the one in which we live today. Is that a correct understanding of how Bauböck is proceeding, and if so why has he chosen that approach?

Let me be clear. I am not arguing that Bauböck ought to transform his essay on democratic inclusion into a general discussion of global justice. Rather I am trying to get him to clarify what questions he is pursuing and what questions he is setting aside. In particular, I am asking him to explain why he is not pursuing some questions that seem to flow from his own stated concerns. As I noted early on in my comments, I think there can be a tension between the goal of pursuing an analysis with practical relevance and the goal of pursuing an analysis of fundamental principles. I have no objection if someone chooses to accept the constraints of the current international system as a way of limiting the scope of a particular discussion so as to make it more useful for addressing immediate issues. Indeed, I think it is legitimate to set some questions aside simply on the grounds that one cannot discuss everything, even everything relevant to one's topic. But I do think that it is important to acknowledge such restrictions explicitly if that is how one chooses to proceed. I don't see that Bauböck has done this. On the other hand, if Bauböck does actually think that, apart from the problem of external affected interests, the principle of AAI is largely compatible with the way the current global political order assigns power and responsibilities to different polities and orders both the relationships among polities and the relationships between any given polity and members of other polities, and if he wants this assessment to play a role in his analysis, I think he should explain more fully the reasons for his holding this view.

ASC and equality of rights

Turn now to the second principle that Bauböck considers: the idea that being subject to government coercion entitles one to democratic inclusion (ASC). As Bauböck notes, many people use this as a principle for determining who is entitled to citizenship. Bauböck argues that those who are within a polity's jurisdiction are normally subject to its coercive powers in ways that those outside it are not. This does give rise to special claims to inclusion, he says, but not, as some argue, to membership in the political community itself. Rather, those subject to governmental authority are entitled to equal rights and liberties, to equal protection of their rights and liberties under the law, and to opportunities to contest the exercise of governmental authority. Bauböck explores a number of interesting issues in this section (3.2), and I agree with much (though not all) of what he says. I want to focus again, however, on what he leaves out – the questions that he does not pursue and whose non-pursuit he does not explain. I have two concerns in mind: (1) questions about the background economic and social conditions that must be satisfied in order for this sort of democratic inclusion to be meaningful; and (2) questions about the extent to which different categories of people may be entitled to different legal rights because of their legal status within the polity.

In discussing what ASC requires, Bauböck says the following:

> the institutional devices for securing equal protection of the law and opportunities for contestation are conventional and do not have to be newly invented. They include constitutional protection of fundamental rights and judicial review of ordinary legislation by constitutional courts as well as institutionalized complaints and contestation procedures for individuals in courts and ombudsman bodies and, finally, the rights to protest against governments and their decisions through political speech and activities.

On the one hand, I certainly agree that all of these institutional devices are necessary. On the other hand, it seems equally obvious that they are not sufficient. Reading this passage I could not help but recall Anatole France's famous remark about the law forbidding both rich and poor to beg bread in the streets and sleep under bridges at night, thus drawing attention to the limitations of formal equality under the law.

Shouldn't an essay on democratic inclusion say something about the economic and social prerequisites of democratic inclusion, or at least acknowledge that this is an important set of issues that is being set to one side for reasons of time and space and not because they are irrelevant? In my discussion of AAI, I have already tried to indicate why questions about economic arrangements might be relevant to an assessment of the moral legitimacy of the global political order. ASC ought to bring those questions sharply into view within the boundaries of particular polities. It is a longstanding egalitarian critique of liberal theory that it focuses too much on formal rights and so neglects the social and economic conditions that determine how formal rights affect people's lives. I fear that Bauböck's discussion here is open to that critique. Let me add that it is clear from Bauböck's other writings that he accepts the argument that we should be concerned with substantive, not purely formal, equality. So, I regard the absence of attention to this topic in this essay as an oversight rather than a reflection of his actual views. Nevertheless, I think it is worth elaborating the point just a bit further.

Anatole France's comment draws attention to the ways in which the content of the law itself can be discriminatory or unfair because of its differential impact on those subject to it. But even if one focuses only on the protection of fundamental rights – which, to be fair, is Bauböck's primary concern – we cannot ignore questions about the social and economic conditions that determine what those rights mean in practice. I write at a moment when the Black Lives Matter movement has gained prominence in the United States and, to a lesser degree, in other states as well. This movement reminds us that some people have a daily experience of not enjoying equal protection of their most fundamental rights under the law, simply because of the colour of their skin, even though they are formally entitled to equal protection. The problem may be worse in the United States than elsewhere, but it is certainly a serious problem in Canada as well (where indigenous people are also particularly subject to this reality) and I think it is safe to say that neither are European states immune.

Now think also about the role that money can play in determining how formal legal rights function in practice in any arrangement that permits individuals to hire legal representation. If we were really committed to equal rights under the law, we would have to devise mechanisms to ensure that rich and poor were equally secure against (and equally vulnerable to) governmental coercion. From a North American perspective at least, that would entail the development of some new "institutional devices" in addition to those mentioned by Bauböck.

These brief examples only scratch the surface of the ways in which social and economic factors affect democratic inclusion. As in my discussion of the possibility of a radical challenge to the current global political order, I am not arguing here that Bauböck should have addressed questions about the economic and social prerequisites of equal subjection to coercion. Rather, I am asking whether he would agree that these are questions that do flow naturally from ASC as a principle of democratic inclusion, that he should explicitly explain his decision not to address them, and that he should acknowledge the ways in which leaving them aside might qualify any conclusions reached in the essay.

I can address my second concern much more briefly. There is a tendency in discussions of ASC to lump together questions about who is subject to government coercion with questions about who is entitled to legal rights, and to focus on those who are within the territorial jurisdiction of a state. That approach works well enough when what is at issue is the protection of basic liberties such as religious freedom, protection against arbitrary detention, and so on, but it is rather misleading if one tries to ask how legal status should or should not affect the legal rights that a person possesses. Not all legal rights are basic liberties, and even some pretty fundamental legal rights, like the right to work, are normally not granted to everyone who happens to be within the jurisdiction of the state at a particular time, but are allocated on the basis of one's legal status.

Bauböck skims over this problem. At one point he says,

> The duty of equal protection for all within the jurisdiction needs to track the impact of being subject to coercive legislation on individuals' freedom. While tourists will hardly qualify, temporary migrants may experience significant restrictions of their autonomy, especially if they do not enjoy the same freedom of movement and legal protections as long-term residents. (p. 31)

Notice what this obscures. Tourists do qualify for the protection of their basic rights and liberties, but they do not have the right to work or the right to access most social programmes that the state provides. That may be justifiable, but it requires an argument. The very category of "tourist" (or "visitor") serves a function in allocating legal rights, defining those within that category as people who are not entitled to some of the important legal rights enjoyed by residents, including, for example, the right to stay as long as one wants and to seek employment. So, here some contestable background features of the current global order are simply presupposed.

The sentence about temporary migrants seems to suggest that temporary migrants should enjoy the same legal rights as residents. As it happens, I largely agree with this claim but it is hardly uncontested and it requires qualification. In any event, there is a literature advocating sharp differences between the rights of temporary migrants and the rights of residents, and lots of actual programmes that limit the rights of temporary migrants. So, one cannot simply assume that everyone will accept this way of interpreting the requirement of equality under the law.

A bit further on in the section Bauböck says, "From an inclusion perspective the important question is who should be protected and have access to contestation opportunities. If the answer is: all subjected to government jurisdiction, then citizens and non-citizen residents must enjoy these rights equally" (p. 34). He goes on to cite a famous American Supreme Court decision that extended the Fourteenth Amendment to irregular immigrants. But that decision did not entail the conclusion that irregular immigrants were constitutionally entitled to all the legal rights that authorized legal residents enjoy. Leave aside questions of constitutional interpretation. Is the correct moral position for someone committed to equality of rights as a principle of democratic inclusion that irregular migrants should enjoy the same legal rights as permanent residents? I happen to think that it is, but even I add some qualifications to the claim, and I recognize that I am somewhat of an outlier in my view of this question. Lots of people would argue that one can be committed to equality of rights and democratic inclusion without embracing this view of the legal rights of irregular migrants.

As before, I am not arguing that Bauböck should have discussed these issues in his essay. I am suggesting that he should have added a few qualifications to what he did say and noted the existence of a genuine debate about what rights different categories of immigrants should enjoy.

ACS and the importance of self-government

I turn finally and even more briefly to Bauböck's discussion of his third principle, the democratic requirement that all those who have an important stake in citizenship be recognized as formal members of the political community (ACS). As I indicated at the outset, I am largely in agreement with Bauböck's discussion of who ought to have access to legal citizenship in the world as it is today and how that access ought to be provided. As I read the essay, that is the main function of ACS as a principle. Nevertheless, Bauböck also tries to connect ACS to deeper questions and, as with his discussion of AAI, I am unclear about the extent to which he is open to basic challenges to current political arrangements.

There are points in his essay at which Bauböck seems to want to advance a claim about the fundamental moral importance of membership in a self-governing political community. In section 2.1, for example, he distinguishes between justice and legitimacy: "popular self-government is a fundamental and intrinsic value, the pursuit of which must be constrained by requirements of justice, but which is at the same time a free-standing value that cannot be entirely derived from what justice requires. The primary purpose of democracy is to provide legitimacy to coercive political rule through popular self-government" (p. 10). This precedes the discussion of ACS, of course, but it is intimately connected to that principle, as becomes apparent later in the essay in section 3.3 where he says in the course of his discussion of ACS that "membership in a polity is a necessary condition for human autonomy and well-being" (p. 40).

These sorts of statements invite an inquiry into more fundamental questions. Here are some that occur to me. What sorts of powers must a polity have to count as self-governing and why? Are these absolutes or questions of degree? How well does the existing international state system do in providing human beings with the kind of political membership needed for human autonomy and well-being? What are the requirements of justice and how should they constrain the pursuit of popular self-government? What are the other necessary conditions for human autonomy and well-being besides membership in a polity? How well does the existing international state system do in providing human beings with the various conditions required for human autonomy and well-being? Can we imagine better ways of organizing the global political order that would do better in meeting the various requirements of human autonomy and well-being?

Does Bauböck actually intend to raise these questions or would he prefer to rescind the invitation I found in some of his statements? Does the principle of ACS depend upon how those questions are answered? I pose these as genuine, not rhetorical, questions. But the main questions I want to pose to Bauböck in this regard are those I have been pursuing throughout my comments: What questions is the discussion of ACS intended to address? What questions is he leaving aside in this discussion and why is he leaving them aside? If Bauböck addresses my questions about his questions, I think that his readers will gain a much clearer sense of the boundaries of "democratic inclusion".

3

What makes a democratic people?

David Miller

Rainer Bauböck has offered us a fascinating and wide-ranging analysis of a question that is often now referred to as "the democratic boundary problem".[1] How does this problem arise? Before we can begin to discuss how a democracy might function, what decision rules it should use, and so forth, we have to decide how it should be constituted. But on closer inspection, this turns out to raise two questions rather than one. The first is the question of jurisdiction: over what domain is the democratic body we are about to constitute authorized to take decisions? By a domain here I mean a geographical area – a territory – within which the decisions that the democracy is going to take will be applied.[2] Then there is the question of inclusion: who will form part of the relevant demos that makes these decisions, in the sense of being eligible to vote in elections and referendums, stand for office, and so forth? These two questions are obviously intertwined. Indeed one might be tempted to think that by answering the jurisdiction question one has also found the answer to the inclusion question: the demos should be made up of all and only those who fall under the jurisdiction of the democratic unit we are about to create. But, as Bauböck's admirable discussion makes

---

[1] This has already generated a substantial literature. See, for example, Whelan (1983); Arrhenius (2005); Song (2012); Saunders (2012); Erman (2014). My own contribution is Miller (2009).

[2] Of course, the jurisdiction of a democratic body need not be territorially defined – for example a professional association or a trade union can have a democratic constitution. But here we are concerned with democratic institutions in the conventional political sense, and these always have territorial jurisdictions.

abundantly clear, this is far too simple an answer. Both jurisdiction and inclusion pose intractable questions for democrats. Moreover, these questions are not just theoretical. The first arises in practice whenever one state annexes territory that previously belonged to another, altering jurisdictional boundaries, or when a region within a state secedes to form a state of its own. How, if at all, might such domain changes be justified? And the issue of inclusion arises whenever democracies have to decide who among the many people present on their territory at any moment should qualify for full rights of citizenship, as well as who among those currently *outside* the territory might also qualify.

How, then, should we think about these two interrelated boundary problems? Can the same principles guide us towards solutions to both, or do they have to be addressed independently? And which needs to be tackled first? You might think that jurisdiction is the more basic problem: we need to establish the size and the shape of the political unit that will be governed democratically before we can decide who should be entitled to take part in running it. We could, for instance, try to settle the domain question on functional grounds. Suppose our aim is to create a democratic state: then we should form a unit that is neither so small that it cannot carry out the basic functions of a state, whatever those turn out to be, nor so large that it becomes too unwieldy to be governed democratically. We might also appeal to geographical or economic grounds for choosing a particular jurisdictional space. Having sorted out which principles should apply to jurisdiction, we could then go on to tackle the inclusion issue, with at least a strong presumption that all those who fall within a democracy's jurisdictional domain should be included in the demos. However, we could also proceed quite differently. We could begin by asking: what must a group be like if it is to form an effective demos – one that can operate in the way that we hope a democratic body should? In asking this, we make the assumption that not just any randomly selected set of individuals could compose such a body; a collective that is able to work as a viable democracy must have certain essential features – the members must speak a common language or languages, for example. Then, having arrived at principles for constituting demoi, we would settle the jurisdiction question by drawing boundaries in such a way that as far as possible each set of boundaries enclosed a viable demos. If for some reason the As and Bs can't work together democratically, then we should try if we can to give each group their own area of jurisdiction, perhaps even their own state.

The discussion in the previous paragraph might create the impression that we have to solve the boundary problem starting from scratch, in a world where no boundaries yet exist, which is of course absurd. The point, however, is that we do face jurisdiction and inclusion problems in the world as it is, with boundaries already drawn, and then we have to decide in which direction to look for guidance. Suppose for instance we had to adjudicate between possible solutions to the Israel/Palestine problem. We might begin by addressing questions of jurisdiction first, and conclude that, for economic and other reasons, it makes sense to have a single state in the region now covered by the state of Israel and the occupied territories. Having settled that issue, we would move on to consider the composition of the citizen body who should govern it, as well as other questions concerning the institutional form that democracy should take in that area. Alternatively, we might take the composition of the demos as our most basic question, and ask whether Israelis and Palestinians together could form one. If the answer to that question turns out to be "No", then we would approach the jurisdiction issue on the assumption that two separate units – quite possibly two independent states existing side by side – need to be created. My point here is not to suggest that either the one-state or the two-state solution is necessarily to be preferred, but to illustrate how it makes a difference whether the question we first ask is about jurisdiction or about inclusion in the demos.

But where *should* we start? This will depend on how we understand democracy and the values that underlie it. Here we need to draw another distinction. Democracy, uncontroversially, is a way of making political decisions. But we can focus our attention either on the input side of any decision or series of decisions, or on the output side. That is, we can investigate how a decision came to be made, how good or bad the process was that led to that particular decision being reached; or we can investigate the impact that a decision will have on the people being affected by it, asking in particular whether the needs or interests of those people were properly taken into account when the decision was made. From a democratic perspective, both of these aspects should matter. Presumably we want democratic decision procedures to meet certain standards internally. We want the decisions that are reached to be mutually consistent, for example; we want them to be informed by the relevant evidence, where appropriate; we don't want majorities to ride roughshod over minorities within the demos. But we should be concerned about impact as well. Something has gone wrong if a democratic institution, no matter how well functioning internally, takes decisions that may inflict serious harms on people who are not represented in the body that decides. We cannot just assume that good procedures will always take proper account of the interests of those who have no say in the process itself: "no taxation without representation", as the old slogan has it. So both aspects are important, but how we weight them relative to one another may depend on our underlying conception of democracy, as I have argued elsewhere (Miller 2009).

Most of Bauböck's discussion addresses the impact side of this debate: he is trying mainly to pin down the *kind* of impact that will entitle its recipient to participate in a democratic body. I shall shortly be discussing the various answers to the impact question that he canvasses, but first we should observe that he is also sensitive to the issue of functioning. He recognizes that a viable demos must possess certain features, in particular a sufficient degree of stability. This emerges in the course of his very interesting discussion of mobile and sedentary societies. As he notes:

> Democracy also needs a sense of "ownership" and belonging to the polity. It is difficult to imagine how hypermobile populations could be citizens of the territorial polity who authorize the government that issues and implements the laws to which they are subjected. If there is

a relatively sedentary core population, then immigrants can integrate into the society while emigrants can remain connected to it across borders. Where there is no such core, it will be difficult to generate among territorial populations a sense of responsibility for the common good of the polity. (p. 17)

This is important, though I shall later argue that Bauböck does not pursue the idea to its logical conclusion. In particular it exposes for what it is the fantasy that democracy could work on an ad hoc basis, with different constituencies being assembled to decide each issue as it arose. So already we can see that attending to the process side of democracy will place some constraints on the possible answers one might give to the impact question. Solutions to the latter question that are incompatible with the thesis stated in the paragraph above ought to be summarily rejected.

Despite this, Bauböck begins by considering sympathetically the all affected interests (AAI) principle, according to which "all those whose interests are affected by any possible decision arising out of any possible agenda must be included in the demos" (p. 22).[3] Taken literally, this would mean that the demos must be global in scope, since any decision taken by a less inclusive body is liable to affect the interests of at least some outsiders, and Bauböck recoils from this conclusion, arguing that democracy presupposes the existence of a plurality of bounded political communities. Nevertheless, he concedes to the defenders of AAI that "those whose interests are affected by a decision have a democratic claim that their interests be taken into account in the process of decision-making and implementation" (p. 20). It is not entirely clear what is needed to satisfy this claim: do the interests of outsiders have to be *represented* in some way when the decision is taken? There are moments at which this seems to be Bauböck's view. He says "actually affected interests have a claim to voice. They must be heard and taken into account by those

3 For debate about this principle, see Goodin (2007); Näsström (2011); Owen (2012); as well as the works cited in note 1 above.

who take the decision" (p. 24). But this is immediately equated with having a "right to justification of the decision", which seems less to do with having a voice before the decision is made and more to do with the decision itself being such that once taken it can be justified to all those whose interests it affects – a substantive rather than procedural requirement.

Rather than trying to find a version of AAI that renders it consistent with the sedentarist thesis that democracy requires a bounded territory and a relatively stable core membership, it would be better simply to drop AAI altogether as a solution to the boundary problem. It is, after all, highly implausible in the canonical form cited in the previous paragraph. Consider an example. The British Chancellor decides to raise consumption taxes to finance rising health care costs. British consumers have a bit less disposable income and decide to cut back on Mediterranean holidays. This, obviously, has an impact on the livelihoods of the island-dwellers for whom tourism is the main source of income. Perhaps the marginal beach-bar owner will be forced out of business. Should he or she have a voice in the Chancellor's decision? Is the Chancellor even required to justify his decision to the bar owner? I take the answers to these questions to be obvious, but it may still be worth spelling out why. Anyone who sets up a beach-bar on a Greek island must expect that tourist flows will vary significantly from year to year and take appropriate precautions (save in the good years, have a second line of work for the bad years, etc.). They have entered a market, and markets are not only unpredictable in general but are also affected by government decisions (including foreign government decisions) over things like monetary policy and tax rates. Like human beings everywhere, beach-bar owners are responsible agents who need to protect themselves against decisions over which they neither have control in fact, nor are entitled to have it normatively. To have to justify ourselves to everyone whose interests we might affect by our actions would make it impossible for people to act at all, except in the rare cases where what we do is fully self-regarding – that is, has no perceptible impact on anyone other than the agent herself.

Defenders of AAI will protest that I have caricatured their principle by taking a case like the Mediterranean beach-bars. They are concerned with much weightier instances in which governments take decisions that impact outsiders – refugees, climate change, nuclear waste, and so forth. What this reveals, however, is that any plausible claims that might be advanced under AAI are better understood as falling under a Global Harm Principle (GHP), which among other things prohibits countries from causing serious and unavoidable harm to those outside their borders.[4] In contrast to AAI, GHP only considers as relevant cases where interests are affected *negatively*, cases where the setback to interests is *serious* and cases where the setback *cannot reasonably be avoided* by prudent action on the affected agent's part. Where it is likely that a decision will be taken that breaches GHP, there may often be good reason to listen to the voices of those who are liable to be harmed, since they will be best placed to explain how the harm can be averted, or, if that is not possible, compensated for. So there are occasions when people outside of the demos do have a right to be heard by those inside – Bauböck's conclusion is correct, but the principle that delivers it is GHP, not the wildly over-inflated AAI.

Let me turn, then, to the second principle of inclusion that Bauböck considers sympathetically (but ultimately rejects, at least as a comprehensive solution): the principle that all subject to coercion (ASC) by a democratic institution are entitled to participate in that institution. What does it mean to be subject to coercion? As Bauböck's discussion makes clear, he is thinking primarily of the case in which someone is governed by a legal system that uses coercive sanctions, not of isolated acts of coercion. This distinction is important. What lends plausibility to ASC is the thought that a coercively enforced legal system shapes people's lives in a fundamental way, and potentially exposes them to domination. To guard against this possibility, they must be given the opportunity to control how that system operates. The principle does

---

[4] For defences of this principle, including discussion of how "harm" should be understood in a global context, see Linklater (2006) and Vernon (2010: ch. 7).

not imply that whenever anyone is subjected to coercive force, they are entitled to a democratic say in how that force is exercised – a position that quickly reveals its absurdity.[5]

ASC tells us why everyone who is permanently resident in a country and subject to its government ought to be included as an equal participant in democratic institutions. Does it over-extend democratic rights by demanding that every immigrant who intends to stay must be granted full rights of citizenship immediately? Here we see why, in thinking about the democratic boundary problem, it is important to keep both the question of impact and the question of how democratic procedures are likely to operate in full view. When democracies require a period of some years of residence to elapse before immigrants can apply for citizenship, they do so (presumably) on the basis that new arrivals need to learn something about the politics of the country they are joining before they are given the responsibility of casting their votes. No doubt some will be prepared for this sooner than others, but a uniform residence requirement operates in the same way as a uniform age requirement for voting – as a rough indicator of when somebody is likely to be sufficiently competent to perform as a citizen in a democracy. So ASC can't be treated as providing necessary and sufficient conditions for inclusion; it needs to be used in conjunction with other principles, such as the presumptive competence principle just sketched. Nevertheless it carries a good deal of the weight, and in particular, as Bauböck emphasizes in the later stages of his essay, provides the best rationale for giving everyone who is resident in a local community voting rights in that community, regardless of their citizenship status.

What guidance can ASC provide in the case of those who are *not* resident in the relevant jurisdiction? As Bauböck says, it awards rights

---

[5]   "Imagine, for instance, that Ben and Jerry knock on my door and ask to enter my house, eat the dinner I was in the process of preparing, and then have sex with me ... I brandish a pistol and warn them that I will not hesitate to shoot if either of them puts so much as one foot inside my house ... Could Ben and Jerry rightfully object that, insofar as they were subjected to coercion, they were entitled to an equal vote as to what my decision should have been? Presumably not ..." (C. Wellman in Wellman and Cole 2011: 97).

to those who are temporarily abroad but expected to return (since their lives overall will be shaped by the policies of the home government), but not to those who have emigrated on a permanent basis: if they are allowed to remain citizens with the right to vote, it must be on some other basis. Somewhat mysteriously, he also claims that ASC will grant rights to "coerced emigrants who have been driven into exile by a non-democratic predecessor regime. In these cases, the situation of individuals is comprehensively marked by subjection to coercion that they have experienced in the past and this creates an ongoing duty of protecting their rights" (p. 31). What is the argument here? People in this position will have a choice, under the current democratic regime, either to return home or to remain in the countries in which they have been exiled. If, despite the offer of readmission, they choose to stay where they are, then ASC grants them rights in *that* jurisdiction, since those are the laws that now and in the future will shape their lives. How can the fact of past coercion by country A – the forces that drove them into exile – justify A awarding them rights of participation in the present?[6] ASC is restrictive towards those who do not currently fall within a government's jurisdiction, and this seems correct.

There is controversy, however, about the case of immigrants who are refused entry under the prevailing immigration policy. Is this an exercise of coercive jurisdiction, and does that mean that prospective immigrants are entitled to a say in the formulation of immigration law, if not over other issues? This position has been defended by Arash Abizadeh especially, though the claim about the coercive nature of immigration law has been widely accepted (Abizadeh 2008).[7] I have

---

[6] Perhaps the thought is that the present regime has inherited from its predecessor a special responsibility towards the exiles. It is not clear, however, why this would not be discharged by an offer of return, on favourable terms and with instant access to citizenship. Governments do also acknowledge a continuing responsibility towards their émigrés, in cases where the émigrés suffer bad treatment in the countries to which they have moved, but this seems to apply regardless of the reasons for emigration, and is not usually thought to justify extending voting rights.

[7] Among others who claim that border controls are coercive are Carens (2013: ch. 12), Blake (2013) and Hidalgo (2014).

subjected it to critique elsewhere (Miller 2010; 2016: ch. 4). In brief, I suggest (a) that not all coercive interventions give rise to democratic rights (see note 6 above); and (b) in the case of immigration policy, it is important to distinguish between the policy itself being coercive, and coercive means being used to enforce it. When people are prevented from entering a country by immigration controls, a significant opportunity is often being denied them, but it does not follow that their lives are being shaped and potentially dominated by the legal system of the country they are trying to enter in the same way as those who are already living under that system. So why should exclusion per se, independently of the means used to enforce it, be regarded as coercive?

Without signing up to the Abizadeh position, Bauböck wants nonetheless to say that the relationship between the state and at least some of those who want to immigrate can be described as coercive. However, the argument at this point morphs into the somewhat different thesis that states have a special responsibility to protect migrants "who have stronger claims to admission to this country than anywhere else" (p. 36). He does not elaborate on how such special claims are established, but let's assume that the migrant is someone who applies to state S for asylum, or simply washes up on its shores. I agree that physical presence of this kind does give state S a special responsibility to protect the migrant's rights, and in some cases this would mean granting her admission. But the argument here has nothing to do with coercion. What gives the migrant a claim is her specific *vulnerability* to S, not the fact that S is coercing her. So it is hard to see how ASC can be applied to such a case.

The limitations of ASC as a general solution to the democratic boundary problem, however, are best brought out by considering a case touched on briefly by Bauböck, one in which what is effectively a colony is incorporated into the metropolitan state in such a way that its inhabitants are given voting rights as citizens of that state. The example he cites is Algeria prior to independence in 1962, but one could also instance Ireland during the nineteenth century, when its voters sent MPs to Westminster. If we assume (contrary to fact) that every adult member of those territories had been awarded voting rights, then ASC would have been fully satisfied. As Bauböck says, the lesson here is that "a democratic principle of membership must link individual inclusion claims to collective self-government claims in order to avoid a status quo bias" (p. 30). But to do that we need some prior way of identifying Algeria and Ireland (rather than Algeria-in-France and Ireland-in-Britain) as the proper units of self-government, and ASC, as a principle of individual inclusion, is of no help here.

So what does Bauböck suggest instead? He proposes the all citizen stakeholder (ACS) principle as the main plank of his theory of democratic inclusion, with AAI and ASC both relegated to supporting roles. The best succinct statement of ACS is found in another of his papers: "Those and only those individuals have a claim to membership whose individual autonomy and well-being is linked to the collective self-government and flourishing of a particular polity" (Bauböck 2015: 825).[8] Since this principle is presented as having the capacity to solve problems that neither AAI nor ASC can deal with adequately, we can assume that it is intended to provide an account of democratic membership that explains *both* why it would be wrong to deny voting rights to, say, women in Britain *and* why it would be wrong to re-annexe Ireland and govern it as a region of Britain. In other words, it can provide answers to questions of both inclusion and jurisdiction as I identified them at the outset. So it must be read so as to mean not merely that individuals have a claim to membership in whatever polity happens to govern them at any moment, but to membership in a polity that enables them to "link" their own autonomy and well-being to the collective autonomy of the polity as a whole. Bauböck's answer to the Algeria question will need to show that Algeria-in-France did not qualify as a polity of that sort; ACS would require Algeria to be both independent and democratic.

Moreover, this has to be demonstrated without recourse to two positions that Bauböck explicitly rejects: nationalism and voluntarism. He

---

[8] I find this version more helpful than the slightly different formulation on p. 49 of the present essay.

cannot, in other words, reject Algeria-in-France on the ground that Algeria forms a nation separate from France, and is entitled on that ground to self-government, or on the grounds that the inhabitants of Algeria had never consented to being governed by France. As he puts it, "political legitimacy in a democratic polity is not derived from nationhood or voluntary association but from popular self-government, that is, citizens' participation and representation in democratic institutions that track their collective will and common good" (p. 41).

I shall return later to Bauböck's rejection of nationhood as a basis for jurisdiction, but first I want to try to unpack these formulations of ACS. What kind of link is being postulated here between "individual autonomy and well-being" and "the collective self-government and flourishing" of the polity? Let me explore two possible answers. According to the first, the link in question is utilitarian. Individuals' interests will only be properly protected when they enjoy collective self-government with appropriate jurisdiction. This answer has some plausibility if we look at the examples I have been using. Britain and France governed Ireland and Algeria, respectively, less well than they might have been governed by institutions that were closer to the people and better informed about local conditions. But how far does it generalize? Can we be confident that when larger units break into two or more pieces, the new units always do a better job of protecting "individual autonomy and well-being" than their more inclusive predecessors? Do Slovaks enjoy more of these goods now than they did when Czechoslovakia was still intact? Or should we conclude that there was no sound case for that state to dissolve? If we acknowledge that it is sometimes legitimate for jurisdictional boundaries to be redrawn so that they align better with the physical habitation of a distinct "people", then the utilitarian way of reading Bauböck's link won't deliver that verdict.

The other possibility is that the link between individual and collective should be understood as psychological. People won't have a sense that they are free and flourishing unless they can identify with their government and see their own freedom as dependent upon the collective freedom of the people. This psychology seems to be what fuels many independence movements, for example. But if ACS understood in this way is also to serve as a principle for deciding upon individuals' rights to be included in the demos, it will yield some paradoxical results. Bauböck himself gives a relevant example, though I shall challenge his use of it. Consider a closed monastic order whose members have little interest in what is going on in the secular world beyond the cloister walls except so far as it interferes with their chosen way of life. Their overwhelming interest is in being left alone by the state. Bauböck claims that "even the members of reclusive monastic orders will be better off as citizens of a democratic polity than as stateless persons or as subjects of autocratic rule" (p. 41). But if this is indeed true – and there is certainly some reason to doubt it – it is not because the monks see any intrinsic value in belonging to a "self-governing political community". They do not connect their own flourishing, and the autonomy and flourishing of their religious community, with any wider version of collective self-government. Any benefits that come to them from inhabiting a democracy are purely instrumental. Do they therefore fail to qualify as "citizen stakeholders" and might they be excluded from voting rights under ACS? Or for a different example, consider those members of the cosmopolitan elite who are rich enough that swapping jurisdictions would at most be a mild inconvenience for them. They have no emotional or other psychological stake in the flourishing of any particular political community (so long as they can get their money out if it collapses). Should they too be disenfranchised under ACS?

This argument can be run in the other direction as well. Consider a passionate Francophile who lives outside of that jurisdiction and cannot for legal or practical reasons move to the country she adores. Nevertheless she follows the news avidly, celebrates when the French team triumphs on the football field and is deeply disturbed by events such as the Charlie Hebdo massacre. She seems to fall within the scope of the ACS principle as laid out above. But we might be unconvinced that such a psychological link, however strong, should be a qualification for rights of citizenship. Now in all these cases it would be possible to bite the bullet, and argue for enfranchising the non-resident Francophile and disenfranchising the monks and the disengaged sports stars and finance capitalists. But unless Bauböck is prepared to accept this, the psychological reading of the link postulated in ACS must be abandoned.

Perhaps there is some third way of reading ACS, and the connected idea of a "citizen stakeholder", that would yield plausible answers both to the jurisdiction question and to the inclusion question. But until this is provided, our verdict must be that there is no single principle that will do the job. Indeed Bauböck reaches a similar conclusion at the end of his essay, arguing that AAI, ASC and ACS all have some contribution to make to the general inclusion question, with different rights going to different constituencies in accordance with the demands of each principle. But if a pluralist approach to democratic legitimacy is correct, this opens the door to a reassessment of the nationalist principle that Bauböck firmly rejects, since we no longer expect that, or any other principle, to be doing all the work that needs to be done. So I should like to end these comments by reflecting on nationality as a source of democratic legitimacy, in the light of Bauböck's critique.

Bauböck concedes that his position resembles liberal nationalism in treating membership in a political community as prior to subjection to government and its decisions. But he argues that a nationalist principle of inclusion will be unable to deal satisfactorily with immigrants and other minority groups, since it requires that "admitting new members to the political community must serve the purpose of nation-building" (p. 39). Depending on the circumstances, this might mean selecting immigrants on cultural grounds, or closing the borders altogether. Now it is true that liberal nationalists will want immigration policy to be shaped in part by a concern for the preservation of national cultures, and this is likely to mean imposing restrictions on the numbers who enter, as well as pursuing active integration policies that seek to familiarize new arrivals with the culture and institutions of the country they are joining. But to say that immigration must "serve the purpose of nation-building" is an exaggeration; immigration policy must be *compatible* with nation-building, a much weaker condition. Moreover, liberal nationalists regard national culture as sufficiently flexible that it can accommodate the distinctive cultural contributions of national minorities and immigrants. The nation that is in the process of being built can be inclusive of these groups.

Bauböck is not committed to an open borders principle; nor does he say that we should judge principles of inclusion only according to the numbers of people who will be let in by following them. If following principle A has the consequence that fewer immigrants are admitted but those who are let in are better integrated, while following principle B would admit more but integrate them less well, is it obvious that B is to be preferred to A?

When it comes to national minorities, ACS is said to be sensitive to their claims. Democratic legitimacy may require that the state be defined constitutionally as "plurinational", and these minorities granted territorial autonomy. Where these conditions are not met, Bauböck says, internal minorities "have remedial rights to self-determination that may result in the formation of autonomous territories or new independent states" (p. 43). So it seems that, after all, he is committed to a principle of national self-determination, albeit not necessarily one requiring that the nation should control a state of its own. A national minority is something more than just a territorially concentrated population. Although he does not spell it out, Bauböck must assume that it has a political identity of its own that demands constitutional recognition and political arrangements through which it can exercise collective autonomy. But it is inconsistent to claim this for national minorities without recognizing that the same must hold for majority nations. What is true of the Basques and the Welsh must also be true of the Spanish and the British: a legitimate government for these peoples must be one that grants them an adequate measure of self-determination.[9]

---

[9] In a footnote, Bauböck claims that he endorses secession only as a remedial measure, and denies that there can be "a primary right to self-determination". But there is something quite puzzling about this. How can self-determination be claimed as a remedy unless the group in question has a right to self-determination that had previously been violated? It would be rather like saying that I have no primary right to own property, but I do have a remedial right to take back stolen possessions.

So long as it is applied flexibly, the nationality principle provides good answers to questions of jurisdiction and boundary-drawing. This is true even in cases where people's political identities are complex, and the jurisdictional solution needs to mirror this complexity, allowing for minorities within minorities and so forth.[10] It is less successful as a principle of individual inclusion: it is not acceptable on democratic grounds to make citizenship rights dependent upon a person's national identity – though it *is* acceptable, I believe, to forge links between the two by means of citizenship education for native-born and immigrants alike, whose purpose is in part to encourage recipients to identify with the nation. It needs, therefore, to be used in conjunction with a principle such as ASC which grants citizenship rights to everyone who is permanently resident in a society, and thereby subject to the life-shaping effects of a coercive legal system. But whereas ASC by itself has nothing to say about the conditions for an effective democracy, other than that everyone who lives under it must be given the vote, the nationality principle underlines the role of a shared identity in creating social and political trust, thereby facilitating the accommodations and compromises that are essential if democratic decisions are to be accepted as authoritative by all concerned.

Earlier in the essay I cited, approvingly, a passage from Bauböck in which he argues that democracy requires a "core" population who are sedentary and think of themselves as "owning" the polity. They will acknowledge "duties of solidarity" towards one another and have "a sense of responsibility for the common good of the polity". To meet these conditions, however, it is clearly not enough for people simply to coexist side by side over time, since otherwise we would not witness conflict-ridden societies where near-neighbours are unable to cooperate to build a life together. The missing element, clearly, is that the people in question identify with one another as compatriots, recognize a common inheritance which may involve responsibilities as well as

---

[10]   I use Kashmir as a pertinent case study in Miller (2014).

rights, and feel an obligation to their successors to leave the society in at least as good a shape as they found it. If we accept this – and I think Bauböck does – then the main issue is the kind of identity that is needed to perform this role. In the real world, the answer at least for the liberal democracies is nationhood, but it is a legitimate topic for research how far existing national identities can be "thinned" so that they become more accessible to newcomers. My own reading of the evidence is that we may face a tradeoff between thicker and more motivationally powerful forms of national identity and thinner and weaker, but more inclusive, forms (Miller and Ali 2014). Whatever the right answer, however, questions about identity are unavoidable, and this it seems to me is the missing ingredient in Bauböck's otherwise compelling discussion of democratic legitimacy.

References

Abizadeh, Arash 2008. "Democratic Theory and Border Coercion: No Right to Unilaterally Control Your Own Borders." *Political Theory* 36: 37–65.

Arrhenius, Gustaf. 2005. "The Boundary Problem in Democratic Theory." In (ed.), *Democracy Unbound*, edited by Folke Tersman. Stockholm: Stockholm University: 14–29.

Bauböck, Rainer 2015. "Morphing the Demos into the Right Shape: Normative Principles for Enfranchising Resident Aliens and Expatriate Citizens." *Democratization* 22: 820–839.

Blake, Michael 2013. "Immigration, Jurisdiction, and Exclusion", *Philosophy and Public Affairs* 41: 103–130.

Carens, Joseph 2013. *The Ethics of Immigration*. Oxford: Oxford University Press.

Erman, Eva 2014. "The Boundary Problem and the Ideal of Democracy." *Constellations* 21: 535–546.

Goodin, Robert 2007. "Enfranchising All Affected Interests, and Its Alternatives." *Philosophy and Public Affairs* 35: 40–68.

Hidalgo, Javier 2014. "Freedom, Immigration, and Adequate Options." *Critical Review of International Social and Political Philosophy* 17: 212–234.

Linklater, Andrew 2006. "The Harm Principle and Global Ethics." *Global Society* 20: 329–343.

Miller, David 2009. "Democracy's Domain." *Philosophy and Public Affairs* 37: 201–228.

Miller, David 2010. "Why Immigration Controls are not Coercive: A Reply to Arash Abizadeh." *Political Theory* 38: 111–120.

Miller, David 2014. "Debatable Lands." *International Theory* 6: 104–121.

Miller, David 2016. *Strangers in Our Midst: The Political Philosophy of Immigration.* Cambridge, MA: Harvard University Press.

Miller David and Sundas Ali. 2014. "Testing the National Identity Argument." *European Political Science Review* 6: 237–259.

Näsström, Sofia 2011. "The Challenge of the All-Affected Principle." *Political Studies* 59: 116–134.

Owen, David 2012. "Constituting the Polity, Constituting the Demos: On the Place of the All Affected Interests Principle in Democratic Theory and in Resolving the Democratic Boundary Problem." *Ethics and Global Politics* 5: 129–152.

Saunders, Ben 2012. "Defining the Demos." *Politics, Philosophy and Economics* 11: 280–301.

Song, Sarah 2012. "The Boundary Problem in Democratic Theory: Why the Demos should be Bounded by the State." *International Theory* 4: 39–68.

Vernon, Richard 2010. *Cosmopolitan Regard: Political Membership and Global Justice.* Cambridge: Cambridge University Press.

Wellman, Christopher and Phillip Cole. 2011. *Debating the Ethics of Immigration: Is There a Right to Exclude?* Oxford: Oxford University Press.

Whelan, Frederick 1983. "Prologue: Democratic Theory and the Boundary Problem." In *NOMOS 25: Liberal Democracy*, edited by J. Roland Pennock and John W. Chapman. New York: New York University: 13–47.

4

Republicanism and the all subjected principle as the basis of democratic membership

Iseult Honohan

Introduction

In his illuminating essay Rainer Bauböck advances a comprehensive approach to the question of how to determine membership of a democratic political community, that takes into account alternative theoretical principles, a variety of kinds of contemporary membership claims, and the complexities of current multiple levels of political structures.

He identifies his all citizen stakeholders (ACS) approach as broadly republican, concerned with individual and collective self-government by those who have a stake in the polity's future because of the circumstances of their lives. "Citizens are stakeholders in a democratic political community insofar as their autonomy and well-being depend not only on being recognized as a member in a particular polity, but also on that polity being governed democratically" (p. 41). Thus the essay combines arguments associated with membership of the demos with others concerning the grounds for citizenship.

Bauböck proposes that ACS is better able than two other principles advanced in democratic theory – the all affected interests (AAI) and all subject to coercion (ASC) principles – to subsume a range of justified claims to membership. Those norms are depicted not so much as wrong but as incomplete to cover all claims for democratic inclusion. They "cannot be accepted as comprehensive answers to the democratic boundary problem, since they fail to provide a principle for the legitimate constitution of such polities and claims to inclusion in them" (p. 27).

Thus they are to be seen less as rival alternative justifying principles for defining the demos than as complementary to the more comprehensive citizen stakeholder approach.

Thus, in his account, each principle has a particular focus – on interests, on protection and on citizenship – that is appropriate at different levels:

> Those whose interests are affected by a decision have a democratic claim that their interests be taken into account in the process of decision-making and implementation. Those who are subjected to the jurisdiction of a polity have a democratic claim to equal protection under the law. And those who have a legitimate stake in participating in the self-government of a particular polity have a democratic claim to be recognized as citizens. (p. 20)

In my response, I do not attempt to provide anything like a systematic alternative account of democratic membership to that proposed by Bauböck, who has developed a unique theoretical account that gives due consideration to a dense array of both normative and empirical factors at multiple levels. I simply sketch the lineaments of an all subjected account of the demos that provides for republican self-government. This aims to redeem the power of the all subjected principle to define the demos, and suggests that there is more continuity between the demos based on this principle and that referring to citizenship stakeholders.

There is a great deal that can be accepted in Bauböck's account, including many of the framing assumptions of the discussion. My queries arise mainly from the way in which the theoretical principles justifying claims to membership of the demos are characterized and distinguished, and in particular how the all subjected principle is seen in terms of a purely protective neo-republicanism, which is distinguished from the democratic republican self-government of citizenship stakeholding. I re-examine the interpretation of the neo-republican non-domination account that Bauböck associates with the all subjected principle. I suggest that, if we see the underlying problem of subjection to coercion as domination, this focuses on continuing subjection, and requires more than protection. Moreover, when domination is interpreted in terms of the imposition of arbitrary will rather than a failure to track interests, neo-republicanism lends itself to an emphasis on self-government. The connection between non-domination and autonomy leads beyond domination to the kind of self-government among related individuals that Bauböck associates with his citizenship stakeholder account. On this basis, I propose an account of ASC that focuses on continuing subjection to a political authority, which, if it is not to be dominating, requires secure protection and facilitates autonomy, personal and political. I argue that a modified version of the all subjected principle escapes a number of the criticisms levelled at it, and provides a clear basis for membership of the demos. Finally, I offer future continuing subjection as a more defensible basis for birthright citizenship while ensuring the continuity of the democratic political community. This may be seen less as a criticism of Bauböck's analysis than as a qualification, strengthening the case for the all subjected principle as a clear principle of membership, and revealing not just complementarity but a greater continuity between ASC and ACS from a republican perspective.

The framing assumptions outlined by Bauböck that I am taking as agreed and will not discuss further include the following: Democracy is independently valuable, not just a means to justice. For both empirical and normative reasons, there will be a plurality of democratic polities, which will, in foreseeable practice, be territorial – that is, they will take the form of bounded spaces within which political power is exercised over human beings and laws applied to them. In territorial states, the best proxy for subjection is residence.[1] Democratic politics needs continuity over time, and thus depends on a relatively sedentary (but not static) population, or is more difficult to realize with hypermobility between polities. Furthermore, accepting the existence of borders does not mean accepting that those borders are necessarily sites of control.

---

[1] While a case can be made that citizens abroad are subject in certain respects, whether this justifies membership of the demos is a matter of debate (Owen 2009, 2012).

Likewise, I accept that there are good empirical and normative reasons why the demos cannot be defined on the basis either of a pre-political entity such as the nation, or of voluntary consent, as in the social contract tradition. Largely involuntary in membership, the political community is less than the political expression of a pre-political people, but more than an association or agreement on procedures. Furthermore, I also adopt a republican approach in which individual autonomy is connected with participation in collective self-government.

Turning to the principles proposed as criteria for membership of the demos, I accept the argument that the all affected principle cannot define the ground for the protection of rights or membership of the political demos, though it does provide good reasons for requiring states to take into account the interests of all those significantly affected by political decisions.

Interpreting the all subjected principle

As presented by Bauböck, the all subjected principle provides for protection of the rights of those who are subject to coercion. "The ASC principle captures the idea that the democratic legitimacy of government coercion depends on securing equal liberties for all whose autonomy it restricts" (p. 28).

This is interpreted in terms of interference with individuals and failure to track their interests, as presented in the neo-republican account of non-domination articulated in particular by Philip Pettit (Pettit 1997, 2012). This requires that there be institutional constraints on government and that those subjected have the opportunity to contest exercises of power over them, but it does not constitute self-government. On this account, the people are like editors rather than authors of government, or, as Bauböck puts it, government is accountable to, but not authorized by them. From his perspective this is a serious drawback for the claim that the all subjected principle should be the basis of the demos: "This shortcoming makes neo-Roman republicanism a somewhat limited perspective for a comprehensive theory of democratic inclusion, but one that has elective affinity with the ASC principle and is well suited to provide normative support for it" (p. 34). For him, non-domination could be achieved by a paternalistic government which tracked the interests of those subjected, and it does not require democracy at all.

Our attention is drawn to the fact that this diverges from an older republican tradition in which individual autonomy and collective self-government are linked, and the people authorize – not merely check – government. While bringing participation in collective self-government to the fore, that tradition has encountered some hostility because of the tendency to identify "the people" as a unitary subject that may threaten to dominate individuals and minorities.

Before considering the possibility of reformulating the conception of the people in the self-government tradition, I unpack the interpretation of neo-republican non-domination and its implications for democracy. This unpacking suggests that the requirements of non-domination are not as separate from republican self-government as they may at first appear. We may first of all say that domination is indeed expressed in terms of interference, but it is not just a matter of particular interference. If it were a matter of particular cases of interference in interests, it would fit better with the all affected principle – and indeed connections with, and similarities to, that principle have been identified by others – and contestation could be seen as appropriate for affected interests (e.g. Näsström 2011: 122, n. 5). But, as Bauböck correctly assesses, "vulnerability to arbitrary interference is a condition in which individuals find themselves as the result of exposure to coercive government institutions rather than to negative externalities of particular decisions" (p. 34); it thus provides normative support for ASC.

Thus there is more to non-domination than the protection of interests against specific interference. It opposes the condition of subjection to coercion that renders arbitrary interference always possible. But there has been some indeterminacy between interests and will in expressions of neo-republican theory. The emphasis in Pettit's account of domination has varied between the failure to track interests and the imposition of an arbitrary will (Markell 2008; Lovett 2010). An emphasis on tracking interests may not require democratic self-government – or requires only a weaker version of democracy. As Pettit puts it, "[d]emocracy is not inherently a collective matter, then; it is not inherently a matter of active control, and it is not inherently the sort of system that confines decision-making to sites that are available to public scrutiny and influence" (Pettit 2000: 140).

This account of republicanism, in which non-domination is closely linked to non-interference, is compatible with a kind of protective liberal politics – dealing with negative freedom, albeit a more secure negative freedom. Thus, on this basis, Bauböck judges that "ASC is rooted in a liberal conception of democracy as the system of political rule that is most likely to guarantee fundamental rights" (p. 48). Likewise he sees it, like liberal politics, as dealing mainly with individual–state relations rather than relations of self-governing citizens.

But Pettit has at some points expressed what is at stake in domination not as a failure to track a range of interests, but as the continuing threat of the imposition of the arbitrary will of another. Then what non-domination realizes is not tracking the interests of subjects, but removing the power of that continuing threat.[2] In the first instance, this amounts to the replacement of mastery by "non-mastery" (Pettit 1997: 22). This requires more than liberal institutional protections constraining government, guaranteeing and publicly recognizing the equal status of citizens; it also depends on mutual recognition by citizens of one another as equal and of non-domination as a common good that can only be realized collectively, depending on citizens internalizing the value of non-domination as well as having the standing to contest laws and policies (Pettit 1997). While Pettit defines the institutional

---

[2] That this is specifically within relationships of dependence is made clear in Lovett's reformulation of domination: "Persons or groups are subject to domination to the extent that they are dependent on a social relationship in which some other person or group wields arbitrary power over them" (Lovett 2010: 119).

provisions this requires mainly in terms of constraints on government, other theorists of non-domination have argued that more substantial political power of the people or their representatives relative to rights-protecting institutions is required for non-domination (Maynor 2003; Bellamy 2007).

It may be argued further that the point of non-domination, or non-mastery, is to allow for individual autonomy. Non-domination may be seen then as an essential precondition for personal autonomy. Pettit sees this as beyond the domain of politics, maintaining that non-domination is compatible with personal autonomy and that republican institutions facilitate this indirectly, but argues that personal autonomy does not have to be a concern of republican politics: "people can be trusted to look after their own autonomy, given that they live under a dispensation where they are protected from domination by others" (Pettit 1997: 83).

As domination precludes the exercise of individual and collective autonomy, non-domination may be seen as the condition for autonomy. Autonomy, moreover, like non-domination, cannot be exercised individually, or understood in purely private terms. Thus political autonomy can be seen as a natural extension of personal autonomy, or, as Habermas puts it, private and public autonomy are "equiprimordial" or equally fundamental:

> In the final analysis, private legal persons cannot even attain the enjoyment of equal liberties unless they themselves, by jointly exercising their autonomy as citizens, arrive at a clear understanding about what interests and criteria are justified and in what respects equal things can be treated equally and unequal things unequally in any particular case. (Habermas 1994: 113)

If we follow this line of thinking, we move beyond the protection of interests to participation in collective self-government. There seem, then, to be two alternatives in considering non-domination as the basis of ASC: we can interpret it in terms of interests, in which case it collapses back into AAI, or in terms of facilitating autonomy, when it leans towards a stronger norm of participation in collective self-government.

Reconsidering a republican account of the all subjected principle

If self-government is seen as entailed by the need for non-domination, and to realize autonomy among those who are interdependent, we may propose a modified republican formulation of the all subjected principle, in which the demos is composed of those who share a wide range of multiply reiterated interdependencies, which have been significantly shaped by their subjection to a common authority. They have not constituted themselves voluntarily as a demos, but have been thrown together historically; they share not only a common past, but also (putatively) a common future; they are faced by issues that can only be addressed, and goods that can only be realized, collectively. If they can act collectively as citizens they may be able to determine their future – to be part-authors, if not wholly in control of their lives. They become a demos through the practice or even the open possibility of collective public interaction (Honohan 2002: 266).

But Bauböck identifies certain obstacles to ASC as the basis for determining membership in a self-governing citizenry. First and foremost, this seems to root self-government only in subjection, and cannot identify the links that make a people a candidate for self-government. It involves a circular argument that the demos is constituted by the impact of the government that can only be constituted by the same demos.

The ASC principle, it is argued, allows prior subjection to be the determinant of the shape of the political community. It lacks a "conception of political membership linking individual inclusion claims to collective claims to self-government and a conception of political community that is not limited to sovereign states" (p. 30). But, it may be argued against this, continuing exposure to political authority does have the effect of framing interdependence in such a way as to make self-government between people necessary. Within states over time, interdependencies grow, making individual personal and political autonomy more inter-dependent on others than before. Even in the contemporary context of globalization, the authority of bounded states has the effect of creating multiply reiterated relations of interdependence.

The second issue is that ASC involves an inherent bias towards existing boundaries. This is true, but there may be reasons to be biased towards existing boundaries – in the way in which, as I have noted, they come to determine all kinds of interdependencies, and constitute the demos who have a future together and the possibility of collectively determining it. We may accept them also, as many theorists have done, in the absence of a convincing alternative principle on the basis of which a demos can constitute itself.

But a further issue arises – that it is not clear that all forms of subjection justify inclusion in the demos. Bauböck poses the problem cases of the U.S. occupation of post-World War 2 Germany and the Algerian independence movement. In these cases, he points out, the subjection involved could not be seen as requiring or being remediated by inclusion in the demos of the sovereign state. But in the German case, the temporary nature of the subjection may be thought to ground the need for protection and contestation rather than inclusion.[3] Moreover, if we formulate the demos of collective self-government in terms of those whose multiple relationships of interdependence have been shaped by subjection to a state, it does not follow that its bounds will be identical to those of that sovereign state. Not all boundaries create a single people, but a democratic people may be created by subjection within a boundary. In the case of Algeria (and other colonies), the grounds for the demos could be thought to reflect the fact that Algerian subjection to France was different from that of French citizens in France. Algeria could not be seen as part of the same web of reiterated interdependencies as those in metropolitan France. Likewise, although two colonies remote from one another might have common cause, this does not mean that their subjection to a single colonial power made them a single demos. A colony without statehood may be a candidate for self-government because the people there have become increasingly interdependent through their subjection within a bounded polity. The grounds lie in their need for autonomy rather than their capacity, and do not depend

---

[3] Germany's constitution as a demos may be seen as following from its political unification in the nineteenth century, but that is not essential to the argument here.

on their constituting a prior "people" in the conventional sense. Rather than being irredeemably backward-looking, this account of the demos based on the all subjected principle balances backward- and forward-looking elements.

Thus the possibility of a people's collective self-government does not depend (unlike the approach of Stilz that Bauböck criticizes) on their "history of political cooperation by sharing a state ... in the recent past" or their demonstrable capacity to "reconstitute and sustain a legitimate state" today (p. 30, quoting Stilz 2011: 591) so much as that they find themselves in the circumstances where collective action is required for the possibility of self-government.

On this view the demos is a relatively stable set of people who face a common predicament, share common risks and common goods, who may realize – or fail to realize – the possibility of securing non-domination and jointly exercising some collective control over their lives. Accordingly this interpretation of ASC reveals what Bauböck sees as a necessary "correspondence between individuals' interests in autonomy and well-being and the collective interests of all citizens in their polity's self-government and flourishing" (p. 41). It does not involve an essentialist view of "the people" (pre-political or otherwise), who constitute a unitary body with a single will.

Even if citizens of self-governing polities are initially constituted through common subjection, their coming to authorship in self-government can be thought of as an incremental possibility.[4] While my account may still be seen as "statist" in the sense that it arises from former subjection to a state and accepts a starting point of existing borders, it does not imply that it is impossible to go beyond these borders; rather it acknowledges that the state remains one of the strongest determinants of continuing subjection and interlocking interdependencies.

---

[4]　This incremental justification may be compared with similar accounts of social contract theory as recognizing as legitimate states that acquire emergent consent over time (e.g. Hampton 1998, who identifies the possibility of moving from a weak consent to government – convention consent – to active support of a particular form – endorsement consent). See also Pettit's more narrowly focused discussion of a constituting and a constituted people (Pettit 2012: 285–190).

As Bauböck points out in section 4.1, the possibility of domination between and across states may call for political authorities at higher and lower levels.[5]

Among other difficulties identified with ASC as the basis of inclusion in the demos is the fact that it may be over-inclusive in several ways. First, it does not exclude temporary visitors and tourists, who are subject as long as they are present in the country. But temporary rather than continuing subjection does not constitute the same threat of domination as longer-term residence, and requires protection rather than membership of the demos. The possibility of voluntary exit reduces the risk of domination. But the longer a person is resident the greater may be the costs of leaving and the risk of domination; thus long-term residents generally need a voice and membership of the demos (Lovett 2010; Benton 2014).

This does indeed, as Bauböck notes, lead logically to mandatory citizenship for long-term residents. He sees residence as an appropriate basis for the local political demos, but not for membership of the larger political community, where people should be able to choose whether to acquire a new citizenship status. There are convincing arguments, however, that mandatory citizenship can be justified on the basis that citizens' capacity for self-determination and their realization of common goods are undermined if many of those linked in interdependencies subject to the state do not have a political voice.[6] This is not just a matter of individual protection. As de Schutter and Ypi have argued, it creates an unfair asymmetry in the distribution of political obligations between citizens and immigrants; non-citizen long-term residents are

---

[5] The idea of domination (more than simple subjection at a point in time) supports the proposal for multilevel citizenship – as the larger unitary polities become, the more risk of domination of minorities within those states (p. 59); maintaining or extending the devolution of power to local and regional levels, and also calling for the creation of supranational institutions and polities where the threat of domination prevents collective decision-making or action (p. 60). "The dispersal and pooling of sovereignty at substate and suprastate levels reduces the risk of political domination within states and enhances opportunities for democratic self-government beyond the state" (p. 57).

[6] This may be seen as parallel to the suggestion that the inclusion of non-resident citizens without a real connection to the demos undermines citizen self-government.

(willing or unwilling) free riders, weakening the possibilities of self-government (de Schutter and Ypi 2015).[7] Having a say where one is subject to coercion, in relations of interdependence and cooperating with others in shaping the future common life should not be a matter of choice. If dual or multiple memberships become increasingly accepted by states, this reduces the difficulties with respect to mutual obligations between independent states.

Finally, is the claim of ASC undermined by the fact that, at least on an expanded account of what counts as subjection, it suggests that those coerced by migration laws should be part of the demos that determines those laws? (Abizadeh 2008). On the one hand, it can be argued that migration laws sufficiently dominate those who have good reasons to migrate to justify at least consideration of their affected interests and, arguably, a range of protections and contestation (Honohan 2015). But, however significant for individuals and their life chances, if the coercion involved does not add up to continuing subjection, it may not provide grounds for full inclusion in the existing polity (though this also may call for a polity at higher levels).

When it comes to necessary inclusions, Bauböck acknowledges that the ASC principle can clearly include those who may not easily be seen as active political participators, for example those with cognitive limitations and very young children, who are subjected and share a common future in the state. On certain accounts of autonomy and political capacity, perhaps, it might be thought that they are less easy to include. But, while they may differ in capacity for autonomy or participation in self-government, it is important first that they are not subject to domination, and that their opportunity to participate in proportion to their (hitherto seriously underestimated) capacity for autonomy be facilitated.

---

[7] This roughly corresponds to just one of de Schutter and Ypi's arguments – that based on equal burden-sharing, including a duty to become part of the demos: "Preserving public goods needs political management. And the latter is in turn difficult without a collective 'we' that is required to mobilize politically in order to uphold common institutions" (de Schutter and Ypi 2015: 241). They develop three other arguments, based on affectedness, equal citizenship and stability that I do not rely on here.

Birthright citizenship and the continuity of the political community

Bauböck acknowledges that, unlike AAI and ASC, ACS does not immediately provide a clear ground for including newborn children. But he justifies their inclusion as needed to fulfil the conditions for continuity of a self-governing polity over time. He sees birthright citizenship (both ius soli and ius sanguinis) as a better way to establish this continuity than basing citizenship on residence (while allowing also for adjustments through naturalization and voluntary renunciation in response to mobility in later life).[8] Birthright citizenship allocates membership to new generations that are born without the need for potentially divisive individual decisions or determinations in each case, and makes citizens aware that they are part of an intergenerational community. This is, he says, at least compatible with ACS.[9]

He rejects the argument that birthright citizenship is analogous to inherited property rights. But, even if citizenship is not appropriately seen as property, it could be said that awarding birthright citizenship facilitates the transmission of privilege in the interest of the continuity of the polity. On some views children entering society should logically be seen as similar in all significant respects to immigrants entering (or seeking to enter) as strangers (e.g. Brezger and Cassee 2016). I suggest that the all subjected principle, understood as future-oriented interdependence in continuous subjection, for which residence is a proxy, provides a more defensible ground for birthright citizenship.

Forward-looking interdependence in subjection to authority can ground provisional ius soli membership for those born in the state, depending on continuing residence, and conditional ius sanguinis membership for those born to citizens abroad, retained only if residence

---

[8] The alternative would be to allow membership only at majority.
[9] Bauböck acknowledges that there is more to said here, however: "Birthright citizenship is certainly not a sufficient answer to this challenge, but it may be a necessary one once we consider the alternative of grounding all political memberships on residence" (pp. 88–9).

in the state is subsequently established (cf. Honohan 2015). There are many practical reasons for granting citizenship at birth rather than postponing it until adulthood. These include the need of children for protection and the chance to live and move with their families while they are children, even if (arguably) they are not eligible to be members of the demos until adulthood.

Conclusion

Bauböck's work has established clearly that we have to deal with questions not just of inclusion or exclusion from the demos, but with a whole panoply of full and partial claims for membership in the demos, to citizenship and to access of various kinds, ranging from consultation through protection to participation in self-government, and that these arise at multiple levels. The citizenship stakeholder account allows for recognition of this panoply of claims. It facilitates their incorporation by articulating the grounds for membership at a more general level of abstraction. Nonetheless, it requires considerable interpretation and specification in more concrete cases.

This discussion suggests that the appropriate images for thinking about the terrain of democratic membership are neither a flat landscape with separate states demarcated by linear boundaries, nor radiating circles of those whose interests are affected to diminishing degrees with distance, nor even a three-dimensional terrain of occasional supranational hills and many deeper subdivisions within states. On reading this essay, we might conclude that the complexity of member-ship claims needs geological images of layered structures, with multi-dimensional and cross-cutting tectonic plates that overlap partially but not fully.

Both Bauböck's and my accounts recognize a difference between the membership of the active demos and the citizenry: "A stakeholder conception does therefore suggest a distinction between the *demos*, consisting of all those who have the franchise, and the *citizenry*, composed of all who have a stake in being members of a transgenerational political community" (p. 46). The bundle of rights and duties we conventionally associate with citizenship may be subject to certain kinds of disaggregation. On my account, the protections of citizenship may need to be applied more widely and in a more capacious time-frame than membership of the demos. Thus while ACS provides a general account of grounds for membership at the most abstract level, and is pluralist in seeing different principles as appropriate at different levels, the all subjected account here may define membership of the demos more clearly on the basis of a single principle, but the account of citizenship needs to be pluralist, mainly by building in a temporal cushion with respect to subjection. Even when there is no firm basis for membership of the demos, individuals need protection, and to maintain family and other connections within states, for example. Citizenship may, for practical reasons, be retained with a lag when an individual citizen moves to another country, be awarded with a time-lag after arrival as a permanent immigrant resident, and be held conditional on residence for children born in the country or to citizens.

I have suggested that the all subjected principle provides grounds for determining membership of a republican political community for those interdependent in continuing subjection to a political authority. This account has much in common with the citizenship stakeholder account based on a legitimate stake in participating in the self-government of a particular political community. But it may be argued that the clearest and most significant stake in membership derives from continuing subjection, and that the all subjected principle provides a clearer criterion for membership of the demos, and can ground an account of republican self-government of the kind that Bauböck endorses.

References

Abizadeh, Arash. 2008. "Democratic Theory and Border Coercion: No Right to Unilaterally Control Your Own Borders." *Political Theory* 36 (1): 37–65.

Bellamy, Richard. 2007. *Political Constitutionalism: A Republican Defence of the Constitutionality of Democracy.* Cambridge: Cambridge University Press.

Benton, Megan. 2014. "The Problem of Denizenship: A Non-domination Framework." *Critical Review of International Social and Political Philosophy* 17: 49–69.

Brezger, Jan and Andreas Cassee. 2016. "Debate: Immigrants and Newcomers by Birth – Do Statist Arguments Imply a Right to Exclude Both?" *Journal of Political Philosophy* 24 (3): 367–378.

de Schutter, Helder and Lea Ypi. 2015. "Mandatory Citizenship for Immigrants." *British Journal of Political Science.* 45 (2): 235–251.

Habermas, Jurgen. 1994. "Struggles for Recognition in the Democratic Constitutional State." In *Multiculturalism*, edited by C. Taylor and A. Gutmann. Princeton: Princeton University Press: 107–148.

Hampton, Jean. 1998. *Political Philosophy.* Boulder: Westview.

Honohan, Iseult. 2002. *Civic Republicanism.* Abingdon and New York: Routledge.

Honohan, Iseult. 2015. "Limiting the Transmission of Family Advantage: Ius Sanguinis with an Expiration Date." In *Bloodlines and Belonging: Time to Abandon Ius Sanguinis?*, edited by C. Dumbrava and R. Bauböck. Florence: EUI Robert Schuman Centre for Advanced Studies: 32–34.

Lovett, Frank. 2010. *A General Theory of Domination.* Oxford: Oxford University Press.

Markell, Patchen. 2008. "The Insufficiency of Non-domination." *Political Theory* 36 (1): 9–36.

Maynor, John. 2003. *Republicanism in the Modern World.* Cambridge: Polity.

Näsström, Sofia. 2011. "The Challenge of the All Affected Principle." *Political Studies* 59 (1): 116–134.

Owen, David. 2009. "Resident Aliens, Non-resident Citizens and Voting Rights." In *Citizenship Acquisition and National Belonging*, edited by G. Calder, P. Cole and J. Seglow Basingstoke: Palgrave: 52–73.

Owen, David. 2012. "Constituting the Polity, Constituting the Demos: On the Place of the All Affected Interests Principle in Democratic Theory and in Resolving the Democratic Boundary Problem." *Ethics and Global Affairs* 5 (3): 129–152.

Pettit, Philip. 1997. *Republicanism: A Theory of Freedom and Government.* Oxford: Oxford University Press.

Pettit, Philip. 2000. "Democracy, Electoral and Contestatory." In *Designing Democratic Institutions*, edited by I. Shapiro and S. Macedo.. New York: New York University Press: 105–142.

Pettit, Philip. 2012. *On the People's Terms: A Republican Theory and Model of Democracy.* Cambridge: Cambridge University Press.

Stilz, Anna. 2011. "Nations, States, and Territory." *Ethics* 121 (3): 572–601.

5

Metics, members and citizens

Will Kymlicka and Sue Donaldson

Rainer Bauböck's essay argues persuasively that our account of democratic inclusion needs to be more complex than is usually recognized. Whereas most authors attempt to identify a single fundamental principle of democratic inclusion – whether it is the all affected interests principle or the all subjected to coercion principle or some social membership/ stakeholder principle – Bauböck shows that there are different types of polities with different principles of inclusion, and that the appropriate principles for inclusion at one level depend in part on the principles operative at other levels. Birthright citizenship at the national level, for example, makes possible both residency-based citizenship at the local level and derivative or nested citizenship at the federal level, just as the latter two modes of citizenship help to correct potential injustices or forms of domination generated by birthright citizenship at the national level.

We are in broad agreement with Bauböck's general story about the need to complicate theories of democratic inclusion by recognizing multiple principles of democratic inclusion tied to multiple types of polity. The aim of this commentary is to push his project one step further, by adding another layer of complexity to our thinking about democratic inclusion. We will focus on a range of cases that fall outside our normal assumptions about who is eligible for, or capable of, citizenship, including children, people with cognitive disabilities and domesticated animals.

What members of these groups have in common is that they are members of society, in a sociological sense – living out their lives as part of a transgenerational "core" community, engaging in intersubjective communication, participating in cooperative activity, abiding by social norms – but they lack the capacity to engage in the kind of rational deliberation about political propositions that is widely assumed to characterize democratic citizenship. As Gary Steiner (2013) notes, most theories of citizenship have assumed that citizens have what he calls "linguistic agency" – the ability to articulate, understand, evaluate, negotiate and commit to abstract linguistic propositions regarding the terms of social cooperation with their fellow citizens.[1] But in reality, many members of society are not linguistic agents. Where do they fit in our theory of citizenship?

Bauböck does not say much about such groups, and what little he says, we will argue, is inadequate. In this respect, he follows much of the Western political tradition, which has systematically ignored the rights and status of social members who are not capable of deliberative political speech. We will argue that these cases raise a fundamental challenge to our theories of democratic inclusion, not just about who is included, but also about what it means to be a citizen and how to characterize the underlying moral purposes of citizenship.

To foreshadow, our argument is that these cases reveal a deep tension within democratic theory between two models of citizenship: what we call a "membership model", which defines citizenship in terms of social membership; and a "capacity contract", which defines citizenship in terms of capacities for particular kinds of political agency.[2] The former entails that children, people with cognitive disabilities and (we will argue) domesticated animals count as citizens; the latter entails they do not. Most theorists appeal to both, and then seek to square the circle by

---

[1] We realize that "linguistic agency" can be defined more expansively, in ways that would recognize many animals as linguistic agents. As discussed below, members of these groups are certainly *communicative*. We are using the phrase "linguistic agency" to isolate the capacity shared by many humans, and no non-human animals of which we are aware, for engaging in a process of discursive reason-giving about abstract propositions.

[2] We take the phrase "capacity contract" from Clifford (2014). The contract language is misleading if it suggests a voluntary agreement. It is used here, rather, in the same sense that theorists talk of "the racial contract" (Mills 1997), "the sexual contract" (Pateman 1988) or the "settler contract" (Nichols 2013): as a deeply embedded social logic that structures our institutions and practices in hierarchical terms.

creating various subordinate forms of membership-without-citizenship. Bauböck's argument can be seen as a version of this strategy.

We will argue that there is no way to square the circle: the two models are simply contradictory, requiring us to choose between them.[3] We will also argue that, confronted with that choice, liberals should simply abandon the capacity contract. This would not, by itself, require rejecting the basic structure of Bauböck's model, with its three distinctive principles for the three distinctive forms of polity. Indeed, it would strengthen it, by providing a clearer and more defensible account of both the circumstances and purposes of citizenship.

The membership model

Current debates in political philosophy on democratic inclusion arose initially in response to the problem of what Michael Walzer called "metics" – the existence of large numbers of immigrants who had settled long term in European countries, such as the Turkish *Gastarbeiter* in Germany, yet who were not eligible for citizenship. Indeed, even their children, born and raised in the country, were sometimes ineligible for citizenship (Walzer 1983). Walzer argued compellingly that this was an injustice. These long-time residents were clearly members of society, not just in the sense that they paid taxes and obeyed the law, but in the deeper sense that they had made a life in their new society and formed a dense web of social ties. In the case of their children, this was often the only home they knew. Yet they were treated as aliens and outsiders. Walzer argued this was both unjust and undemocratic.

This initiated a search within political philosophy to specify more precisely the principle that grounds a right to citizenship for metics. For many theorists, the first reaction was to appeal to some version of the all affected interests principle: metics are entitled to citizenship because

---

[3]   Toby Rollo suggests that the tension between the capacity contract and the membership model is one of the most "intractable problems in political theory" (Rollo 2016: n.p.).

their interests are affected by the decisions of the state in which they live. But on sober second thought, it became clear that this principle is problematic. The set of individuals who are affected by political decisions varies from issue to issue in ways that make it impossible to develop a stable demos. For example, while all of our decisions are likely to affect some foreigners, the set of foreigners affected by an environmental policy is likely to be different from a trade policy – just as these policies affect some but not all residents within the country – leading to ever-changing boundaries of inclusion on a case-by-case basis. In Bauböck's words, "letting affected interests determine the boundaries of the demos would create indeterminate or ephemeral demoi that are structurally incapable of ruling themselves" (p. 11).[4]

Whether the all affected interests principle can be salvaged from this criticism is an ongoing debate in the literature (e.g. Goodin 2007; List and Koenig-Archibugi 2010; Saunders 2011; Koenig-Archibugi 2012; Song 2012). But in any event, it is clearly a misdiagnosis of the original problem of the metics. In fact, it arguably replicates that injustice, by putting metics on a par with foreigners, as prima facie outsiders who might nonetheless qualify for inclusion on particular decisions because they have affected interests. The Turks in Germany are not just saying that they are affected by this or that public policy of the German government, but that they are members of the public in whose name the state governs. They are part of German society – they belong there and have made a life there. It is the failure to recognize this fact of social membership that creates the injustice – not the failure to take into account some discrete interest affected by a particular German policy. If Germany adopts an industrial policy that has spillover pollution costs for people in Poland or Denmark, that is a harm to affected interests for which

---

[4] Moreover, taken to its logical conclusion, the all affected principle seems to entail a single global demos. After all, my interests are affected, not just when choosing between two options, but also when those options themselves are selected to be the focus of choice: what Bauböck calls the "agenda-setting" power (p. 22). And if we have a right to be part of the demos whenever agenda-setting powers might affect us, we quickly reach the idea of a single global demos – see Goodin (2007).

some sort of accountability and remedy is required.[5] But permanently relegating a portion of German society to the status of non-citizen metics is a very different type of injustice, for which a different remedy is required. The all affected interests principle has nothing useful to say about addressing this type of injustice.

In response to this defect of the all affected interests principle, other theorists have proposed the "all subject to coercion" principle as a basis for grounding rights to citizenship for metics. This seems closer to the mark, since it focuses not just on incidental or unintended impacts on interests of discrete policies, but on a more direct relation of governing. The Turkish metics are not just affected by German policies, but are governed by them. But this too doesn't quite capture the injustice of the metics' situation. After all, even short-term tourists or visitors are subject to the law, and so would seem to qualify for rights of inclusion under the all subject to coercion principle.[6] Yet the whole point of the metics example is that it is wrong for the German government to treat them as if they were visitors or tourists, rather than as full members of society. It is no response to this problem to say that even if they are just visitors, they still have democratic rights. That leaves untouched the fundamental injustice of being treated as an alien or outsider in the society where one has made one's life. Insofar as tourists are subject to coercion they may well have rights to equal protection of the law and to contest the arbitrary exercise of power, but that is different from the right of members of society to inclusion in the demos.

The case of the metics shows that citizenship is not ultimately about being affected by particular decisions or being subject to particular laws, but about *membership* in a self-governing society. People living in foreign societies are affected by our decisions, and tourists visiting our society are subjected to our laws, and these facts are politically consequential – we

---

[5] See Bauböck pp. 25–26 for helpful suggestions about the appropriate remedy for these external impacts.

[6] And on the other hand, it seems to provide a pretext for colonization of other societies, so long as one then grants citizenship to the colonized.

need to be held accountable for these impacts and these exercises of power. But citizenship is about being a member of a self-governing society. In short, citizenship should track social membership.[7]

We can call this the membership model of citizenship, which ties citizenship to an ethos of membership. To be a citizen is to be a member of the society (or "the public" or "the people") in whose name the state governs, and one central function of citizenship is precisely to acknowledge this membership, to acknowledge who belongs here, who has made a life here, and who therefore has a right to shape the terms of our shared social life.

Many passages in Bauböck's text can be seen as endorsing this membership model. He says that we are "social animals" (p. 40) who have a stake in membership as such which is different from a stake in the protection of a particular policy interest or a particular legal right. Because of the kind of social animals we are, we thrive as members of an intergenerational community, bound together by ideas of belonging to, and ownership of, a bounded society. We are not a "merely functional aggregates of individuals who happen to share an interest in a particular political decision" (p. 11). Rather, we make a life for ourselves in a particular society, develop social ties within that society, and our well-being is pervasively tied up with the shared norms that govern the scheme of social cooperation, and with how we are treated by our fellow members. Citizenship is an acknowledgement of this "stake in membership": it affirms that we are members of this inter-generational community, and that, as such, we have a right to shape its social norms and to co-author its laws, as well as a responsibility for its long-term future.[8]

---

[7] The locus classicus for this social membership model is Carens (2005, 2013).

[8] Some commentators argue that this picture of the importance of membership in bounded societies is increasingly obsolete in an age of mobility, but we share Bauböck's view that individual mobility is possible and valuable because it takes place on a terrain structured by the operation of bounded societies with a "relatively sedentary core population" (p. 17). In this sense, the enduring importance of social membership is one of the "circumstances of democracy" (pp. 7–18).

As we said, many passages in Bauböck's text can be read as supporting this membership model, which we take to be the most compelling account of democratic inclusion. However, in other places he backs off this view, and suggests that social membership is not a sufficient condition for political membership. In various places,[9] he implicitly suggests that belonging to the "public" or the "demos" is qualitatively different from belonging to "society" or "community", and suggests that one's interest in being recognized as a member of society is not sufficient for being recognized as a citizen. The net result, as we will see, is that he condones creating a new set of metics. Most of the original metics – such as the Turkish *Gastarbeiter* – may be included as citizens on his account, but a whole new set of members of society are rendered ineligible for citizenship. These passages are puzzling, and at odds with the liberal and democratic impulses that otherwise inform his account. We will return to these passages below, but let us first spell out the broader implications of the social membership model.

Inclusive membership[10]

While the migrant workers in northern Europe were the initial case that stimulated recent work on democratic inclusion, a moment's reflection would reveal that they are not the only group that is relegated to the status of metics within contemporary democracies. There are many other groups that are clearly members of society but who are denied the rights of democratic citizenship. Consider children, who form around one-third of the population of any given society. Or consider people with cognitive disabilities, who number in the millions in some countries.[11] They are clearly members of society. They are born into a

---

[9]   Including in his commentary on Joseph Carens in Bauböck (2015).
[10] The following section draws on ideas we have developed in other work (e.g. Donaldson and Kymlicka 2016a).
[11] And with ageing populations, living longer lives, the number of people with various forms of dementia will increase.

society, participate in its social relationships, share in the benefits and burdens of social cooperation, and live their lives within its territorial boundaries. And this fact of social membership is acknowledged in nationality law: children and people with cognitive disabilities typically have the formal status of citizenship or nationality by birth. They are not foreigners or stateless. Yet these members of society are denied substantive citizenship, and are disenfranchised (universally in the case of children, to varying degrees in the case of people with cognitive disabilities). As members of society, they are typically accorded certain rights to protection (against harm) and provision (of public services), but they are denied the rights to participate in democratic shared rule which defines modern accounts of citizenship.[12] (This denial of political rights has come under increasing scrutiny, and is directly challenged by the UN Convention on the Rights of Persons with Disabilities.)

An even more striking case concerns domesticated animals. They too are members of society, at least according to most standard sociological definitions of sociality (i.e. intersubjective recognition, communication, trust, cooperation, compliance with shared norms). Domesticated animals share a social world with us, and play a vital role in our schemes of economic production and social cooperation, a reality which is now widely acknowledged (and studied) by sociologists and anthropologists (Peggs 2012). They too live and die within our societies, and they too belong here. Having been taken out of the wild and bred over centuries to be dependent on us, they have no other home. In that sense, domesticated animals are, sociologically speaking, members of our societies, whose fate is entirely tied up with how they are treated under our social norms and institutions. They would therefore seem to qualify for citizenship under a membership model that ties citizenship to being a member of

---

[12] Commentators often talk about a "3P" model of citizenship rights – protection, provision and participation – which should apply to all members of society (see, for example, Quennerstedt 2010). In reality, most children and people with cognitive disabilities are at best accorded a 2P model, without participation rights. And since domesticated animals have the status of property in law, they are denied all three, lacking legal recognition of personhood or membership even in the thinnest sense.

society.[13] Yet, virtually without exception, theorists of citizenship have excluded animals, often in the very same sentence that they exclude children and people with cognitive disabilities,[14] relegating them to the status of metics.

One might think that this exclusion is inevitable because members of these groups simply are unable to engage in some of the core practices of citizenship, such as jury duty, voting or public political deliberation. But from a membership perspective, this gets things backwards. We don't start with some received view about essential citizenship practices and then ask who qualifies for citizenship in virtue of being able to perform these practices. Rather, we start from some account of who is a member of society – in Bauböck's terms, who has a "stake in membership" – and then ask how to organize politics to enable all members to enact their citizenship. If not every member of society is able to vote or to engage in public reason, then we need to find alternative ways of enabling those members to have a say in the governing of society.

In fact, important work has already been done in imagining how to extend democratic citizenship to children (Moosa-Mitha 2005; Rehfeld 2011; Bacon and Frankel 2014), and to people with cognitive disabilities (Francis and Silvers 2007; Arneil 2009; Clifford 2014; Davy 2015). These experiments in democratic inclusion have emerged, partly in response to the mobilization of advocates, but also in response to recent changes in international human rights law, which emphasize that both children and people with cognitive disabilities have a right to a say in matters that affect them – that is to say, rights to participation, and not just rights to protection and provision.[15]

---

[13] For a detailed defence of this argument, see Donaldson and Kymlicka (2011: chs 4 and 5) and Kymlicka and Donaldson (2014).

[14] Among many such examples, see Hobbes: "Over natural fools, children, or madmen there is no law, no more than over brute beasts; nor are they capable of the title of just or unjust, because they had never power to make any covenant or to understand the consequences thereof" (*Leviathan* II.xxvi.12).

[15] See note 12 above for the 2P versus 3P model of citizenship.

Implementing this right to a say is obviously a major social and political challenge, but the basic idea should not be particularly mysterious. After all, children and people with cognitive disabilities are clearly wilful individuals, with strong preferences about the sorts of activities and relationships in which they would like to engage. They are also quite communicative about these preferences. They may not communicate through reasoned propositions, but they have a host of other communicative strategies for expressing their preferences and negotiating relationships (e.g. utterances, body language, demonstrative actions). And they are capable of forming trusting relationships with others who can create the social conditions under which alternative activities and relationships can be safely explored. An individual's subjective response to these alternatives can then be observed and analysed, and those subjective responses can in turn be incorporated into collective decision-making. There is nothing particularly mysterious about any of this, all of which takes place on a daily basis, and various societies have explored how to connect these everyday potentialities for communication and voice into the broader political process – that is, how to enable democratic citizenship. As Hartley notes of people with cognitive disability, while they may lack the capacity for linguistic agency, they certainly have what she calls the "capacity for engagement" (Hartley 2009), and wherever this exists, possibilities for democratic engagement exist.

And once we accept this possibility in the case of children and people with cognitive disabilities, there is no conceptual obstacle to applying it to domesticated animals as well (Meijer 2013; Donaldson and Kymlicka 2016a). All of the facts that make democratic citizenship possible for young children and people with cognitive disabilities – facts about individual wilfulness, communication, trust, engagement, dependent agency and the structuring of choice situations – are also at play in our relations with domesticated animals. (Indeed, animals could not have been domesticated had they lacked these capacities for interspecies sociability.)

In any event, this is the logic of the membership model: we start with an account of who is a member of society, and we ask how to enable all members of society to participate in shaping the shared norms that govern our life together. This is a vision of a truly democratic society, one in which democratic values animate the governing of social life.

The capacity contract

Unfortunately, Bauböck does not follow this logic. On his story, membership in the demos is not a right of social membership, but a privilege restricted to those who possess certain sophisticated cognitive capacities for rational deliberation. Indeed, on a more careful read, his argument that as "social animals" we have a "stake in membership" in "transgenerational human societies" turns out to have little to do with social membership in the sense described above (i.e. making a life for oneself within a particular society, developing social ties within that society, complying with social norms, participating in schemes of social cooperation that determine the distribution of burdens and benefits). Rather, his argument isolates a much more specific interest of certain people – namely, linguistic agents – in being members of a specifically political association that is defined by certain deliberative practices. Only people who are able to participate in these deliberative practices qualify for membership in the demos.

The result is that, on Bauböck's model, a gulf emerges between those who are merely members of society, and those who are members of the demos who govern society. In the case of children and people with cognitive disabilities, he says that we can still use the honorific "citizens" to describe them, in the sense that they are co-nationals with a right to belong. But he then insists that citizenship in this sense is not a right to democratic inclusion: not all "citizens" are members of the demos with rights to participate or to co-author the shared norms of society (p. 46). Only linguistic agents are members of the demos – that is, only they are entitled to democratic citizenship. Others have some sort of shadowy pseudo-citizenship – that is, something other than the kind of democratic citizenship that tracks membership in the demos.[16]

In this respect, Bauböck implicitly endorses what Stacy Clifford calls a "capacity contract", by which some members of society are deemed to be naturally governed by others (Clifford 2014). According to the capacity contract (democratic) citizenship should be limited to those who are by nature capable of ruling, while all others are relegated to some subaltern status, such as semi-citizenship (Cohen 2009) or wardship (or, in the case of animals, property).

This capacity contract runs very deep in the Western political theory tradition, dating back at least to Aristotle, who famously explained that man is a "political animal" because of his "gift of speech":

> Now that man is more of a political animal than bees or other gregarious animals is evident. Nature, as we say, makes nothing in vain, and man is the only animal who she has endowed with the gift of speech. And whereas mere voice is but an indication of pleasure or pain, and is therefore found in other animals (for their nature attains to the perception of pleasure and pain and the intimation of them to one another, and no further), the power of speech is intended to set forth the expedient and inexpedient, and therefore likewise the just and unjust. And it is a characteristic of man that he alone has any sense of good and evil, of just and unjust, and the like, and the association of living beings who have this sense makes a family and a state.[17]

---

[16] For a similar manoeuvre of defining democratic citizenship in terms of the capacity for linguistic agency but then granting honorific citizenship to others, see Hinchcliffe (2015). Bauböck's decision to extend the honorific "citizen" to children and people with cognitive disabilities, even though he denies they are members of the demos, muddies the conceptual clarity of his argument. Having introduced this distinction half-way through the text, one would need to go back through his entire text and ask, each time that the word "citizen" appears, whether he is referring to "mere" citizenship without rights to participation, or to the full democratic citizenship that entails membership in the demos, or to both. We leave this as an exercise for the reader, but we think several passages trade on the ambiguity.

[17] Aristotle, *Politics*, in Hutchins (1987: 446). On the foundational significance of this view for the Western philosophical tradition, see Franklin (2011), Steiner (2013) and Wadiwel (2015).

For Aristotle, only those with "the power of speech" to "set forth the just and unjust" can be party to a political relationship or members of a political community. Humans who lack this power, like other animals, may have "the perception of pleasure and pain", but they are incapable of articulating and deliberating their interests and claims in abstract propositional form and are therefore disqualified from being "political" animals.

This idea is so embedded in our philosophical tradition and political imagination that we have trouble thinking outside of it. There is growing acceptance that domesticated animals share a social world with us, just as we have no hesitation in accepting that children and people with cognitive disabilities share social membership with us. But as Gwendolyn Blue and Melanie Rock note, we seem incapable of accepting that they can be part of *the public*:

> Developments in social theory over the past few decades have unsettled deeply entrenched assumptions about what constitutes the human by exposing the tenuous divisions that separate humans, non-human animals and technologies and, in turn, affording a more active role to non-human entities in the constitution of social worlds. The concept of the public, however, remains persistently, stubbornly, and somewhat curiously entrenched in anthropomorphic imaginaries. Within and outside of academe, it is commonplace to suppose that publics are purely human and that publics arise from the unique human capacity for symbolic communication. (Blue and Rock 2014: 504)

Noortje Marres and Javier Lezaun make a similar observation about our inability to understand politics outside of linguistic agency:

> The idea that language is the central vehicle of politics – that language, in fact, founds and sustains the difference between human politics and the lives and quarrels of those (beasts or gods) who exist outside the polity – is so deeply ingrained in our preconceptions of the political that it is almost impossible to imagine a public, particularly a democratic one, not constituted primarily by acts of discursive deliberation. We have only

to think of a term such as "public sphere", and the careful delimitation of the kinds of activities conducive to its emergence that defines its use in contemporary democratic theory, to grasp the difficulty of coming up with a political vocabulary that is not premised on disembodied "voice" and linguistic exchange. (Marres and Lezaun 2011: 492)[18]

And we should note that virtually every single textbook in political philosophy published in the past thirty years implicitly or explicitly endorses the capacity contract, and the restriction of the public to linguistic agents.[19]

Given this enduring legacy, it is hardly surprising that Bauböck ends up recapitulating the central terms of the capacity contract. But in our view it remains puzzling, and at odds with the spirit of inclusion that otherwise informs his work. It resolves one case of metic exclusion but in the process creates another one, and indeed an even larger one.

It is not easy to discern what precisely is Bauböck's argument for denying that all members of society should be members of the demos. In places, he suggests that what distinguishes the demos as a political association from the rest of social life is the activity of "self-government".[20] Self-government is the purpose of political association, and only rationally deliberating linguistic agents have a stake in the activity of self-government. But talk of self-government cannot justify the capacity contract. After all, the linguistic agents whom Bauböck empowers to rule society are not just governing themselves. He is not proposing that linguistic agents form a club that would govern its members according to their own rules about deliberation, in the way that a chess club might

---

[18] We should note that while we endorse these calls to conceive "more-than-human" publics, we do not endorse the "new materialist" or "actor network theory" approach which elides the distinction between wilful agents and non-sentient life forms (e.g. Latour 2005; Bennett 2009). Our remarks here are restricted to non-human animals. And while many non-human animals have affected interests that need to be taken into account, we believe that it is primarily domesticated animals with whom humans share the "circumstances of democracy", including the fundamental facts of sociability and capacity for engagement.

[19] See Donaldson and Kymlicka (2016b) for a more systematic review.

[20] Also in Bauböck (2015).

govern itself. Rather, he is saying that linguistic agents have the right to *exercise state power*, and thereby govern society. The power of the state, which on a social membership model belongs to all members of society, becomes the property of the subset of linguistic agents.[21] In this sense, the capacity contract does not grant a right of self-government to linguistic agents, but something quite different – it grants a right to rule over others. (The right to rule over others is in fact at the heart of the capacity contract.) It is difficult to see how this can be justified in terms of a right to self-government.

So what, then, explains this "persistent" and "stubborn" clinging to the capacity contract? There are undoubtedly several factors, which we discuss elsewhere (Donaldson and Kymlicka forthcoming). But it is worth noting that the historical origins for the capacity contract are fundamentally illiberal and undemocratic. For Aristotle, the function of politics was to display a series of gender, class, racial and species supremacies: politics was where men revealed themselves to be superior to women, the propertied revealed themselves to be superior to slaves, the Greeks revealed themselves to be superior to barbarians, adults revealed themselves to be superior to children, and humans revealed themselves to be superior to animals. This affirmation of hierarchy, and exclusion of the inferior, was the point and purpose of politics: politics was where we display our exalted status. For Aristotle and his latter-day acolytes, mere members of society are just the backdrop or the stage on which exalted agents exercise their unique (male, propertied, Greek, human) powers. Medieval and Renaissance philosophers maintained this perfectionist preoccupation, although they tied it to Christian doctrines about humanity's distinctive place in divine creation: organizing politics around rational speech appropriately marked our favoured position as made in God's image, above other animals.

---

[21] Bauböck says that "it is the larger transgenerational society that collectively governs itself and not the subcategory of adults who have the capacity ... to vote or hold public office" (p. 46). But in fact he provides no account of how anyone outside that subcategory can take part in collectively governing society, and on the contrary he explicitly states that only this subcategory forms the demos. Here again, the conceptual argument is muddied by the equivocation between mere citizens and democratic citizens.

Needless to say, there is nothing liberal or democratic in any of this, and most contemporary political theorists officially disavow this Aristotelian legacy. For contemporary theorists, the function of politics is not to express species essences or divine providence, but to ensure that the distribution of the benefits and burdens of social cooperation is just, and to ensure that the exercise of political power over the governed is legitimate. But if so, then it is very difficult to understand why we should maintain the capacity contract, rather than rejecting it as a deeply illiberal inheritance. Both justice and legitimacy would seem to push us in the direction of the membership model of citizenship. Children, people with cognitive disabilities and domesticated animals may not engage in the forms of rational speech that Aristotle and Aquinas viewed as definitively human, but they clearly comply with social norms and carry the burdens of social cooperation, and they are clearly subject to the exercise of political power. They therefore have a stake in shaping our social norms, and if our concern is with justice and legitimacy rather than with exalting species essences, these facts of social participation and political subjection should be sufficient to warrant rights to participate. As we discussed earlier, this is in fact the direction that real-world reforms are taking, as new models of how to enable the engagement of children, people with cognitive disabilities and domesticated animals are continually being explored.

On Bauböck's model, by contrast, our duty to support and enable the political participation of our fellow members of society depends on whether they fall above or below some stipulated threshold of cognitive or linguistic competence. For those who fall above, we have strong duties not just to permit the exercise of their linguistic agency, but also to support it, including translation services or Braille or hearing aids, as well as rights to information and access. But if they fall below this threshold, then it appears we have no obligation to make any effort to solicit their subjective good or to be responsive to it when making collective decisions. Above the threshold, they are active citizens with strong claims to public support for their democratic agency; below the threshold, they are passive wards with no claims on public support for their democratic agency.

It is difficult to see any justification for this differential treatment.[22] The linguistic and cognitive capacities of society's members vary across multiple dimensions, all of which are continua. In our view, a truly democratic society would seek to support the political agency of all its members, wherever they fall on these continua, rather than finding ad hoc or arbitrary thresholds to empower some and exclude others. The capacity contract is not only arbitrary, but also generates politically pernicious myths and prejudices. Since every long-term member of society who complies with social norms and bears the burdens of social contribution would seem to have a prima facie claim to democratic citizenship, defenders of the capacity contract are prone to trivialize the contributions, burdens and the extent of their political subjection of the excluded. In order to justify excluding children, people with cognitive disabilities and domesticated animals from democratic citizenship, there is pressure to hide the unpleasant truth about the caste and metic status of these members of our society. Some theorists claim that children and people with cognitive disabilities inhabit a "separate but equal", or even a privileged, status. Theirs is allegedly an honoured and protected status of social membership, freed from the burdens and responsibilities of democratic citizenship. This is reminiscent of old anti-suffragist arguments about how much women (allegedly) stood to lose by coming down off their (supposed) pedestals to be recognized as grubby democratic citizens. In all of these cases, the commitment

---

[22]   This arbitrary differential treatment reveals the fallacy in Bauböck's claim that we need to keep animals out of citizenship in order to preserve a commitment to equality ("challenging this [human–animal] political boundary … might do great harm to the idea of *equality* of membership that is fundamental to democracy", p. 47). This not only ignores the reality that there are already plural and group-differentiated forms of membership, but it also ignores the fact that it is a commitment to the capacity contract that ruptures the idea of equality of membership. The capacity contract preserves the appearance of equality of membership by expelling all members who do not fit a pre-ordained vision of citizenship that was defined by and for some subset of members. As we have seen, it preserves an image of equality in self-government by granting rights to govern over others. This is not self-government by equal citizens: it gives some the right to rule over themselves and others. This is a Procrustean victory for equality.

to exclude or segregate certain members from citizenship generates cognitive pressure to redescribe their exclusion as a beneficial form of pastoral care and protection, ignoring the realities of burdens, harms and subjugation.

We can see this peeking through in Bauböck's text, where he says that "there is nothing degrading about treating children as children" (p. 46). But we would argue that "treating children as children" is degrading if it means subjecting them to arbitrary power, or trivializing their responsibilities, their work and their contributions, as is widespread in our society (Such and Walker 2005; Lister 2007).[23] Moreover, membership in transgenerational political communities is very much part of the "animal condition", despite Bauböck's assertion otherwise (p. 47). Domesticated animals are almost certainly more subject to political regulation than humans: where they can live or move, what they can eat, whether they can reproduce, and when and how they are killed, are all minutely regulated by the state (Smith 2012).

That defenders of the capacity contract systematically obscure the realities of power, burden and contribution should not be surprising, since these are the bases of claims to citizenship on the membership model. Since the membership model says that individuals are owed citizenship in virtue of enduring participation in schemes of social cooperation that are subject to collective governance, defenders of the capacity contract are more or less compelled to deny or trivialize the extent to which children, people with cognitive disabilities and domesticated animals are subject to power or engage in contribution.

---

[23] Bauböck acknowledges that "treating children as children" may include "responsibilities to allow them to participate in all decisions concerning them" (p. 46). But, as we noted earlier, he provides no account of how anyone other than neurotypical adults can take part in collectively governing society (see note 21 above). In any event, his apparent exception for children rests on the logic that we owe them participation not in virtue of what they are – not in virtue of their interests or membership *as children* – but in virtue of what they will become (adult citizens). This privileging of children's "becoming" over their "being" is precisely the idea that children's rights advocates rail against, since it accords no recognition of the importance of the quality of a child's life as such, in their childhood years (see Arneil 2002). And if we accept that children are owed participation because of their being, not just their becoming, then we have no grounds to exclude animals.

We can't review here all of the intellectual hoops and gymnastics that defenders of the capacity contract undertake to justify their position,[24] but we would suggest the time has come for political theorists to simply abandon the capacity contract. Given the stubborn persistence of the capacity contract, and the cultural and intellectual barriers standing in the way of dismantling it, we are not surprised by its appearance in Bauböck's essay. And we welcome the fact that, unlike most political theorists, he at least flags the issue as one that needs to be acknowledged. More importantly, we believe that Bauböck's work in articulating multiple principles of democratic inclusion tied to multiple types of polity could prove extremely fruitful for thinking about the democratic challenges facing more-than-human political communities. Different kinds of human and animal communities inhabit overlapping territories in complex ways, without necessarily forming shared societies. For example, many non-domesticated animals have interests that are affected by our decisions while not being subject to human governance to any significant degree, let alone being part of a shared demos. Some animals living in remote wilderness areas, for example, are not subject to coercion, but may be affected by human activity such as pollution, climate change or aircraft flight paths. We have duties to take their affected interests into account, but not to include them in the shared demos. Other non-domesticated animals, by contrast, are subject to extreme state violence and coercion. Consider the rodents, pigeons, foxes and countless others who are poisoned, spiked, gassed, shot and ripped apart according to the laws of the human community. As Bauböck notes, justice demands that those subject to the coercive force of the law must share equal protection of the law – and we would argue this should apply to urban wildlife – but

---

[24] Of course, one obvious explanation for its persistence is that political theorists have a pre-theoretical commitment to excluding non-human animals from the demos, in order to continue to enjoy the "flow of pleasures" that is generated by their caste status (Wadiwel 2015), and simply work backwards to find theoretical premises that will generate this result, regardless of the tensions and contradictions this creates for their theories. Whether animals are to be included or excluded is not something to be resolved by appeal to independently justified political principles: rather, we select political principles on the basis of whether they will keep animals out.

here again, being subject to the law does not automatically translate into membership in the demos. Domesticated animals, on the other hand, are genuinely members of our society, and so have a genuine stake in membership in a mixed human–animal political community (as we argued above).

In short, once divorced from the capacity contract, Bauböck's distinctions between "all affected interests", "all subject to coercion" and "all citizen stakeholders" can help us to better understand the diverse patterns of human–animal political relations. Furthermore, Bauböck's concept of nested polities can help us address some of the challenges raised by the fact that humans and non-human animals share spaces and territories in ways which do not neatly line up with the nature, extent or density of governance and social relationships. He may or may not approve, but we will certainly make use of Bauböck's nuanced theory of the complex matrix of polities and democratic principles in order to push forward a new model of democracy that includes all members of society, in all their profuse diversity.

References

Aristotle. 1987. *Politics*. In *The Works of Aristotle*: Volume 2, edited by Robert Hutchins. Chicago: Encyclopaedia Britannica.

Arneil, Barbara. 2002. "Becoming Versus Being: A Critical Analysis of the Child in Liberal Theory." In *The Moral and Political Status of Children*, edited by David Archard and Colin M. Macleod. Oxford: Oxford University Press: 70–96.

Arneil, Barbara. 2009. "Disability, Self Image, and Modern Political Theory." *Political Theory* 37 (2): 218–242.

Bacon, Kate and Sam Frankel. 2014. "Rethinking Children's Citizenship: Negotiating Structure, Shaping Meanings." *International Journal of Children's Rights* 22: 21–42.

Bauböck, Rainer. 2015. "From Moral Intuition to Political Change: On Joseph Carens' Theory of Social Membership and Open Borders." *Political Theory* 43: 393–401.

Bennett, Jane. 2009. *Vibrant Matter: A Political Ecology of Things.* Durham: Duke University Press.

Blue, Gwendolyn and Melanie Rock. 2014. "Animal Publics: Accounting for Heterogeneity in Political Life." *Society and Animals* 22: 503–519.

Carens, Joseph. 2005. "The Integration of Immigrants." *Journal of Moral Philosophy* 2 (1): 29–46.

Carens, Joseph. 2013. *The Ethics of Immigration.* Oxford: Oxford University Press.

Clifford, Stacy. 2014. "The Capacity Contract: Locke, Disability, and the Political Exclusion of 'Idiots.'" *Politics, Groups, and Identities* 2 (1): 90–103.

Cohen, Elizabeth. 2009. *Semi-citizenship in Democratic Politics.* Cambridge: Cambridge University Press.

Davy, Laura. 2015. "Philosophical Inclusive Design: Intellectual Disability and the Limits of Individual Autonomy in Moral and Political Theory." *Hypatia* 30 (1): 132–148.

Donaldson, Sue and Will Kymlicka. 2011. *Zoopolis: A Political Theory of Animal Rights.* Oxford: Oxford University Press.

Donaldson, Sue and Will Kymlicka. 2016a. "Rethinking Membership and Participation in an Inclusive Democracy: Cognitive Disability, Children, Animals." In *Disability and Political Theory*, edited by Barbara Arneil and Nancy Hirschmann. Cambridge: Cambridge University Press: 168–197.

Donaldson, Sue and Will Kymlicka. 2016b. "Locating Animals in Political Philosophy." *Philosophy Compass* 11 (11): 692–701.

Donaldson, Sue and Will Kymlicka. Forthcoming. "Expanding the Boundaries of Citizenship." In *Oxford Handbook of Citizenship*, edited by Ayelet Shachar, Irene Bloemraad, Maarten Vink and Rainer Bauböck. Oxford: Oxford University Press.

Francis, Leslie and Anita Silvers. 2007. "Liberalism and Individually Scripted Ideas of the Good: Meeting the Challenge of Dependent Agency." *Social Theory and Practice* 33 (2): 311–334.

Franklin, Julian. 2011. "Animal Rights and Political Theory." In *Oxford Handbook of the History of Political Philosophy*, edited by George Klosko. Oxford: Oxford University Press: 756–769.

Goodin, Robert. 2007. "Enfranchising All Affected Interests, and Its Alternatives." *Philosophy and Public Affairs* 35 (1): 40–68.

Hartley, Christine. 2009. "Justice for the Disabled: A Contractualist Approach." *Journal of Social Philosophy* 40: 17–36.

Hinchcliffe, Christopher. 2015. "Animals and the Limits of Citizenship: Zoopolis and the Concept of Citizenship." *Journal of Political Philosophy* 23 (3): 302–320.

Hobbes, Thomas. 2010. *Leviathan.* Revised Edition, edited by A.P. Martinich and Brian Battiste. Peterborough: Broadview Press.

Koenig-Archibugi, Mathias. 2012. "Fuzzy Citizenship in Global Society." *Journal of Political Philosophy* 20 (4): 456–480.

Kymlicka, Will and Sue Donaldson. 2014. "Animals and the Frontiers of Citizenship." *Oxford Journal of Legal Studies* 34 (2): 200–219.

Latour, Bruno. 2005. *Reassembling the Social: An Introduction to Actor-Network-Theory.* Oxford: Oxford University Press.

List, Christian and Mathias Koenig-Archibugi. 2010. "Can There Be a Global Demos? An Agency-Based Approach." *Philosophy and Public Affairs* 38 (1): 76–110.

Lister, Ruth. 2007. "Why Citizenship: Where, When and How Children?" *Theoretical Inquiries in Law* 8 (2): 693–718.

Marres, Noortje and Javier Lezaun. 2011. "Materials and Devices of the Public: An Introduction." *Economy and Society* 40 (4): 489–509.

Meijer, Eva. 2013. "Political Communication with Animals." *Humanimalia* 5 (1): 28–52.

Mills, Charles. 1997. *The Racial Contract.* Ithaca: Cornell University Press.

Moosa-Mitha, Mehmoona. 2005. "A Difference-Centred Alternative to Theorization of Children's Citizenship Rights." *Citizenship Studies* 9 (4): 369–388.

Nichols, Robert. 2013. "Indigeneity and the Settler Contract Today." *Philosophy and Social Criticism* 39 (2): 165–186.

Pateman, Carole. 1988. *The Sexual Contract.* Cambridge: Polity.

Peggs, Kay. 2012. *Animals and Sociology.* London: Palgrave.

Rehfeld, Andrew. 2011. "The Child as Democratic Citizen." *Annals of the American Academy of Political and Social Science* 633: 141–166.

Rollo, Toby. 2016. "Feral Children: Settler Colonialism, Progress, and the Figure of the Child." *Settler Colonial Studies.* Published online 29 June 2016, http://dx.doi.org/10.1080/2201473X.2016.1199826, accessed 25 May 2017.

Quennerstedt, Ann. 2010. "Children, But Not Really Humans? Critical Reflections on the Hampering Effect of the '3Ps'," *International Journal of Children's Rights* 18 (4): 619–635.

Saunders, Ben. 2011. "Defining the Demos." *Politics, Philosophy and Economics* 11 (3): 280–301.

Smith, Kim. 2012. *Governing Animals: Animal Welfare and the Liberal State*. Oxford: Oxford University Press.

Song, Sarah. 2012. "The Boundary Problem in Democratic Theory: Why the Demos should be Bounded by the State." *International Theory* 4 (1): 39–68.

Steiner, Gary. 2013. *Animals and the Limits of Postmodernism*. New York: Columbia University Press.

Such, Elizabeth and Robert Walker. 2005. "Young Citizens or Policy Objects? Children in the 'Rights and Responsibilities' Debate." *Journal of Social Policy* 34 (1): 39–57.

Wadiwel, Dinesh. 2015. *The War Against Animals*. Amsterdam: Rodopi.

Walzer, Michael. 1983. *Spheres of Justice: A Defense of Pluralism and Equality*. New York: Basic Books.

6

Populus, demos and self-rule

David Owen

Rainer Bauböck's work on popular sovereignty, citizenship and the demos problem is an important touchstone for contemporary political, and especially democratic, theory. Grounded in attention to both the theoretical and empirical circumstances of individual and collective political agency, Bauböck offers a highly sophisticated and, in many ways, compelling approach to thinking through the philosophical and political challenges of citizenship and democracy in a global landscape characterized by a plurality of peoples, types of polity, multilevel governance and migration (internal and transnational). In this essay, I aim to put some pressure on the relationship between *populus* (i.e. the citizenry) and *demos* (i.e. those entitled, in one way or another, to participate in the decision-making process) in Bauböck's account. Put another way, I accept Bauböck's argument that the all citizenship stakeholders (ACS) principle is the best available principle for determining the composition of the citizenry but, in a particular and specific sense, reject the claim that it thereby also demarcates the demos.

Demos principles and citizenship

It is an important strength of Bauböck's argument that his account articulates complementary relations of the all affected interests (AAI) principle, the all subjection to coercion (ASC) principle and the all citizenship stakeholders principle. His position is summarized thus in section 3.4 of his essay. It is, however, an equally important feature of his argument that it draws attention to the normative political challenge that this argument poses for contemporary polities. In addressing Bauböck's argument, I will begin by developing the claim that ACS specifies who is entitled to be a part of the populus, a citizen of the polity, but not who is entitled to be a member of the demos. In this section, I advance this argument by distinguishing different types of membership of the demos and focusing on what I will call the *authorial* membership of the demos. In the following section, I argue that we have reason to distinguish between *populus* and authorial membership of the *demos* in addressing the issues identified by Bauböck and that doing so is normatively consequential for Bauböck's argument.

One way of thinking about the general structure of Bauböck's account and the differentiation of the three principles that he identifies as relevant to the demos problem is in terms of three distinct types of membership of the demos:

> AAI demarcates the scope of *discursive* membership of the demos, that is, those entitled to voice or representation of their interests in the decision-making process.

> ASC demarcates the range of *editorial* membership of the demos, that is, those entitled to contest the government's decisions.

> ACS demarcates the limits of *authorial* membership of the demos, that is, those entitled to authorize the government's decisions.

However, if we compare this schema with Bauböck's own account, we find that rather than demarcating the scope of *authorial* membership of the demos, ACS identifies persons who have a legitimate claim to citizenship as membership in a self-ruling polity and, as Bauböck acknowledges, not all of those who satisfy ACS will be included in authorial membership of the demos. Specifically, Bauböck identifies two groups who he takes to be rightfully excluded from the franchise: persons who lack the capacity to vote or stand for election and persons who are stakeholders but whose stakes do not stand in the appropriate relationship to the polity. Let us address each in turn.

Bauböck distinguishes between citizens included in, or excluded from, authorial membership of the demos in terms of their capacity to participate:

> Even if the link between individual autonomy and collective self-government need not imply that citizens have a *duty* to participate actively in the political life of the polity, it does imply that they must have the *opportunity* to do so. But this opportunity in turn depends on their *capacity* to participate. The citizenship status of minor children or cognitively disabled persons might then be in jeopardy under this conception whereas AAI and ASC would have no difficulty in arguing for their inclusion. (pp. 44–45)

He argues that, for example, if "there is no democratic way of providing children below a certain age with opportunities for participating in electoral politics" (pp. 45–46), they can be legitimately excluded. Why, then, should children, especially newborn or very young children, be included as citizens at all? After all, one way to identify the populus and authorial membership of the demos is to exclude children from citizenship until they meet the relevant capacity threshold. Bauböck's rejection of this seemingly theoretically neat solution is grounded in an appeal to "the conditions for continuity of a self-governing polity over time":

> Newborn babies are attributed citizenship not just because we regard them as future citizens. If this were the case, one might as well wait until they have reached the age of majority and consider them until then subjects within the jurisdiction who have a claim to equal protection. The reason why we recognize them as citizens is that political communities are transgenerational human societies. The status of membership in such communities is acquired at birth and does not depend on age-related cognitive or other capacities. In democracies, it is the larger transgenerational society that collectively governs itself and not the subcategory of adults who have the capacity and opportunity to vote or hold public office. Minor children are citizenship stakeholders because of their belonging to a transgenerational political community. (p. 46)

However, this appeal to a transgenerational political community is, on Bauböck's own account, limited to some types of polity (e.g. states) and not others (e.g. municipalities). This point is reflected in the fact that ACS justifies birthright citizenship (supplemented by naturalization) for states, but residence-based citizenship for municipalities. Should children be citizens of states but not of municipalities? It is not clear why this should not be the case, especially as national citizenship would offer protection from domination for children who are citizens, while children who are not citizens would be entitled to *editorial* membership of the demos at both local and national levels. This criticism operates within the terms of Bauböck's argument, but we may also question these terms. There are two issues here. The first concerns where any capacity threshold should be drawn; the second whether a capacity threshold should be drawn.

On the first, it is notable that Bauböck appeals to the age of majority in relation to voting rights but no criteria for the identification of this age are offered. In principle, Bauböck could, I think, endorse the account of "franchise capacity" offered by Lopez-Guerra in which all who are capable of experiencing their exclusion from the franchise as an injustice ought to be enfranchised (Lopez-Guerra 2014: 71) rather than, say, a form of input minimalism which hangs on the epistemic claim to protect the quality of electoral outcomes (ibid.: 63–69). However, the significant issue is the second. Bauböck rightly holds that "giving parents proxy votes that they can cast on behalf of their minor children looks more like a violation of the one-person-one-vote principle in favour of a particular category of adults than a vehicle for children's participation in the polity" (p. 45), but this is hardly the only option. Consider an alternative in which all enfranchised persons also have a second "proxy" vote cast for candidates on a separate children's list who have a limited number of reserved seats in the legislature and whose role is to act as advocates for the interests of children and who have a qualified veto power (e.g. a power to refer back and require a supermajority for the bill to pass) over legislation that directly affects the interests of children as children. The inclusion of all voters acknowledges that the interests of children are not the sole domain of parents and that the vast majority of people stand in both general and agent-specific obligations of care towards children (e.g. older siblings, cousins, aunts and uncles, grandparents), while the limited number of reserved seats and particular powers provides conditions for the effective representation of the interests of children, not least since in each successive election a new group of voters who have been represented by these special representatives will be able to hold them to account for their performance. (One could experiment with weighting votes inversely to the number of elections since the voter acquired franchise rights, or would have done so if a citizen from the age of majority, so young voters' votes weigh more heavily than those of aged voters.) The point here is that it is not clear to me that Baubock requires the appeal to transgenerational political community that would distinguish children's citizenship rights at national and municipal levels of governance; rather, he could tie citizenship to voting rights with a generalized distribution of "proxy" votes for children across the enfranchised citizenry. The political representation of the interests of children is a tricky political challenge but not obviously an insurmountable one – and while the case of children is, in certain respects, a special case among those excluded on capacity grounds, this does not entail that one could not develop related democratic proposals in other cases.

The second case is rather different. In his discussion of the problem of the over-inclusiveness of an unlimited ius sanguinis rule, Baubock argues that third generation emigrants should not acquire citizenship at birth and continues:

> It is more consistent with the birthright character of national citizen-ship to let it expire for the distant descendants of emigrants through non-acquisition at birth instead of depriving first or second generation holders of this status on grounds of long-term residence abroad and acquisition of a foreign citizenship. It seems, however, reasonable to exclude second generation emigrants who have never resided in the country from voting rights, even if they retain a lifelong citizenship status. Since voting rights are anyhow not acquired at birth but only

around the age of majority, the concern about over-inclusiveness of an external franchise can be easily taken into account by tying the external franchise to a condition of prior long-term residence in the country; this would include not only first generation emigrants but also second generation returnees, while the children of emigrants who have never resided in the country would never acquire the franchise instead of being deprived of a birthright status. (pp. 69–70)

Apart from confirming Bauböck's appeal to the age of majority, this passage argues that the over-inclusiveness problem for an external franchise can be dealt with if the franchise is restricted to first generation emigrants and second generation returnees who have lived in the "home" state for some significant period prior to, respectively, emigration or re-emigration. There are two issues here. The first is that it is not clear what status Bauböck is ascribing to expatriate voting rights. The second concerns the non-identity of citizenship and authorial membership of the demos. I'll address these in turn.

In earlier work explicitly addressing the external franchise, Bauböck (2007) argues that expatriate voting is neither required nor forbidden by justice. Consider two sets of remarks. In the first, Bauböck reiterates the stakeholder principle:

> The notion of stakeholding expresses, first, the idea that citizens have not merely fundamental interests in the outcomes of the political process, but a claim to be represented as participants in that process. Second, stakeholding serves as a criterion for assessing claims to membership and voting rights. Individuals whose circumstances of life link their future well-being to the flourishing of a particular polity should be recognized as stakeholders in that polity with a claim to participate in collective decision-making processes that shape the shared future of this political community. (ibid.: 2422)

This passage suggests that stakeholders have a legitimate claim to participate, although this does not rule out either that the reach of this claim (i.e. the extent of participation it legitimates) may vary or that it may defeated by other legitimate concerns. In the second set of remarks, Bauböck comments:

In a stakeholder conception of democratic community, persons with multiple stakes need multiple votes to control each of the governments whose decisions will affect their future as members of several *demoi*. This applies, on the one hand, to federally nested *demoi* where citizens can cast multiple vertical votes on several levels and, on the other hand, to the *demoi* of independent states with overlapping membership. (ibid.: 2428)

This gestures to a stronger view, namely that the stakeholder principle supports a requirement of inclusion in authorial membership of the demos for stakeholders, where we may surmise this requirement would be legitimately subject only to (a) the basic constraint that such inclusion does not threaten the stability of the state (i.e. its capacity to reproduce itself as a self-governing polity over time); and (b) feasibility constraints. Bauböck does not adopt this stance, remaining content with the view that expatriate voting is permissible but not required (although acknowledging the normative salience of existing state practices of expatriate enfranchisement as having constructed reasonable expectations which it would be unjust to frustrate given the normative permissibility of the practice). Overall, the most one can say is that, for Bauböck, the stakeholder principle broadly supports a presumption in favour of such rights for first generation migrants, while acknowledging that this presumption can be supported or defeated by a wide range of factors relating to the specific circumstances of the polity and the conditions that support its stable reproduction (Bauböck 2007).

The implication of this argument is that first and second generation emigrants are rightfully included in the citizenry but *may* be in the case of first generation emigrants and *should* be in the case of second generation emigrants excluded from the authorial membership of the demos. Recall that Bauböck also argues that third generation emigrants should be excluded from the citizenry:

It is obvious that third generation emigrants will generally not have a sufficiently strong stake in a grandparent's country of origin to claim citizenship, unless their parents have themselves renewed their links to this country through taking up residence there. In the case of second

generation return ... the next generation of children born abroad are
again second generation emigrants and qualify for citizenship based on
their ties to parents who are themselves strongly linked to the country
awarding the status. (p. 69)

The implication is that what legitimately includes second generation
emigrants in the citizenry is that they do have a "sufficiently strong stake",
but what legitimately excludes second generation emigrants from voting
rights is that they don't have the same kind of stake as residents (or first
generation emigrants). Recall at this point that the notion of stakeholding
appeals to the relationship between individual autonomy and well-being
on the one hand, and the collective autonomy and well-being of the
polity on the other hand. ACS specifies that all whose autonomy and
well-being are linked to the collective self-government and flourishing
of a polity have a claim to citizenship. In this statement, stakeholding is
being treated as a non-scalar property (i.e. what matters is being inside
a given boundary, not how far inside you are). However, stakeholding
can also be treated as a scalar property in which our concern is how
much, how densely, how intensely, a person's autonomy and well-being
are linked to the collective self-government and flourishing of a polity.
This matters because it enables the setting of stakeholding thresholds
internal to the general stakeholder boundary above which it will be
treated in a non-scalar way – and this is what Bauböck is doing in
restricting membership of the authorial demos to a subset of the general
class of stakeholders. His explicit rationale for maintaining this exclusion
claim runs thus:

> Members of this so-called second immigrant generation still have a
> plausible interest in their parents' citizenship, and virtually all democratic
> countries therefore have external jus sanguinis provisions in their citizen-
> ship laws. Yet a right to acquire citizenship status at birth need not
> entail a right to vote. Benefits of external citizenship, such as diplomatic
> protection and the right to return to, and to inherit and own property
> in, the country of citizenship reflect interests of a slightly different kind
> than those that ground a right to political participation. The former

refer to potential interests that a second generation external citizen may activate over the course of her life, whereas the latter should presuppose that some of these interests are currently active. (2007: 2426)

There are good reasons for advancing this distinction. For example, it is clear from the standpoint of a concern with individual autonomy that even though both resident and expatriate citizens are subject to the political authority of the state, the former are more comprehensively subject to the coercively enforceable authority of the state. Similarly, if we consider individual well-being it is entirely plausible that the well-being of resident citizens (and first generation emigrants whose identities were constituted through residence in the "home" state) is likely to be more densely dependent on the autonomy and well-being of the polity than the well-being of second generation emigrants. In this respect, the general notion of "stakeholding" is still playing the pivotal normative role but – and this is the point I would stress – ACS is now revealed as a principle for determining membership of the citizenry and not authorial membership of the demos. ACS is presented as a necessary but not sufficient condition of authorial membership of the demos.

At this stage in my argument, I need to introduce another set of distinctions in relationship to the concept of the demos. These relate to the kind of political decision-making in question (rather than the modes of relationship to decision-making that I have already distinguished in terms of discursive, editorial and authorial membership of the demos), and we can in general distinguish executive, legislative and constitutional demoi depending on the political system.[1] For current purposes, it is the distinction between legislative and constitutional demoi that is pertinent. The salient normative difference between these demoi is that the judgements of the constitutional demos structure the fundamental terms of political association and, hence, the foundational commitments and character of citizenship as membership of the self-ruling polity,

---

[1] We would also have to add "judicial" for polities in which judicial positions are subject to election.

whereas the decision-making of the legislative demos addresses ways of structuring relationships between persons subject to the territorial jurisdiction and/or political authority of the state within the terms set by the constitutional rules and norms. This distinction matters for two reasons. First, it makes clear the priority of the constitutional demos for popular sovereignty, that is, for the people to be conceived as self-ruling. Second, even if there are legitimate reasons for some citizens – for example, second generation expatriate citizens – to be excluded from the legislative demos, these reasons do not apply to the constitutional demos since constitutional decisions are (a) collectively binding on all citizens and (b) constitutive of what, fundamentally, comprises one's political status as a citizen. For this reason, the authorial membership of the demos for constitutional decision-making should include all citizens regardless of their location.

Consider two examples. The first is the UK referendum on membership of the EU. Since the access to EU citizenship of UK citizens is derivative of their UK citizenship, this decision has clear and significant implications for the legal status of UK citizens living elsewhere in the EU but it also changes the legal position of UK citizens living outside of the EU. Even if we set this issue of legal status aside though, it fundamentally concerns the nature of the political association to which citizens belong and the terms on which they relate to one another and to others. This second point is clearly made by the second example, the 2004 Irish referendum on whether to abolish their unconditional *ius soli* rule in respect of citizenship acquisition. In this case, the proposed change would not have direct effect on the rights of any individual Irish citizens given that the existing ius sanguinis rule would be unaffected by such a change, but it would significantly change who had an automatic right to acquire Irish citizenship and hence the nature of the political association. In this respect, popular sovereignty requires that all citizens can express the judgement concerning this foundational aspect of Irish political community. These examples propose key test cases for Bauböck because if he holds that second generation immigrants can rightfully be excluded from authorial membership of the demos for constitutional decision-making, then he ought to exclude them from citizenship. (This would be compatible with giving them a distinct quasi-nationality status such as a right to accelerated naturalization conditional on a period of residence.) If, however, he wants to sustain their claim to citizenship, then he ought *either* to drop the claim to legitimate exclusion of second generation emigrants from voting rights *or* acknowledge that there is reason to distinguish the authorial composition of the constitutional demos and the legislative demos.

I think that the best option for Bauböck is to distinguish between the authorial composition of the constitutional demos and the legislative demos, not least because doing so would allow him to avoid a further problem to which his argument is otherwise subject. This problem is what elsewhere (Owen 2011) I have called the *arbitrary demos* problem and concerns the fact that if one holds the view, as Bauböck does, that expatriate voting rights in relation to legislative (or executive) elections are permissible rather than required or forbidden, one must still address the question of *who* is entitled to determine whether or not expatriates are included in the national franchise. To resolve it, what is required is a principled (i.e. non-arbitrary) basis on which to determine who is entitled to decide on this question. Here the fact there is one type of decision by any polity which not only binds all citizens irrespective of residence but also directly concerns their very status as citizens, namely constitutional laws that specify the entitlements and obligations of citizens – such as, for example, laws on nationality and expatriate voting rights – is critical. Moreover, because constitutional rules concern the character of citizenship itself, to deny any citizen or group of citizens the right to participate as an equal authorial member of the democratic community in the decision-making process is to deny their status as a citizen; it is to subject them to an alien form of rule. The only legitimate basis for such constitutional decisions as decisions on expatriate voting is, thus, that all citizens are entitled to authorial inclusion irrespective of their residential status (although this does not rule out that considerations of feasibility and cost may legitimately allow the requirement that votes are cast within the territory of the home state).

If this is cogent, ACS not only demarcates those entitled to citizenship, but it also simultaneously identifies those who are entitled to authorial membership of the constitutional demos as the keystone of popular sovereignty. This may be compatible with the legitimate exclusion of some citizens from authorial membership of the demos for legislative (or executive) elections. Acknowledging this point, however, raises a further question. If legitimate inclusion in the citizenry is not a sufficient condition of authorial membership of the legislative demos, is it a necessary condition?

Demos problems

The argument thus far has involved what may appear to be a minor refiguring of Bauböck's account but, as this section will attempt to illustrate, the claims advanced provide the conceptual space to advance normative reasons that offer a significant challenge to Bauböck's argument. To begin to make this case, I shall return to his critical incorporation of AAI and ASC principles into the architecture of his account.

While rejecting AAI as a principle for demarcating the scope of authorial membership of the demos, Bauböck presents it as having a role to play in his overall account of democratic legitimacy as a principle addressed to policy decision-making:

> Tracking affected interests requires taking these into account in decision-making, not after that decision has already been taken. Affected interests thus have a claim to be included in the process of deliberation that precedes the decision and not only the process of implementation that follows it. In other words, actually affected interests have a claim to voice. They must be heard and taken into account by those who take the decision. They form the relevant public for political decisions. Those whose interests are affected by democratic decisions, no matter whether they are citizens, subjects or completely outside the jurisdiction, have a right to justification of the decision that respects them as autonomous sources of valid claims. (p. 24)

In my terms, Bauböck presents AAI as demarcating the scope of discursive membership of the demos. However, notice that, as Bauböck rightly states, this is not simply a right to speak but also a right to be listened to and have one's interests taken into account by authorial members of the demos. Put another way, for one's speech acts to be communicative acts within the discursive demos, the relevant conditions of deliberative uptake must be met. Since this cannot be presumed, the right to justification entails a right to contest decision-making that participants in the demos can reasonably take to have failed to meet the relevant conditions of deliberative uptake. Such an institutionalized right of contestation is practically necessary for assurance that deliberative process will give due regard to the interests of all affected non-resident non-citizens. What is contested here is not the outcomes of deliberation as such but rather the processes that gave rise to these outcomes. Internal to discursive membership of the demos, then, is a contestatory right. Another way to put this point is that discursive membership of the demos entails a particular process-focused form of editorial membership of the demos addressed to policy decision-making.

If we turn now to ASC, we can note that Bauböck's rejection of ASC as a principle for determining the authorial membership of the demos notes rightly that "it is systematically biased towards existing boundaries" (p. 29), before going on to advance the powerful challenge that ASC cannot account for the intuition that while it is legitimate for the U.S. to occupy Germany after World War II, it would have been entirely illegitimate for it to annex it. Or, again, in colonial contexts, it would have been entirely inadequate to respond to national liberation movements with the offer of equal citizenship in the imperium (as Bauböck's example of France and Algeria makes clear).

This argument strikes me as providing compelling reason for ASC to be rejected as the principle for determining claims to membership of the people who have a right to collective self-government in such contexts. This is why I endorse Bauböck's argument that ACS best identifies those who have a claim to membership of a self-governing people, a populus, and to citizenship in the polity that they (are entitled to) constitute. But notice that this is just to say that ACS appropriately identifies those who are entitled to authorial membership of the constitutional demos – it does not determine anything about authorial membership of the legislative demos. The rejection of ASC as a principle for determining membership of the populus does not entail its rejection as a principle for demarcating authorial membership of the legislative demos – and there are compelling reasons why we may wish to adopt it for this role.

Consider the classic argument provided by Robert Dahl for the "Principle of Full Inclusion" which can be stated thus: "The demos must include all adult members of the association except transients and persons proved to be mentally defective" (1989: 129), where "adult members of the association" refers to "all adults subject to the binding collective decisions of the association" (ibid.: 120). As Lopez-Guerra helpfully notes, Dahl's specification of criteria of democracy can be summarized thus:

> (1) governments must give equal consideration to the good and interests of every person bound by their laws (principle of intrinsic equality); (2) unless there is compelling evidence to the contrary, every person should be considered to be the best judge of his or her own good and interests (presumption of personal autonomy); therefore (3) all adults [who are not merely transients (1) and are not shown to be mentally defective (2)] should be assumed to be sufficiently well-qualified to participate in the collective decision-making processes of the polity (strong principle of equality). (Lopez-Guerra 2005: 219, my insertion)

In the context of a territorial state, Dahl's account implies that any competent adult who is habitually resident within the territory of the state and, hence, subject to the collectively binding laws and policies of its government is entitled to full inclusion within the demos.[2] Such

---

[2]   Although Dahl talks of the Principle of All Affected Interests, I agree with Lopez-Guerra (2005: 222–225) that since it is being governed that is the normatively relevant issue for Dahl, the relevant principle is that of being *subjected to* rule rather than *affected by* rule. For defences of the all affected principle, see Shapiro (2003) and Goodin (2007).

an argument can be taken to underwrite Walzer's claim that the denial of full political rights to habitual residents amounts to *citizen tyranny* (Walzer 1983: 55).[3]

Dahl's argument is built in two stages. The first stage offers reasons for supporting the Strong Principle of Equality and hence democracy against other forms of rule; the second stage moves from this principle to the Principle of Full Inclusion as a way of specifying the composition of the demos. The Strong Principle of Equality can be stated thus:

> All members are sufficiently well-qualified, taken all around, to participate in making the collective decisions binding on the association that significantly affect their good or interests. In any case, none are so definitely better qualified than the others that they should be entrusted with making the collective and binding decisions. (Dahl 1989: 98)

To ground this principle, Dahl appeals to two further claims. First, the Principle of Intrinsic Equality expresses the claim that governments must give equal consideration to the good and interests of every person subject to their laws. This principle is not itself sufficient to ground the claim to democratic government expressed in the Strong Principle of Equality since it does not entail that equal consideration is best or only realized through democratic rule. Hence Dahl introduces a second claim, the Presumption of Personal Autonomy, which states: "In the absence of a compelling showing to the contrary everyone should be assumed to be the best judge of his or her own good or interests" (ibid.: 100). Whereas the Principle of Intrinsic Equality is a universal moral claim that expresses the claim to equal treatment of all those subject to a scheme of rule and hence their fundamental interest in being treated as an equal, the Presumption of Personal Autonomy is a *prudential* claim. As Dahl notes:

---

[3] Walzer links this claim to one in which the polity has the right to determine its own entry criteria as an element of its right to self-determination; for an excellent analysis of the difficulties that this conjunction generates, see Bosniak (2006).

> To reject it as a presumption for individual and collective decisions,
> however, we would have to believe *not only* that (1) some substantial
> portion of adults are quite unable to understand, or are not sufficiently
> motivated to seek, their most fundamental interests, *but also* that (2)
> a class of paternalist authorities could be counted on to do so in their
> behalf. (Ibid.: 101)

Dahl reasonably appeals to our political history to indicate that we can
have little confidence in (2), but we can helpfully develop the grounds
of this prudential claim by drawing on arguments proposed by Cristiano
in response to this question of whether my fundamental interest in
being treated as an equal may be better advanced if those more enlightened than I have the power to determine laws and policies under which
I should live. As Cristiano comments:

> The epistemic access that each person has to her own interests and
> the cognitive biases that interfere with their understanding of others'
> interests (along with the idea that equality involves advancing those
> interests) suggest that the epistemic differences between persons on
> these matters is not likely to be very great and that a person's interests
> will be neglected if they do not participate ... And, of course, there is
> always a lot of disagreement among even the enlightened about what
> equality and interests require. (2015: 248)

On the basis of this argument, Cristiano notes that "given the setback of
these fundamental interests [through exclusion from the demos], each
person whose interests are set back in this way will have reason to think
that she is not being treated as an equal" and, since each person has a
fundamental interest in being recognized as an equal whose interests
count equally with others', this interest "cannot be met if this person
lives in a world that can be seen by others to be treating them as equals
but which she cannot see to be treating her as an equal" (ibid.: 248).
Cristiano's argument thus helps to clarify further how the relationship
between the Principle of Intrinsic Equality and the Presumption of
Personal Autonomy suffice to ground the Strong Principle of Equality.

The next step is to note that we require criteria to determine who has a rightful claim to membership of the demos in order to draw normatively salient distinctions between democratic states and states which restrict membership of the demos to any particular group (e.g. white men). In the light of the foregoing arguments, one attractive-looking response to this requirement is to offer a categorical principle according to which everyone subject to a government and its laws has an unqualified right to membership of the demos (Dahl 1989: 124). Dahl's objection to this categorical principle is that it elides the problem posed by competency issues. Although he acknowledges that criteria of competency are defeasible, Dahl, like Bauböck, holds that in the case of young children and the severely cognitively disabled who are unable to meet the minimal criteria required for personal autonomy (i.e. pursuing, revising or rejecting conceptions of the good or seeking their fundamental interests), exclusion from the demos is justified.[4] It is notable that it is in his discussion of competency issues that Dahl also addresses the exclusion of transients:

> Suppose France is holding an election on Sunday and I, an American, arrive in Paris on Saturday as a tourist. Would anyone argue that I should be entitled to participate in the election, much less acquire all the other political rights of French citizenship? I think not. On what grounds could I properly be excluded? On the grounds that I am unqualified. (Ibid.: 128)

This is a problematic argument, however, as Dahl comes to recognize. Suppose I can demonstrate that, having studied French politics, I am fully aware of the issues: then the objection that matters is not that I am unqualified but rather that, as a transient visitor to the state, I may not be subject to the laws that my participation helps to bring about.

---

[4] I referred earlier to Lopez-Guerra (2014: 71), who has advanced an argument that we can relate to Dahl's and Cristiano's argument by drawing attention to the fact that denial of franchise to a person is susceptible of producing injustice. Lopez-Guerra's suggestion is that only habitual residents who are incapable of experiencing disenfranchisement as an injustice in these senses can legitimately be excluded from the franchise.

If I had voting rights, I would be involved in authoring collectively binding decisions to which, presumptively, I would not be subject (ibid.: 354–355, n. 11) There are thus two legitimate forms of exclusion from the demos on Dahl's account: first, exclusion on incompetency grounds and, second, exclusion on "presumptive non-subjection" grounds. It is the combination of these considerations that leads Dahl to reject categorical principles of inclusion in favour of the conditional principle that he terms "the Principle of Full Inclusion".

This type of general argument concerning democracy as a form of rule provides prima facie reason for the inclusion of all non-transitory residents in the legislative demos. However, Bauböck can respond that when democratic rule is mediated through the political form of the state, the implication of this argument is that non-transitory residents should be entitled to citizenship and ACS acknowledges this claim. The key issue here is that whereas ASC simply requires that non-transitory residents be enfranchised, ACS requires that they be granted access to citizenship. It is certainly an advantage of ACS that it has this entailment; however, our question is whether this legitimates the exclusion of non-transitory residents who choose not to acquire citizenship from the legislative demos.[5]

The claim that such exclusion is illegitimate has been acutely put by Angeli's discussion of the condition of a resident non-citizen. Angeli's argument has two elements. The first draws attention to the fact that, in the conduct of her life, the resident non-citizen is required to navigate

> a dense and complex network of legal norms that is "backed up by coercive measures that implicate the liberal principle of autonomy". Her profession, her private aspirations and other dimensions of her life are "matters that the legal system influences at every turn – by recognizing

---

[5]   Two alternative views are available. The first denies that non-transitory residents should be entitled to choice, arguing that citizenship should be mandatory (Rubio-Marin 2000). The second acknowledges Bauböck's argument for the choice to naturalize being voluntary but draws a distinction between citizenship and membership of the legislative demos and argues that the latter should be mandatory (Owen 2011). Here I focus only on the second.

(or not) different rights and liberties, by carving out specific rules of property and contract, and so on." … [In] a territorially organized legal system coercive constraints are virtually omnipresent in the life of resident people. And it is precisely the density and pervasiveness of coercion that causes liberal political theorists to worry about the extent to which residents are capable of leading an autonomous life and not a life according to other people's understanding of what is valuable and worth doing. (2015: 89)

We can link this argument back to Dahl's and Cristiano's argument that the denial of rights of membership of the legislative demos will almost inevitably lead to one's life being shaped and constrained by "other people's understanding of what is valuable and worth doing" even if they are making good faith efforts to acknowledge one's own interests. Angeli's second step is to note that this is particularly problematic in respect of coercive laws and policies over which there is widespread disagreement. Thus, whereas an important range of laws – such as those protecting basic human rights or establishing neutral conventions for the coordination of basic activities (driving on the left or right, for example) – command widespread agreement among the inhabitants of democratic states, much else is subject to significant degrees of substantive moral and political disagreement. Hence, Angeli argues: "When disagreements about the legitimacy of coercive measures occur, democratic processes provide a solution. These processes offer the potential for residents to express their wills on roughly equal terms and to accord each other's views and interests respect" (ibid.: 90).

Granting all residents the right to participate in democratic practices and institutions involves recognizing that these kinds of disagreements over the legitimacy of coercive laws must be settled by those who are subject to them.

It may be objected that this undermines the self-rule of the national citizenry, but there are two responses to this objection. The first is that the fundamental condition of self-rule is met by the fact that authorial membership of the constitutional demos is reserved for citizens. The second is that, on Bauböck's own account, the democratic legitimacy of popular self-rule requires that laws and policies track the common good of all subjected to them – and, as the above arguments show, determining and tracking the common good requires the inclusion of resident non-citizens as authorial members in the legislative demos. Does this undermine the transgenerational political community by weakening incentives for resident non-citizens to naturalize? We might say, rather, that it supports the conditions of genuine consent by weakening an instrumental reason for resident non-citizens to naturalize.

Conclusion

In this essay I have endorsed Bauböck's proposal of ASC as the best principle, under contemporary political conditions, for determining access to national citizenship. I also welcome his incorporation of AAI, ASC and ACS into an account of democratic legitimacy – a move that significantly advances the debate concerning political membership and the demos problem in contemporary political theory. My critical aim has been to argue that ACS in determining who is entitled to citizenship and, hence, to authorial membership of the constitutional demos does not thereby determine who is entitled to authorial membership of the legislative demos and that we have good reason to endorse ASC as the appropriate principle for playing this role. I have also shown that this has practical implications. In contrast to Bauböck's account, all non-resident citizens have a claim to be included in constitutional referendums and all long-term resident non-citizens have a claim to be enfranchised in national elections.

References

Angeli, Oliviero 2015. *Cosmopolitanism, Self-determination and Territory.* Basingstoke: Palgrave.

Bauböck, Rainer 2007. "Stakeholder Citizenship and Transnational Political Participation." *Fordham Law Review* 75 (5): 2393–2447.

Bosniak, Linda 2006. *The Citizen and the Alien*. Princeton: Princeton University Press.

Cristiano, Thomas 2015. *The Constitution of Equality*. Oxford: Oxford University Press.

Dahl, Robert 1989. *Democracy and Its Critics*. New Haven: Yale University Press.

Goodin, Robert 2007. "Enfranchising All Affected Interests and Its Alternatives." *Philosophy and Public Affairs* 39 (1): 40–67.

Lopez-Guerra, Claudio 2005. "Should Expatriates Vote?" *Journal of Political Philosophy* 13 (2): 216–234.

Lopez-Guerra, Claudio 2014. *Democracy and Disenfranchisement*. Oxford: Oxford University Press.

Owen, David 2011. "Transnational Citizenship and the Democratic State." *Critical Review in Social and Political Philosophy* 14 (5): 641–663.

Rubio-Marin, Ruth 2000. *Immigration as a Democratic Challenge*. Cambridge: Cambridge University Press.

Shapiro, Ian 2003. *The Moral Foundations of Politics*. New Haven: Yale University Press.

Walzer, Michael 1983. *Spheres of Justice*. New York: Basic Books.

7

Stakeholder theory won't save citizenship

Peter J. Spiro

Introduction

Rainer Bauböck's "Democratic Inclusion: A Pluralistic Theory of Citizenship" is characteristically incisive. In this essay and elsewhere (e.g. Bauböck 2003, 2007), he has liberated normative political theory from the girdle of territorial boundary conditions. If ever it was, it is obviously no longer possible to posit a world of perfectly segmented national communities. For normative theory to remain relevant, it has to acknowledge the mismatch between borders on the map and the boundaries of human community. Bauböck's work offers a rigorous defence of citizenship and the state against the new architectures of globalization.

It's as good a defence as can be offered. But political theorists do not the state make. Membership in the state remains supremely important; by far the most important associational attachment of individuals. But there are cracks in the edifice. Bauböck confronts the territorial leakiness of state-based communities. But the assault on the state is more insidious than he can safely concede.

This essay interrogates Bauböck's stakeholder model as a matter of theory and highlights possibly unsustainable empirical assumptions behind it. It is unclear what binds citizens together in the stakeholder state. There is a suggestion of shared purpose, but it is not apparent what that purpose consists of beyond the collective maintenance of a safe space, democratically self-governed. That seems a weak reed on which to support the heavy lifting of the liberal state. The intergenerational qualities of citizenship are central to Bauböck's analysis. Although those intergenerational qualities serve the interests of both the state and liberal conceptions of justice, it is not clear that they are necessary to community or that they can independently generate the kind of solidarity necessary to sustaining citizenship as we know it.

Bauböck understands that citizenship persists only where boundaries exist and where populations remain relatively sedentary. States and citizenship cannot survive a condition of hypermobility. Whether the globe remains sedentary is an empirical question. There is strong evidence in the numbers that sedentary conditions continue to exist. But the trend is to greater mobility, and it may be that some state of greater mobility, short of extreme mobility, will pose greater challenges to the state than Bauböck allows. I use the archetypes of diaspora communities to critique his position on citizenship inside and outside the territory of the state. Diaspora communities may be disconnected from the political community of their state of residence even as they maintain a strong intergenerational connection qualifying as stakeholder citizenship in the homeland.

Non-state communities will also compete with citizenship in the state. These communities also comprehend the boundary and diversity conditions on which stakeholder citizenship is premised. They may also have broad jurisdictional reach. Unlike state-based communities, non-state communities have largely retained discretion to set their own membership criteria. That advantages them as locations for associative activity. What is old is new again, this time fuelled by material changes in communications. Meanwhile, community at the local level supplies some indirect evidence that community can exist in conditions of greater mobility. This possibility contradicts Bauböck's insistence on birthright citizenship and transgenerational community, both of which appear necessary to citizenship in independent states. Both phenomena will tend to contribute to stronger community but only where they are supported by sociological ties. In the case of diasporas and other forms of transnational communities, those ties will sometimes suffice to sustain solidarities in the absence of territorial presence.

At the same time, material developments challenge the binary quality of citizenship. Social attachments are increasingly scalar, something that citizenship's in/out form has difficulty processing. Citizenship law is no longer well equipped to sort inauthentic claims from authentic ones. The scalar nature of attachment also challenges citizenship's equality condition. To adapt to variable levels of membership, citizenship might have to abandon equality. But it is not clear what remains of citizenship without equality, since equality is located at its ideological core. The spaces we inhabit do not have to be the ones that are represented on the world map. The transformation, and its implications for citizenship, may only become legible in the longer term. But surely we are not in an equilibrium state. Stakeholder citizenship may not be radical enough for the times.

Community formations

What is the stake that holds citizenship together?

"Stakeholder citizenship" is an appealing Goldilocks label. On the one hand, the theory frames citizenship as something more substantial than the thin gruel of constitutional patriotism, under which a common faith in constitutional democracy putatively binds the citizenry. On the other, it is not unrealistic in the way of the methodological statism that has characterized autarkic liberal theories of citizenship, much less the gluey and oppressive ethno-cultural versions of national community. It is inclusive in the context of a system that (mostly) slots individuals into one or two but not all of many different polities. It takes account of movement among states, liberal autonomy values, the continued dominance of territorially based governance and the possibility (up to a point) of non-territorial identity. Stakeholder citizenship promises a taste that's just right for the new world.

The key, of course, is how the stake behind stakeholder citizenship is defined. Bauböck sets down the requirement that citizens "must be able to see themselves and each other as members of a transgenerational political community whose government institutions have to track the collective will of the citizenry" (p. 63). The vision is a self-consciously republican one. "Citizens are stakeholders in a democratic political community insofar as their autonomy and well-being depend not only on being recognized as a member in a particular polity," Bauböck writes, "but also on that polity being governed democratically" (p. 41). Those who have a shared interest in self-government will also have a shared interest in the "flourishing" of that polity.

Does that suffice to build the social solidarity necessary to sustain a state? (Words like "solidarity" and "bonds" go missing in describing stakeholder citizenship, where "collective will" and "common good" are centred.) I admit to being instinctively sceptical of republican theories of citizenship as an American old enough to have lived through the mid and late twentieth century – a period of contentious but genuinely engaged self-governance – who must now suffer today's appalling spectacle of national politics with few entry points for responsible participation. Self-situated contingencies aside, there are systematic reasons to be suspicious of any theory of citizenship that hinges mostly on process. In this respect, stakeholder citizenship is a thicker variant of constitutional patriotism. Constitutional patriotism is grounded in a kind of faith in constitutional democracy. Stakeholder citizenship adds a material element – the individual and collective interest in self-governance. Both are elementally civic, with no social or cultural referents.

Stakeholder citizenship has the advantage, at least, of a bounded element. Territory, unlike belief in constitutional democracy, is distinctive, and physical presence is singular. It is a common interest in self-governance in a particular shared space that defines stakeholder citizenship. Although stakeholder citizenship makes allowances for movement, conceding the continuing attachment of first generation emigrants, it remains territorially driven. Absence from the homeland territory eventually results in the curtailment of transgenerational transmission. Those who establish residence in state territory should be afforded access to citizenship after some reasonable period.

The theory is mostly decoupled from examples or empirics. I understand that parsimony is a disciplinary characteristic. But it seems fair game to test the theory against developments on the ground. Stakeholder citizenship processes diaspora populations better than ethno-cultural conceptions of citizenship. Diasporas are a challenge nonetheless. As a community that defines itself in part (possibly in larger part) in relation to another state, the question is how it relates to the state of residence. There is reason to be sceptical of the proposition that the interest in self-governance in the state of residence will establish a community. Of course, individuals have an interest in public order and non-interference with their autonomy. But as long as they are undisturbed in the governance of their own community (typically through non-state institutional channels), it is not clear that they have a self-governance interest in the community defined in terms of the state, much less its "flourishing".

Bauböck anticipates a variant on this objection with the example of apolitical individuals and the monk in the monastery; that they, too, will be better off as citizens of a democratic polity (p. 41). I wonder to what extent that is true for those who, like monks, exist in communities insulated from the state, so long as they are allowed to go about their business as monks behind the monastery walls (a capacity now protected by substantive, exogenously imposed human rights more than procedural, internally generated self-governance – more on that below). The same could be true among diaspora populations whose identities are more tied to their place of origin and who can (in concentrations) confine interactions to other diasporans. So long as the state maintains some level of order and doesn't interfere with their own self-governance, these kinds of insulated communities may not have an interest in self-governance at the level of the state.

The volitional element of stakeholder citizenship acquired after birth, reflected in the theory's preference for naturalization at will over automatic naturalization (pp. 37; 66), does not nullify the objection. In the conventional narrative, naturalization evidenced a commitment to the state of naturalization. Typically coupled with termination of homeland citizenship, this template correlated with the citizenship discourse of "loyalty" and "allegiance". Naturalization was a solemn exercise, not always but on average, framed as a "new political birth", in the words of one mid-nineteenth-century U.S. official (Spiro 1997). If only because of the perceived impossibility of multiple nationality, naturalization would have been more likely both to reflect and accelerate membership in the adopted national community. The transferred attachment was singular. The naturalized citizen would have had a clear interest in the "flourishing" of that community because he wouldn't have any other.

Today, much less can be read into the agency of the act of naturalization. Naturalizing citizens are now enabled to naturalize for purely instrumental reasons (Spiro 2007a). Now that multiple nationality is widely accepted, the cost of naturalization has been reduced. A correspondingly lower level of benefit will suffice to incentivize naturalization. Citizenship acquisition cannot be taken to represent strong commitment. The pervasiveness of multiple nationality itself reduces the commitment. Retention of original citizenship makes sentimental and material attachment to country of origin more competitive with attachment to country of naturalization. Naturalizing citizens are less likely to be all-in. Indeed naturalization has become an exit strategy. Empirical research is identifying some long-time residents who are naturalizing in their state of immigration only at the time they decide to retire back in their country of origin, by way of ensuring re-entry rights (Gilbertson and Singer 2003; Mateos forthcoming).

Of course, naturalizing citizens (along with long-term residents) will still have an interest in protected autonomy. They might even have an interest in collective self-governance insofar as that autonomy is threatened. Will they have an interest in the "flourishing" of their new national community? Maybe, maybe not. That could depend on the relative strength of alternative attachments to national and non-national communities and the capacity of those communities to provide alternative safe spaces. Participation in self-governance activity may give rise to a shared identity. Or such participation could entrench a sense of persistent alienation. One does not need to look very hard for examples of this phenomenon.

Beyond political community

Here is another way of putting it: citizens may not have that much interest in collective self-governance in states. The security imperative that was once so central to state function (providing a safe space against hostile competitor states) has dissipated. Terrorism creates security needs, but the battle lines do not coincide with state borders and the defence does not require mass, state level mobilization. The redistributive capacity of states may also be waning. As the state retreats, citizens may thus have little or no stake in self-governance. This poses a challenge to the territorial inclusiveness of stakeholder citizenship. It seems no response to say that these citizens don't understand their real interests. Their lack of interest in collective self-governance, much less the flourishing of the state, may be completely rational. The opting out applies most obviously to new territorial entrants, who will never have opted in, but over the long run it will apply to others as well.

Political membership may be decentred in a way that Bauböck's theory cannot process. In an Arendtian move, Bauböck posits the "extreme precariousness" of those who lack membership in a particular political community. "To put it positively: membership in a polity is a necessary condition for human autonomy and well-being" (p. 40). Defined narrowly as participation in democratic self-government at the level of states, this seems both empirically doubtful and possibly condescending to the many individuals who live self-fulfilled, post-political lives. In the United States, for example, many people have checked themselves out of the political process, and for good reason. The level of enmity is high. Rent-seeking abounds. Legacy ideological and institutional constraints severely limit the possibilities for constructive action. Politics is a waste of associative energy.

This may reflect frayed underlying community. In a national frame, solidarities have dissipated. The New Yorker may not feel much in common with the Alabaman. The thinning common identity explains the inability to undertake compromise and sacrifice in the spirit of a shared project – to reach across the aisle, in American political parlance.

The exercise of engaging in political self-governance based on territorial boundaries cannot by itself shore up the crumbling edifice. Politics cannot compensate for an absence of shared non-political identity. Bauböck is surely correct that "humans are social animals" (p. 40). But people do not need to locate their need for community in national political community, which is increasingly artificial and non-organic. In the range of community choice, individuals may see a higher probability of meeting their social needs in non-state communities. There are many people finding fulfilment behind the monastery walls these days. These communities may be gated, literally or metaphorically. But, then again, so are states. As Bauböck observes, the boundary condition is necessary to stakeholder citizenship. It is also satisfied in the context of other forms of membership.

Behind the (non-state) walls, politics continues. This will be obvious to all of us in the many facets of our associative existence. Family, faculty, church, club: there are always differences of opinion on the best ways to enhance community prosperity, from the micro level on up. There is literally no community in which all members "[share] the same interests, a single collective identity as members and the same ideas about the common good" (p. 8). All bounded communities thus also satisfy Bauböck's diversity condition. Whether that diversity will exceed the diversity of community defined by the modern territorial state is contingent. Walzer posits that "A citizen, we might say, is a man whose largest or most inclusive group is the state" (Walzer 1982: 218). This is a cornerstone fallacy of liberal nationalism. The citizen of a small state who is also a Catholic will find a larger, more inclusive group in the non-state community. The Catholic Church excludes those who aren't church members. But consistent with the boundary condition, states exclude non-members as well. They are not essentially more inclusive.

States, it is true, tend to have a greater reach in terms of jurisdiction. They are not issue-specific demoi, as Bauböck puts it (pp. 11–12). But nor are many non-state communities. The regulatory breadth of communities, state and non-state, is also contingent. States are constrained in their reach in various ways. Just as bye-laws set association rules, constitutions and other governing instruments set the limits of state power. In terms of effect on everyday life, state rules may be less intrusive than the rules of the non-state communities of which citizens are members. Religions set comprehensive standards of conduct, some subject to institutional supervision, all (for believers, at least) subject to enforcement by an authority higher than the state. Educational institutions widely regulate behaviour, especially for students, backed by various enforcement tools including expulsion. Professional communities and employers impose ethical rules not demanded by the state. The state may have powers of coercion that are not available to non-state communities, but state enforcement is idealized. There are many contexts in which enforcement of state-based rules is anaemic or non-existent, their regulatory ambition pretentious. The Mormon Church's tithing requirement, for example, enjoys better compliance than compliance with state-based tax obligations (Spiro 2007b).

The state has historically done a better job than other institutions at protecting autonomy, serving as the meta-association that enables other forms of associations. However, today we can query state performance along this metric, too. It is not just in failed states that states are falling short of their obligations to protect. As noted above, autonomy protection by itself doesn't suffice to maintain meaningful community. Autonomy norms are no longer generated by domestic political processes in any case. Human rights obligations require states to provide territorially present individuals with such protection. Whether or not human rights norms are effective as an empirical matter is somewhat beside the point. The requirement to provide the safe space is the result of inter-community engagement, not intra-community interaction on a republican model. States increasingly serve as an administrative servant of the global system.

States are even becoming constrained by international law in their membership practices, something that hardly computes in a Walzerian equation (Spiro 2011). "Access to citizenship" points to citizenship for habitual residents as a baseline from which to perfect other rights. It also looks to apply non-discrimination norms to citizenship practice, a radical departure from the historical discretion afforded sovereigns respecting membership. To the extent states are required to extend citizenship to some they would otherwise reject, this further detaches citizenship from social membership. It is not always clear how stakeholder citizenship accounts for the rights-advancing dimension of citizenship. For example, Bauböck justifies birthright citizenship in part as a mechanism for reducing statelessness (p. 71). Ditto for the presumption of lifelong membership. In neither case is it clear how the membership rule correlates to the stakeholder theory. What about the cases in which advancing rights and recognizing stake are decoupled? There is a whiff of reverse-engineering here. The rights-advancing practice is validated even where the connection to stakeholding is non-obvious. In any case, foisting members on states will do them no good as locations of community.

Other forms of community are less constrained in their membership practices. It is a cornerstone of free association that non-state communities can pick and choose among prospective members. Domestic law may impose constraints, but these constraints are usually qualified. In the United States, for example, a university may discriminate on the basis of race so long as it does not accept government funding. Non-state communities may also expel members at will, a capacity largely denied states under international law. The continuing latitude of non-state communities to determine their membership boundaries contributes to their growing strength relative to states, whose own membership practices are increasingly set by exogenous agents.

What local citizenship teaches us

Local territorial membership also supplies a useful vehicle for interrogating stakeholder citizenship. Local citizenship implicates the necessary spatial aspects of our existence. Leaving aside the very rich, for whom the concept of habitual residence has become antiquated, most of us have a place where we spend most of our time. We remain sedentary in a national frame as well as a global one. In that place we have clear material interests – in police and fire protection, primary and secondary education, utilities, infrastructure and other matters typically within local jurisdiction. It is at the local level that one might more expect a collective interest in self-governance and a higher incidence of political engagement. (Republican theorists since Rousseau have always been more sanguine about the possibility of republican government on the small scale.) The stake in stakeholder citizenship seems more apparent at the level of the locality than that of the state.

In most states, membership at the local level takes the form of ius domicili. This makes sense, to the extent that the stake will largely correlate with territorial presence. Compared with national citizenship, territorial spillovers of local government will be of a lower order. Most localities have no extraterritorial jurisdiction, which reduces a potential disconnect between residents and those whose interests are affected. (A persistent exception is presented by the case of non-resident property owners.) The lack of extraterritorial jurisdiction nearly eliminates the disconnect between residents and those subject to coercion. The absence of territorial spillovers may also justify the non-practice of local citizenship for non-residents.

Bauböck does not expressly disparage local citizenship on these terms. To the extent local citizenship qualifies as stakeholder citizenship, it comes across as a stepchild variant. It is not clear why this should be so. The fact that local citizenship is automatic, with no exercise of will on the individual's part, might be taken to diminish its solemnity. But we have seen above that volition, to the extent it is exercised instrumentally, may reflect no commitment on the individual's part. The opposite is also true. The lack of a volitional element does not necessarily evidence lack of commitment, especially when no mechanism is offered for exercising such volition. (Locating oneself in a local community reflects a kind of volition – voting with one's feet – but it is overdetermined.) Many local residents/citizens are passionately committed to their subnational jurisdiction, with a transparently expressed ambition for its "flourishing". In these respects, the stakeholder label applies.

The stake can be decoupled from a stake in the state in which the locality is situated (Spiro 2009). Bauböck asserts that we "cannot make sense of claims to inclusion in the city of Florence, the region of Tuscany or the European Union without describing first the different nature of these polities and their relations with the Italian state" (p. 51). I am not so sure. One can be a sociological member of a locality or a region without being a sociological member of a national state. This is the logic of non-citizen voting in local elections. Although membership in localities and regions (and of course the European Union) is formally tied to national citizenship, they could be decoupled. There is an incipient movement in the United States on the part of some states to extend distinct state citizenship that is not conditioned on national citizenship (Spiro 2010). The primary object is to express solidarity with unauthorized migrant co-residents. But the movement could turn into something more. Some legal migrants may identify strongly with their adopted locality while not identifying at all with the national community of their new place of residence. The long-time EU-citizen resident of New York may love New York and hate the United States. Territorial identities may move beyond methodologically assimilated nested arrangements. One might even look to deploy Baubӧck's "constellations" in intra-state contexts as well as transnational ones (Baubӧck 2010).

Local citizenship lacks a formal mechanism of transgenerational transmission. But this will not cancel the stakeholder quality of residential citizenship at the local level. People are often sedentary within the state; families remain in localities over generations. Although individuals will not secure local citizenship by birth, birth in a locality will often coincide with subsequent residence.

Transgenerationality, plus or minus

It is not clear why stake should be contingent on transgenerationality in the first place. We are all members of various communities of which our children are not and may not become members. Although our perceived stake (however defined) in those communities may be intensified in the face of a transgenerational element, it is not contingent on it.

It is true that all states provide for transgenerational transmission of citizenship. But that may be a reflection of instrumental value from the state's perspective more than a necessary condition to establishing stakeholder citizenship. The transaction costs of establishing citizenship would otherwise be high. In the past, the mechanisms of birthright citizenship (ius sanguinis and/or ius soli) matched well with social membership on the ground. Most individuals born to citizen parents and/or born on national territory were by that fact set on a trajectory of a life of communal solidarities with other members.

But why transgenerationality is a necessary condition of stakeholder citizenship in the state remains unclear. Transgenerationality by itself is unlikely to generate a sense of shared identity. There is a certain "build it and they will come" flavour to this element of Bauböck's analysis. Alternatively, birthright citizenship is a legacy condition whose historical prevalence makes it appear constitutive to the form. As Bauböck notes, over-inclusion is obvious in some cases, including those in which an expansive ius soli regime extends citizenship at birth to someone who leaves soon thereafter (aka birth tourism) (p. 70). In other cases it will be less obvious, as where individuals are born and remain in a state without perceiving any stake in membership (and perhaps not having one, at least not at the national level) as defined in the stakeholder model.

Bauböck implicitly recognizes the limits of transgenerationality when he calls for extinguishing citizenship for external citizens past the second generation (and cutting off from the franchise the second generation itself). "It is obvious," writes Bauböck, "that third generation emigrants will generally not have a sufficiently strong stake in a grandparent's country of origin to claim citizenship, unless their parents have themselves renewed their links to this country through taking up residence there" (p. 69). So transgenerationality will not suffice to establish a stake in the state-based polity. Territoriality is also a necessary condition.

This result may be under-inclusive. The stake (conventionally defined) for third generation external citizens will be attenuated relative to those who are territorially present. That will be true under alternative theories of citizenship. Their interests will be less affected by homeland governance and they will be less subject to compulsion than those territorially present. It is not as clear why they should be disqualified under the somewhat stylized notion of stake in the theory of stakeholder citizenship. Although the homeland government will have less control over their physical space and physical autonomy, it can constrain autonomy in other ways. There will be many contexts in which external residents feel a stake in membership in the homeland community. There is an increasing fluidity between internal and external communities. Many externally born children are sent home for school, thus sustaining the connection more intensively than in historical migrant trajectories (Smith 2002). Other second generation diaspora members return for good, but their children will be enabled to return to the external residence through ius sanguinis citizenship rules (King and Christou 2010). The flows are not linear and defy conventional narratives.

The diasporas, again, supply the paradigm case in which individuals will feel exactly the sort of stake that Bauböck describes. How else to explain the intense pressure from the diasporas (including many not conventionally categorized as such, under such monikers as transborder or transnational communities) to secure acceptance of multiple citizenship (e.g. Barry 2006; Itzigohn 2012)? There are sometimes material benefits attached to the status with respect to visa-free travel, the capacity to own property, residency rights, and the like. But these benefits will often be marginal, for example for citizens of European states who move to the U.S. or other non-EU OECD states. These individuals will have premium passports when they naturalize in their new state of residence, but many have mobilized nonetheless in places like Denmark and the Netherlands to be enabled to keep their citizenship of origin. An important motivation appears to be passing the status on to children. The Indian diaspora has been extended a status labelled Overseas Citizenship of India. It includes most of the advantages of real citizenship, save the vote. But some in the diaspora are nonetheless demanding full citizenship, and it is not clear that these demands can be resisted in the long term. What better control for the stakeholder theory: a case in which individuals are clearly interested in membership as such, stripped almost entirely of its instrumental advantage. It should not be surprising that other scholars have put "stakeholder" to work in establishing diasporic community (Addis 2012).

The diaspora context, even beyond the second generation, also supplies examples of individuals whose well-being depends on the "flourishing" of their homeland community. The use of the word betrays, I think, an element beyond the procedural citizenship that stakeholder theory suggests. For one's well-being to depend on the "flourishing" of a community, one has to identify with it. Otherwise, functionality will suffice. Identity does not appear central to Bauböck's orientation. But for a community to do the kind of heavy lifting required of the liberal state, some level of identification is required.

In the end, then, the mismatch between territory and political community at the national level is greater than stakeholder theory alone can correct. Within the national territory, increasing numbers will lack the sort of interest in membership and self-government required to sustain a community. Outside, there are growing numbers for whom transgenerational membership is valued even in republican terms.

Citizenship binaries

The problem for stakeholder citizenship may be that the lines are not as sharp as Bauböck would suppose. He highlights blurriness as a deficiency in competing theories of citizenship. I agree that affected interests and amenability to coercion don't work for purposes of delimiting citizenship. But stakeholder theory may suffer the same problem. In this respect, the suggestions above do not need to establish sharp alternative lines, since I am not proposing an alternative theory of citizenship. I just need to show that Bauböck's lines are also blurry.

The problem with all of these theories, and with citizenship as we know it, is that they require the sharp lines. Citizenship has a binary quality – you either have it or you don't. Historically this was not a weakness. The lines on the ground were well marked. The binary aspect of citizenship was well adapted to a world in which states were segmented from each other in both sociological and territorial terms. The binariness was a feature, not a bug. Coupled with exclusivity (the former norm against multiple nationality), the binariness of nationality helped keep national communities distinct where they might otherwise be blurry. Citizenship helped maintain good fences. But it could do that kind of work only on the margins – in border zones and in the context of limited migration. For the most part, nationality wasn't arbitrary. It reflected social attachment.

Today, citizenship no longer serves a border-policing function. Nor could it. The lines have gotten too blurry on the ground. It is no longer clear where one citizenry leaves off and the other picks up. This is reflected in recent acceptance of multiple nationality. That makes the citizenship binary an uncomfortable fit for sociological realities, and not just because there is more overlap among national communities. The problem is that the underlying attachments are more scalar. You can be in for a little or in for a lot, or somewhere in between.

The "genuine links" approach to nationality that sounds in *Nottebohm* is no longer a very useful metric for assessing membership. It doesn't take much to establish a genuine link. International law assumes that birth in state territory suffices, regardless of subsequent history, and Bauböck effectively concedes the point. He would contest ancestry beyond the first emigrant generation. But ancestry would almost certainly qualify for international law purposes, and for good reason. As demonstrated above, many will maintain affective and material interests in the homeland on an intergenerational basis. The problem with the genuine link threshold (as with Bauböck's) is an inability to sort authentic citizenship from inauthentic citizenship. A third generation emigrant might or might not have an authentic tie to the grandparent's homeland. Citizenship law will have difficulty ferreting out instrumentalist claims (Spiro forthcoming). States have incentives to cast the net widely, for reasons of expediency or fairness, so that they do not exclude authentic claims. That leads to acceptance of plural citizenship, which in turns gives individuals little incentive to self-sort. The cost of maintaining additional citizenships will typically be low. Individuals are enabled to maintain citizenship in states to which they have a high, moderate or negligible level of connection.

The result might not be troubling except for the other binary element of citizenship: equality. You are either a citizen or not. If you are a citizen, you have the same status as all other citizens. "The idea of equality of membership," Bauböck notes, "is fundamental for democracy" (p. 47). Citizenship is closely identified with equality. Citizenship without equality loses its essential meaning. In a context in which national communities were sharply segmented, citizenship advanced equality (if only imperfectly) within a group in which all members merited equality. The equality element does not translate well in a world in which not all citizens merit equality even if their citizenship is authentic. Citizenship has trouble adapting to gradations of sociological membership. Equality may no longer be imperative to citizenship. It might not even be appropriate.

Voting rights point to the decoupling of citizenship and equality. As external citizen communities have become more politically active in their homelands, they have demanded and secured external voting rights (Spiro 2003). As suggested above, this evidences stakeholder citizenship in external communities. But the average level of interest and participation will be lower in external communities, reflecting the aggregately lower, more highly variable self-governance interest. (One should pause to remember that self-governance interests will also be variable among territorial residents, and absolute participation may be low, but it is likely to be higher than external participation and interest.) External citizen interests will also tend to be distinctive.

The resulting dilemma lends itself to bespoke arrangements. Many states have created electoral districts for citizens abroad, giving them a direct voice in national legislatures. But these districts have not been apportioned on the same basis as internal ones (Collyer 2013). These schemes abandon the equality premise of one person, one vote; your vote as an external citizen counts less than your vote as a resident citizen. (Interestingly, Bauböck accepts such underweighting, at least where external voters would "swamp" resident ones (Bauböck 2007).) But diluted voting for external citizens makes sense. It is better than the alternatives. To deny external citizens the right to vote altogether would contravene legitimate self-governance interests. To extend full voting power to external citizens would blinker the reduced level of those interests. The result is something other than political equality. Citizenship's equality will be pressured from other directions. Non-citizen residents are now understood to have self-governance interests of their own, and increasingly enjoy local voting rights. Why should they be denied full political equality because they do not want to engage in the loyalty test of naturalization? Meanwhile, plural citizenship will create various citizenship-generated inequalities that are only starting to be legible (Balta and Altan-Olcay 2016; Spiro forthcoming). Especially in developing states, those who also hold premium citizenships will enjoy enhanced life opportunities over their mono-national neighbours (Cook-Martín 2013; Harpaz 2015). To the extent that (inevitably) some have acquired dual citizenship through inauthentic claims, the result will look random. Citizenship was once a badge of equality. It may come to reek of arbitrary privilege.

Conclusion

Citizenship as we have known it cannot process a condition of trans-nationality. This incapacity explains recent work in normative political theory seeking to restore the institution and defend it against oppositional forces. Against the conventional posture, these efforts find progressive theorists calling for limitations on the extension of citizenship. Bauböck's work reflects this trend (e.g. Shachar 2009). His prescription that citizenship not descend past the second external generation, for example, looks to shore up the stake in stakeholder citizenship. So too with increasingly vigorous progressive denunciations of investor citizenship, the rise of which strikes at the core of liberal nationalist ideology (Shachar and Bauböck 2014).

In this response, I have suggested that the republican orientation of stakeholder citizenship does not match the impoverished political landscapes of our time, which have been transformed by community alignments that no longer trace national boundaries. That makes stakeholder citizenship questionable as a normative matter.

Theory aside, states show little interest in scaling back the availability of citizenship on a liberal nationalist basis. Some extensions of citizenship serve instrumental state purposes, ancestral citizenship among them (Barry 2006; Fitzgerald 2008). When citizenship is extended in one direction, the human rights hydraulic demands that it be extended in others (Spiro 2011). Powerful groups develop a vested interest in the availability of citizenship at the same time that extending citizenship typically poses low fiscal costs. Politically, once the citizenship circle is widened, it is difficult to shrink back. The political prospects for reinforcing citizenship's value are low. The incidence of instrumental citizenship will continue to grow, further undermining the empirical premises of stakeholder citizenship.

In other words, the condition is terminal. Bauböck asserts that this is "very bad news indeed" (p. 5). I agree that the decline of citizenship will compound the many instabilities of our time. Perhaps theorists should now turn their sights towards carrying citizenship values forward to novel institutional arrangements.

References

Addis, Adeno. 2012. "Imaging the Homeland from Afar: Community and Peoplehood in the Age of the Diaspora." _Vanderbilt Journal of Transnational Law_ 45: 963–1041.

Balta, Evren and Özlem Altan-Olcay. 2016. "Strategic Citizens of America: Transnational Inequalities and Transformation of Citizenship." _Ethnic and Racial Studies_ 39 (6): 939–957.

Barry, Kim. 2006. "Home and Away: The Construction of Citizenship in an Emigration Context." _New York University Law Review_ 81: 11–58.

Bauböck, Rainer. 2003. "Towards a Political Theory of Migrant Transnationalism." *International Migration Review* 37 (3): 700–723.

Bauböck, Rainer. 2007. "Stakeholder Citizenship and Transnational Political Participation." *Fordham Law Review* 75: 2393–2447.

Bauböck, Rainer. 2010. "Studying Citizenship Constellations." *Journal of Ethnic and Migration Studies* 36 (5): 847–859.

Collyer, Michael. 2013. "A Geography of Extra-territorial Citizenship: Explanations of External Voting." *Migration Studies* 2 (1): 55–72.

Cook-Martín, David. 2013. *The Scramble for Citizens: Dual Nationality and State Competition for Immigrants*. Stanford: Stanford University Press.

Fitzgerald, David. 2008. *A Nation of Emigrants: How Mexico Manages Its Migration*. Berkeley: University of California Press.

Gilbertson, Greta and Audrey Singer. 2003. "The Emergence of Protective Citizenship in the USA: Naturalization among Dominican Immigrants in the Post-1996 Welfare Reform Era." *Ethnic and Racial Studies* 26 (1): 25–51.

Harpaz, Yossi. 2015. "Ancestry into Opportunity: How Global Inequality Drives Demand for Long-Distance European Union Citizenship." *Journal of Ethnic and Migration Studies* 41: 2081–2104.

Itzigohn, José. 2012. "A 'Transnational Nation'? Migration and the Boundaries of Belonging." In *Politics from Afar: Transnational Diasporas and Networks*, edited by Peter Mandaville and Terrence Lyons. New York: Columbia University Press: 181–196.

King, Russell and Anastasia Christou. 2010. "Diaspora, Migration and Transnationalism: Insights from the Study of Second-Generation 'Returnees.'" In *Diaspora and Transnationalism: Concepts, Theories and Methods*, edited by Rainer Bauböck and Thomas Faist. Amsterdam: Amsterdam University Press: 167–183.

Mateos, Pablo. Forthcoming. "The Mestizo Nation Unbound: Dual Citizenship of Euro-Mexicans and US Mexicans." *Journal of Ethnic and Migration Studies*.

Shachar, Ayelet. 2009. *The Birthright Lottery: Citizenship and Global Inequality*. Cambridge: Harvard University Press.

Shachar, Ayelet and Rainer Bauböck, eds. 2014. "Should Citizenship be for Sale?" *EUI Working Papers*. RSCAS 2014/01. Florence: European University Institute.

Smith, Robert C. 2002. "Life Course, Generation, and Social Location as Factors Shaping Second-Generation Transnational Life." In *The Changing Face of Home: The Transnational Lives of the Second Generation*, edited by Peggy Levitt and Mary C. Waters. New York: Russell Sage: 145–167.

Spiro, Peter J. 1997. "Dual Nationality and the Meaning of Citizenship." *Emory Law Journal* 46: 1411–1485.

Spiro, Peter J. 2003. "Political Rights and Dual Nationality." In *Rights and Duties of Dual Nationals*, edited by David A. Martin and Kay Hailbronner. The Hague: Kluwer Law International: 135–152.

Spiro, Peter J. 2007a. "Dual Citizenship: A Postnational View." In *Dual Citizenship in Global Perspective*, edited by Thomas Faist and Peter Kivisto. New York: Palgrave Macmillan: 189–202.

Spiro, Peter J. 2007b. *Beyond Citizenship: American Identity After Globalization*. Oxford: Oxford University Press.

Spiro, Peter J. 2009. "Formalizing Local Citizenship." *Fordham Urban Law Journal* 37 (2): 559–572.

Spiro, Peter J. 2010. "Dual Citizenship as Human Right." *International Journal of Constitutional Law* 8 (1): 111–130.

Spiro, Peter J. 2011. "A New International Law of Citizenship." *American Journal of International Law* 105 (4): 694–746.

Spiro, Peter J. Forthcoming. "The Equality Puzzles of Dual Citizenship." *Journal of Ethnic and Migration Studies*.

Walzer, Michael. 1982. *Obligations: Essays on Disobedience, War, and Citizenship*. Cambridge: Harvard University Press.

Part III

Reply

8

Response to critics

Rainer Bauböck

I feel very lucky that my essay has received such strong and challenging responses, but I also feel the pressure to do justice to my seven critics' thorough comments. Each of them has chosen a different angle of attack. If this were a military encounter, my best strategy might be to let them direct their fire against each other while taking a middle position and ducking my head so that I am not hit by the bullets. Yet this is not a fight but a debate with friends and colleagues whom I admire too much to play such a game.

Instead of replying to each in turn, I will address their comments in the sequence that has provided the structure for my essay. This means that I will not be able to take up all points. However, that approach will allow me best not just to defend my theory, but also to clarify and correct my views where I feel this is necessary. Ideally, I would have liked to rewrite the essay itself, since my critics made me acutely aware of its gaps and weak spots. In a conversation like this one, earlier statements cannot be undone, but they can be modified subsequently when the force of a better argument is acknowledged. I will of course also try to convince my critics in turn. And I sincerely hope that this conversation will continue beyond this book.

The circumstances of democracy

That brings me straight to Joseph Carens's response. Carens's main question is what my question is. Clarifying this is really important for a good conversation. In a nutshell, my question is: Which principles should guide citizens of a democratic polity and their representatives when considering whose interests should count in their political decisions, whom to offer protection, and whom to include in their midst as citizens?

In sections 1 and 2 of chapter 1 I argue that this question can only be meaningfully asked in a bounded polity and that philosophical approaches that try to conjure away political boundaries or aim at delegitimizing them from a critical or ideal theory perspective are misguided. This is not mainly a conceptual point and I acknowledge Carens's critique that I have been less than clear about this. Not too much follows from saying that inclusion conceptually presupposes boundaries. Boundaries can always be stretched to include whatever has been initially left outside: after including all human beings in a global demos, one might consider including animals, all living organisms, or even inanimate things that humans attribute value to and – why not? – immaterial ones such as ideas. My point is rather that questions about inclusion belong to the stuff of which democratic politics is made, just as much as questions about how to deal with a diversity of interests, identities and ideas within a bounded democratic polity.

This seems, then, like an empirical statement and Carens takes me also to task in this regard when he asks whether we cannot imagine a fully insulated society that has never had contact with other human societies and that is still structured democratically. As a philosophical exercise this may be possible but it still seems to me futile given what we know about human history as well as problematic in setting our normative inquiry on the wrong track. Since Carens asks for actual examples of such communities, let's take the case of Iceland, an insulated and until recently ethnically homogenous society that boasts it has the oldest parliament with some continuity until today. Why was that Althing created in 930 AD? In order to bring an end to bloody wars fought between clans through laws that they would adopt jointly to regulate their relations. I suppose that it is only in retrospect and through a statist lens that we anachronistically attribute to the medieval Icelanders the idea of being members of a single self-governing nation or society.

I assume instead that the politics of the Icelandic Commonwealth was shaped by external boundaries between clans and villages just as much as by internal conflicts within these, and that the dualism between internal diversity and external boundaries was present in the minds of those who engaged in law-making and politics as an alternative to war just as much as it was in ancient Athens or Rome. In order to grasp the general features of what I call the sphere of the political, empirical theories should always take this dualism into account. Where one of the two aspects is missing, our conception of political life becomes seriously flawed. One prong of this critique applies to international relations theories that consider states as homogenous entities endowed with a singular will while the other prong attacks theories of democracy that fail to consider how all democracies are constituted through their horizontal or vertical relations to other polities.

Neither is my claim in section 2.1 of chapter 1 that boundaries belong to the "circumstances of democracy" merely an empirical one. Consider whether Rawls's idea that a moderate scarcity of resources is part of the circumstances of distributive justice is an empirical or a normative claim. On the one hand, the suggestion is that moderate scarcity belongs empirically to the human condition because, given the malleability of human needs, their satisfaction always breeds new desires. Is there also a normative content in this idea? It is certainly not that justice commits us to maintaining a condition of moderate scarcity but the other way round: moderate scarcity is the condition under which distributive justice is possible and necessary. Yet this implies also a normative message for theorists (and political ideologists): theories of justice must not ignore this condition by stipulating full satisfaction of all human needs in a communist society as a goal of ideal theory. My proposition regarding external boundaries has a similar normative message for political theories of democracy. These go wrong when they assume – as, for example, does Robert Goodin (2007, 2013) – that a principle of moral equality of all human beings translates into an ideal of a single world polity that includes all humanity and whose internal boundaries represent only second best accommodations to the problem of how to administer such a polity. Instead, we should consider a horizontal and vertical pluralism of autonomous polities as a condition to which democracy responds and under which it becomes necessary in order to legitimize political rule towards free and equal citizens.

My claim is therefore somewhat stronger than a "normative realist" one that answers to the question of how democracies ought to respond to boundary problems in the current international state system. Carens characterizes my approach as interpretive and critical. But I think of it also as normative and aspirational in the sense that I aim to provide feasible inclusion principles for democracy as it should be, not just as it currently is.

I agree with Carens's view that the state system is unjust, as long as this comment is qualified by telling us what exactly is unjust or democratically illegitimate about this system. In my essay I suggest that the current principles of international law allow states to broadly ignore the interests of outsiders who are negatively affected by their decisions. Under my interpretation of the all affected interests (AAI) principle, this provides not only cover for possible *injustices*, which states may or may not commit towards outsiders, but also tarnishes the *legitimacy* of decisions taken by governments that have been democratically authorized by their citizens. Just as a legislature needs to be exposed to the articulation and mobilization of interests inside its territorial jurisdiction before it can legitimately adopt a law that affects such interests, so it must expose itself also to external interests when adopting a policy that affects these. I suggest some institutional remedies for this problem that could help to mitigate it within the current state system, but my critique is more fundamental than this in challenging the dominant interpretation of state sovereignty that underpins the current state system. I should have stated this more clearly than I did.

Carens puts much weight on how the state system contributes to global social injustice. I have little disagreement with him on this point. What I would like to point out is again that we need to distinguish the "background features of current arrangements that are morally problematic" (p. 107) from those that aren't. To my mind, global social injustice is partly generated de iure by the *Grundnorm* of equal sovereignty of states in international law that permits them to resist just claims for global redistribution and to arbitrarily control immigration into their territories, and partly by their de facto unequal power that allows some states to dominate others. It is not, however, a consequence of the fact that states have boundaries demarcating their territorial jurisdiction and special responsibilities for their citizens. The horizontal pluralism of polities is, in my view, a normatively desirable feature of the state system in the sense that it would be wrong to try to overcome it. This may not be obvious from a perspective of global justice, but it seems to me compelling from a perspective of democratic legitimacy of political rule.

I think it is possible to reconcile these two perspectives as long as our standard of distributive justice is a liberal one. Territorial and membership boundaries are certainly responsible for some cross-border social inequality. Wherever polities can decide autonomously about public investments, levels of taxation and spending on welfare programmes, there will be inequality of collective outcomes even if there had been perfect equality of initial resources. This kind of social inequality is democratically legitimate and should not be considered unjust. We should distinguish it from social inequality that is the result of redistribution-blockers for initial resources and of structures of asymmetric domination between states in the current international order.

Since Carens pushes me hard on this point and provides his own vision of a just world with distinct polities, I will take the risk and describe an ideal global boundary structure. In such a structure a plurality of independent states pool their sovereignty partly in larger regional unions and devolve it partly to autonomous regions and municipalities in their territory; submit to institutions of global governance with regard to issues that by their very nature affect all humankind; and keep their borders open for each other's citizens. I do not claim that this ideal world can be derived from the principles of inclusion I defend. It is just one among a larger set of possible ideal worlds that is very different from the state system without either abolishing political boundaries or internalizing them in a single global polity. The set of these possible ideal worlds is defined by the circumstances and conditions of democracy that I analyse in section 2 of my essay. The three inclusion principles that I propose in the third section would fully apply in any of these ideal worlds, which shows that they not only serve as interpretive and critical standards towards the current state system but also as general principles of democracy under ideal conditions. However, none of the three principles can identify a uniquely ideal world within this set. This is not their task. Doing so would require a much more comprehensive theory than I have tried to provide here. The three principles are meant to establish democratic legitimacy through inclusion in a world structured by political boundaries. This is not the same task as achieving global social justice although I would hope that these goals are fully compatible with each other.

Carens asks whether the limits that I impose on my inquiry are those dictated by a concern for feasibility and political relevance. Not quite. My thinking about specific boundary questions, such as national voting rights for emigrant citizens or local voting rights for non-citizen immigrants, has certainly evolved in response to empirical observations about how democratic states themselves have expanded their conceptions of the demos. And I sympathize with the call of utopophobes that political theory, in contrast with moral theory, should always be action-guiding and aim for improving existing political institutions (Frazer 2016). However, in contrast with normative realist inquiries, I recognize the usefulness of ideal theory in setting goals as long as it strengthens our efforts to build routes and bridges that allow us to approximate these goals. Feasibility and practical relevance are concerns that help in designing the bridges, but they are not the borders of our normative maps. The outer limits are those that I have tried to identify as circumstances of democracy: a double plurality that emerges from internal diversity within and external multiplicity of bounded self-governing polities.

The second set of conditions that I have set aside from my main inquiry are what I call the "contexts of democracy": territorial juris-diction and relative sedentariness. These I do not regard as limits for normative theory. If I could, I would like to develop a normative theory of democracy for a world in which jurisdictions are predominantly non-territorial and only a minority of people are sedentary within any set of political borders. I didn't do so in chapter 1 because I suspect that I would end up describing a dystopia rather than an ideal and the exercise might then discourage the building of bridges starting from current conditions.

Including (all?) affected interests

Does my theory rule out global democracy as an empirical possibility or a desirable goal? This depends partly on what we have in mind when speaking of democracy. Let us consider three ideas: democracy as popular self-government, as government directly accountable to citizens, and as a method for making collectively binding decisions. In chapter 1 section 3.4 I try to combine these three ideas with the corresponding inclusion principles into a comprehensive conception of democratic inclusion for democratic polities. Projecting such a comprehensive conception to the global level is in my view deeply problematic. However, this does not rule out a thinner conception of global democracy that relies only on the principle of including affected interests without aiming to build a global government and to forge humanity into a single political community.

Global democracy in this sense should be promoted by including externally affected interests in decisions made by particular governments and by democratizing global governance regimes through the inclusion of non-state actors and policy stakeholders (Macdonald 2008). Globalizing national decision-making and democratizing global decision-making in this way on issues such as climate change, refugee protection, global poverty relief, international criminal justice, trade and finance is not at all the same thing as building global democratic institutions with the power to set their own agenda and take binding decisions on an unspecified range of issues. The latter would only be democratic if there were a global political community that could authorize such a government and hold it accountable.

Carens seems to suggest that, given the seriousness and interrelatedness of the global collective action problems listed above, we should not rule out such a thicker ideal of global democracy. Yet if there were really a need for global government with such wide competences, then democracy itself might no longer be necessary to provide legitimacy for it. Those who value democracy only instrumentally might easily despair at its capacity to stop climate change or to promote egalitarian global justice. If such goals are seen to be of overriding importance then even democracy at world level might be regarded as an obstacle that needs to be removed. Consider a science fiction scenario under which this conclusion would be hard to reject. Suppose Planet Earth faced a hostile invasion by an alien species that threatened humankind with possible extinction but there were sufficient time to prepare for defence. Under these conditions of a global state of emergency, all states and their citizens should be ready to empower temporarily a global government that is free to impose its decisions on states and on private organizations, as well as directly on all individual human beings. The point of this scenario is that global government would be necessary under conditions that would also justify a suspension of democracy. Conversely, in the absence of such conditions the case for thick global democracy remains unconvincing. In other words, I cannot imagine a situation in which a global government with general legislative powers would become necessary *and* would have to meet also democratic standards of authorization and accountability. This dilemma between the conditions for democracy and the conditions under which a need for global government arises does not depend on whether one accepts the familiar Kantian probabilistic argument that a world state is likely to degenerate into anarchy or despotism (Kant 1795/1991).

As Carens rightly observes, I have not defeated the notion of a global polity as conceptually incoherent. But I have suggested an empirical argument that over the course of human history external boundaries have been a constitutive feature of democracy and a normative one against a thick conception of democracy at the global level. As long as coordination between interdependent polities that are not subjected to a global government can effectively address global collective action problems and provide democratic legitimacy for global policies, we should better stick to a pluralistic and thin conception of global democracy and resist the urge to merge humanity into a single demos.

Let me move on to David Miller, who is much more sceptical than Carens about the principle of including all affected interests and wants to "drop [it] altogether as a solution to the boundary problem" (p. 130). While Carens seems to think that the principle may provide some support for a global demos, Miller aims to limit its scope in two ways. First, he regards AAI as grounding at best a substantive right to ex post justification of decisions rather than an ex ante procedural right to representation in the deliberation about the decision. Second, he limits the material scope of externally affected interests that deserve a justification to those covered by a Global Harm Principle (GHP) that "considers as relevant cases where interests are affected *negatively*, cases where the setback to interests is *serious* and cases where the setback *cannot reasonably be avoided* by prudent action on the affected agent's part" (p. 131).

As I acknowledged in chapter 1, my discussion of the all affected interests and all subject to coercion (ASC) principles is certainly incomplete. My intention was to give these principles their due while demonstrating that they fail to answer to the democratic membership question. My main concern was to pave the ground for my multilevel theory of stakeholder citizenship in section 4. Ideally, in a book-length discussion, I should have devoted as much space to further working out the normative implications and real-world applications of the principles of including AAI and ASC. Miller's sharp comments provide a welcome occasion for adding some more substance and also some revisions to my discussion of AAI.

Let me first concede that ex post justification of decisions towards externally affected interests is always necessary and often sufficient. Although Miller is likely to disagree, I think this can be said even of his Mediterranean beach-bar owner affected by the British Chancellor's decision to raise consumption tax to finance British health care with the unintended effect of reducing the number of British tourists and the money they spend abroad (p. 130). There is indeed no justice-based claim of people working in the tourist industry to a constant demand for its services. In cases like these, the justification is entirely generic and does not even have to be delivered to the affected person; it is implied in the UK's right to take decisions that have external effects on markets. If the owner of the beach-bar calls the British Consulate to find out why his business is suffering, he ought to be given an explanation, but there is no duty of the British government to notify him.

Justification needs to be more specific and addressed to those affected where external agents are not merely impacted but coerced. For example, if a government decides on a trade boycott of another country, it is not sufficient to say that, as a participant in global trade, the other country should accept this as a market risk. Yet, it would still be absurd to claim that the trade sanctions against Iran gave that country's government not merely a claim to specific justification (which was actually provided) but to participation in the decision about the sanctions.

In other instances, ex post justification is not enough and ex ante procedural representation is called for. Miller's GHP is a good candidate for identifying such cases, except that it does not take culpability into account. Such a narrower GHP would help us to identify those cases where externally affected interests are affected negatively and seriously and where the affected agent cannot avoid the effects and suffers them unjustly. It seems to me plausible that in such cases the agent's interests ought to be represented in the deliberation before the decision is taken.

David Owen goes a step further. He suggests in his comments in chapter 6, that such inclusion of externally affected interests has a compositional effect on the demos if we distinguish discursive and editorial demoi or modes of membership from authorial ones. As I will discuss further below, I hesitate to use the term "demos" in this broad way because this risks disconnecting discursive and editorial demoi from the citizenry in a way that clouds their sources of legitimacy. However, in terms of substance Owen's distinction seems sound to me.

Let us first consider how democracy operates internally when a decision is on the agenda that is likely to affect the interests of those within the jurisdiction very unequally. In these cases, liberal and pluralistic democracies do not claim that whatever the parliamentary majority decides is legitimate. Instead, the issue ought to be made public prior to the decision so that citizens can form an opinion on it and we expect the government and MPs to listen to experts and consult with organizations that represent the different affected interests. Not every citizen is, or needs to be, involved in this discursive representation of interests. I have doubts whether the conglomerate of those who are should be called a "demos" that in this case would be narrower than the authorial demos that elects the government.

The difference jurisdiction makes is important. What happens more or less spontaneously within a well-functioning democracy, where civil society associations, interest organizations and mass media constantly monitor public policy-making, needs to be brought about in the transnational realm through institutional innovations that make the voices of externally affected interests heard. But this practical difficulty, which results from the way the international state system works, does not support a normative judgement that ex post justification is enough even where externally affected interests meet the criteria of the modified GHP. These interests must be represented before a democratically legitimate decision can be taken. This can be argued on epistemic grounds: those whose interests are affected know better how they are harmed and may also know better how the negative impact could be avoided if the decision were modified. But it can also be argued on grounds of democratic justice: some outsiders have a moral right to participate in democratic deliberations about decisions the consequences of which should not be imposed on them.

Miller seems to agree when he writes that "there are occasions when people outside of the demos do have a right to be heard by those inside" (p. 131). But this has institutional implications for national democracies, which then need to engage in intergovernmental deliberations, invite external delegates to legislative assemblies, build transnational and global governance institutions and defer to their decisions, or submit decisions that affect several polities to comparable degrees to transborder referendums.

These are the kinds of institutional reforms of the international state system that taking a principle of including affected interests seriously would require. Miller rightly rejects the "fantasy that democracy could work on an ad hoc basis, with different constituencies being assembled to decide each issue as it arose" (p. 129). This is indeed the fantasy of authors who regard AAI as a principle for constituting the demos and determining its territorial jurisdiction. Yet once a demos is legitimately constituted, some externally affected interests must and can be included through issue-specific and ad hoc institutional arrangements that extend inputs into democratic decision-making beyond territorial jurisdictions.

Like Miller, Iseult Honohan wants to minimize the role of affected interests, but in her case this is because she defends the republican principle of non-domination that is supposed to do all the work with regard to democratic inclusion. I have strong sympathy for this approach, but there is something important that gets lost. If domination is interpreted as long-term subjection to the arbitrary will of another agent, then it is no longer clear why taking into account the interests of occasionally affected external interests should be necessary at all. One reply to this might be to accept AAI as a *moral* principle while denying that it has anything to do with democratic legitimacy.[1] This is not, however, a good response. As pointed out by pluralist theories of democracy (e.g. Dahl 1989), democracy is not about the aggregation of equally weighted individual interests of citizens, but relies on input by specifically affected interests through the channels of organized representation of interests, such as trade unions and employer federations, non-governmental organizations, campaigns in online and offline public spheres, and so on. These are not deficiencies of democracy that prevent legislators from considering the common good, but essential devices for making legislation responsive towards internal interests affected by policies. As

[1]   I thank Anna Goppel for this suggestion.

I have already pointed out, the problem is that for externally affected interests such channels are less institutionalized, are monopolized by powerful corporate business and global media, are much more effective when used by powerful states, or are blocked altogether because of states' external sovereignty. Opening them up to global policy stakeholders (Macdonald 2008) and pluralizing them is not only a moral requirement, but also one of democratic legitimacy. For each specific policy decision, including affected interests is a moral requirement of justice addressed to the individual legislator or the collective assembly that takes the decision. But including affected interests is also a requirement of democratic legitimacy that calls for institutional responses. If we accept that including affected interests in the deliberation about policies is a condition for democratic legitimacy, then there is no reason why this should apply only to internally affected interests and not to externally affected ones as well.

In chapter 1I attempted to deflate Goodin's global version of AAI by suggesting that agenda-setting powers remain the privilege of representatives of an authorial demos and that only actually affected interests count. In response to Miller I have now added some further specifications. But Miller's GHP still relies on the intuitive moral appeal of AAI and he fails to explain why the way interests affected within a jurisdiction must be taken into account should be fundamentally different from responding to externally affected ones.

Let me add one further concession. I have adopted the standard formula of the principle that refers to including *all* affected interests and often this is meant to imply that all affected interests ought to be taken into account *equally*. As my discussion here has made clear, this is not sustainable for externally affected interests. I can save the "inclusion of all" requirement by extending the principle to the case of generic ex post justifications discussed above. But there is no way a requirement of equal inclusion can be defended. As Miller rightly points out, the degree of affectedness matters. Even a threshold interpretation does not imply that those interests that qualify have a claim to be represented equally. This is not only because stronger degrees of affectedness and harm give rise to stronger representation claims, but also because the appropriate response to such harms depends on the issue and the institutional context. Representing the universal interests of humanity in slowing down climate change will require a different institutional response compared with representing the interests of the people of Tuvalu in finding a new home if rising sea levels submerge their island state.

Even inside a jurisdiction, affected interests are included unequally, partly based on the degree of affectedness, partly on the numbers of those affected. What is problematic is when strongly affected interests are excluded because they lack legal status and voting power or resources for mobilization and when weakly affected interests of small numbers dominate policy deliberations because they have more resources to make themselves heard or to influence decision-makers. The same considerations apply to negatively affected external interests. But in their case the norm of state sovereignty adds another exclusion mechanism that systematically prevents them from being adequately included. And this is precisely where AAI provides a compelling moral critique and points towards feasible political reform.

Subjection or interdependence?

David Miller's comments prompted me to clarify that affected interests cannot be included *equally* and that including *all* affected interests comes at the price of thinning out the corresponding duties and responsibilities of democratic legislators. I claimed in chapter 1 that the principle of including all subject to coercion is more egalitarian than AAI. Yet Carens points out that those subjected to the laws, too, do not necessarily enjoy, or have a claim to, equal legal status and rights. In his approach, it is social membership that counts and this comes in degrees. Tourists, temporary migrants, foreign students and long-term resident foreigners are all subjected to the laws but do not have the same residence status or access to different types of social welfare rights. Doesn't this undermine the egalitarian thrust of ASC?

In response I should make it clear that I do not understand equal protection of the law as entailing equal enjoyment of all legal rights, but rather equal protection of those rights which persons subjected to government authorities can claim based on the kind of subjection to which they are exposed. In other words, equality here refers to protection of rights rather than to substantive rights per se. What is democratically illegitimate – and incompatible with the rule of law – is to subject persons to the same laws in such a way that some are offered full protection and others only some or no protection at all.

This is not meant to be a formalistic response. It would be a mistake to narrow the scope of ASC so that it covers only long-term residents. Tourists are also entitled to protection of their fundamental rights and should be able to contest administrative and judicial decisions that apply to them and restrict their freedom. And, as Carens has argued persuasively, irregular immigrants who are long-term residents have claims to regularization of their status that provides them then with equal legal rights. I suggest in chapter 1 that ASC should even be applied to would-be immigrants turned away at the border who obviously cannot claim most legal rights and certainly not membership in the polity, but who have a claim to protection of their human rights and to justification of their rejection that is a special responsibility of the state agents who exercise coercion over them.

A critical question is which of those statuses that come with restricted legal rights rather than with the full scope of equal protection exist only in a non-ideal world and which would exist in any pluralistic world that is structured by external relations between self-governing polities. Tourists will exist in any such world and their claims to legal rights will differ from those of long-term residents. Irregular migrants will exist only in a non-ideal world in which states are justified in controlling immigration for work and settlement.

My main disagreement in this regard seems to be with David Miller, who draws a distinction between coercion used against would-be immigrants and their vulnerability. On Miller's account, "[w]hat lends plausibility to ASC is the thought that a coercively enforced legal system shapes people's lives in a fundamental way, and potentially exposes them to domination" (p. 131). "When people are prevented from entering a country by immigration controls, a significant opportunity is often being denied them, but it does not follow that their lives are being shaped and potentially dominated by the legal system of the country they are trying to enter in the same way as those who are already living under that system" (p. 134). This limits the scope of ASC in a way that would leave lots of people against whom states use coercion without any claim to protection of their rights. In my view, liberal states have a general duty to justify immigration control. Contrary to most other theorists (Carens 2013; Oberman 2016), I do not ground this duty in a corresponding human right, but in liberal states' duties to promote their own citizens' opportunities for free movement, which creates a reciprocity-based duty to admit other states' citizens to their territory. This does not entail that tourists who are denied entry visas are thereby dominated. The general duty to justify restrictions of free movement is enhanced if those who want to enter can raise specific claims why this state rather than any other should admit them. The weakest claims of this kind might be those referring to economic benefit. If admitting economic migrants would benefit the country of origin, the migrants themselves and the country of destination – in the language of development economists: if there is a "triple win" – then liberal states ought to create immigration programmes for such economic migrants. The claims of would-be immigrants are much stronger if their family members have previously been admitted to the country, and they become imperative if they are refugees who might perish if they were turned away. Coercion and vulnerability are thus not entirely different things, as they seem to be on Miller's account. Instead, the general duty to justify coercive migration control is enhanced by special responsibilities of states for particular migrants and by those migrants' vulnerability. Where the responsibility and vulnerability is strong, migrants' lives are indeed being shaped by a decision to turn them away and they are actually rather than just potentially dominated by the legal system of the country they are trying to enter.

While my disagreement with Miller concerns what one could call the "lower range" of ASC, I have another one with Carens, Honohan and Owen regarding the "upper range". Can ASC – or Carens's principle of social membership – determine a threshold above which *all* those subjected to coercion have an *equal* claim to *all* rights of citizenship, including access to the legal status and to voting in all elections? Iseult Honohan suggests in her comments, and Carens has argued so in his own work (Carens 2013), that all those permanently subjected (as long-term residents) have this claim. This would imply that, at least inside a territorial jurisdiction, ASC does all the necessary work and my stakeholder principle becomes redundant. I will discuss the implications of this view for voting rights in contexts of migration and multilevel democracy below. Here I want to focus on Iseult Honohan's interpretation of ASC that aims to blunt the differentiation from the all citizenship stakeholders (ACS) principle that I have tried to sharpen.

According to Honohan, "the all subjected account … may define membership of the demos more clearly on the basis of a single principle, but the account of citizenship needs to be pluralist, mainly by building in a temporal cushion with respect to subjection" (p. 157). But she also writes that "temporary rather than continuing subjection does not constitute the same threat of domination as longer-term residence, and requires protection rather than membership of the demos" (p. 153). This is exactly my point and the reason why I want to retain a broader version of ASC that focuses on protection separate from a distinct principle that applies to membership claims.

The risk I see is that an exclusive focus on long-term subjection diverts attention from those forms of domination that would-be immigrants, transients and temporary migrants are subjected to precisely because they are (rightly) not seen as having a claim to membership. The most obvious case is refugees who seek admission and whose vulnerability to domination results from the lack of protection offered by their citizenship of origin.

Honohan acknowledges that the value of non-domination that is foregrounded in contemporary neo-republican theories can be interpreted in different ways. Some, like Philip Pettit, put more emphasis on people's interests in protection of their rights by the government to which they are subjected, while others, such as Habermas, Lovett and Honohan herself, emphasize relations of interdependence and the connection between individual and collective autonomy. "There seem, then, to be two alternatives in considering non-domination as the basis of ASC: we can interpret it in terms of interests, in which case it collapses back into AAI, or in terms of facilitating autonomy, when it leans towards a stronger norm of participation in collective self-government" (p. 244).

This seems to me a problematic contrast. First, all three principles (AAI, ASC, ACS) can be restated in terms of political interests, but they refer to interests in different elements of political life: policies, government protection, and membership and self-government. Regarding the three as complementary rather than alternative or reducible to a single principle should help to save republicanism from the charge that it has illiberal implications. In other words, a republicanism focused on self-government must be tamed and enhanced by a liberalism defending the inclusion of affected interests and equal protection of the law also for those who are not members. This should not be difficult for neo-republicans since they can recognize all three principles of inclusion as responding to risks of arbitrary domination. Outsiders who are seriously and innocently harmed by a policy in whose making their interests have not been taken into account are exposed to the arbitrary will of another agent, even if this is not a permanent condition. Persons inside a jurisdiction whose fundamental rights are not protected by the government are dominated even if they do not have a claim to membership. While all three inclusion principles can be endorsed as serving the same goal of avoiding domination and promoting self-government, it does not follow that asserting this goal as a coherent normative ideal of democracy reduces the three principles to a single one. Republicans who think of ASC as a principle that is sufficiently broad to cover all domains of democratic inclusion are as wrong as liberal theorists who regard AAI as the overarching inclusion principle from which all others are mere derivatives (Beckman 2009).

Honohan provides, however, very helpful interpretations of a republican version of ASC. She responds to the question about membership claims by referring to a condition of "future-oriented interdependence in continuous subjection" (p. 155). Such interdependence creates "circumstances where collective action is required for the possibility of self-government" (p. 152).[2] Notice how, in this account of subjection, it no longer serves as the justifying reason why governments that restrict the autonomy of individuals have also to offer these individuals protection of their autonomy. Instead, continuous subjection to coercive government power becomes a condition under which interdependence among people is likely to grow to the point where they consider themselves as members of a political community with a claim to collective self-government. For membership claims, it is therefore interdependence rather than subjection that does the justificatory work. And this is how it should be, since interdependence is another, and possibly better, name for the genuine links that I seek to trace through the citizenship stakeholder principle.

There are, however, still some differences of view that emerge from Honohan's emphasis on residence as the proxy for forward-looking interdependence. In my view, the subjection of residents within a territorial jurisdiction to the same government *may* create the horizontal interdependence that gives rise to a sense of shared membership in a political community, but is not always necessary (as in the case of diasporas participating from distance in projects of national self-determination) or sufficient (as in the case of colonies and occupied and annexed territories).

It is also good to see that sometimes disagreements about the interpretation of principles matter for specific policy recommendations. This proves that political theory is after all sometimes capable of helping citizens and policy-makers think through the normative choices that they face. So here are my disagreements with Honohan's concluding suggestions for specific citizenship policies.

---

[2] See also Honohan (2002).

Honohan endorses de Schutter's and Ypi's (2015) proposal for automatic citizenship attribution to long-term resident immigrants, which is based on the perception of an "unfair asymmetry in the distribution of political obligations between citizens and immigrants" (p. 153). There are indeed many native citizens who are concerned that immigrants free ride on the benefits provided to all residents in their host country. Instead of campaigning for imposing citizenship on immigrants, however, these citizens mostly want to make it harder for immigrants to get permanent residence and to become citizens.[3] This observation does not of course address the normative question of whether immigrants *should* be compelled to become citizens. My response to this proposal is that it is plausible only from an immigration-centric perspective that fails to consider a just distribution of political obligations and rights for individuals with strong political ties across state borders. The non-citizen residents of one state are at the same time the non-resident citizens of another state. We need to consider their claims to membership (including their claims not to be pressed into another membership against their will) in a transnational context rather than a purely national one.

Transnational migrants do not stand in the same relation to their host state as those residents (including second generations of migrant origin) who have obtained their citizenship at birth. Those who argue that automatic citizenship at birth for natives and optional naturalization for migrants is unfair towards the former are inspired by a version of ASC that focuses on long-term residence rather than a stakeholder perspective, which considers how migrants and sedentary citizens are involved in different membership relations. This may be unfair towards Honohan since she considers the transnational context when arguing that the increasing acceptance of multiple citizenship by states "reduces

---

[3] In nineteenth-century France, however, when military service was the main obligation of male citizenship, automatic naturalization at the age of majority of foreigners born in the territory was seen as the right solution (Weil 2002). Today, the thinning out of legal obligations that depend on citizenship status make such concerns less plausible and even the French law of 1889 did not dare to impose citizenship for this reason also on first generation immigrants.

the difficulties with respect to mutual obligations between independent states" (p. 154). Toleration of multiple citizenship would indeed make the consequences of involuntary naturalization less dramatic for immigrants. But it seems to me implausible to assume that countries of origin will then readily accept compulsory recruitment of their emigrants as host country citizens or ought to do so as a matter of justice. It is also not clear that multiple citizenship reduces the difficulties with sorting out citizenship obligations (just think about military service and diplomatic protection). Finally, it seems incoherent to argue that immigrants have to be naturalized against their will in order to equalize the obligations between long-term residents who are equally subjected to government power, while accepting that as multiple citizens immigrants retain additional rights and obligations that native mono-citizens do not share with them. In my view, these normative puzzles can only be resolved by considering from the very start the membership claims of migrants from a transnational rather than from an immigration-and-residence perspective.

Honohan's second policy proposal concerns ius soli and ius sanguinis, both of which she proposes to make conditional upon residence after birth. These suggestions follow indeed coherently from a strong emphasis on residence as the best proxy for continued subjection and therefore, in her view, also for membership claims. For me, the unattractive implications of such reforms cast instead some doubts on the principle from which they are derived.

Both proposals abolish a main feature of birthright citizenship, which is that it is not conditional or provisional once it has been awarded. Instead, in most current instances, it is the parents and not the child who have to meet conditions. In the case of ius sanguinis, this is often a condition that parents must have been born in the country of citizenship in order to transmit it to a second generation born abroad. In the case of ius soli, it is mostly a condition that one of the foreign parents must have resided for some time in the country for the child to get citizenship at birth. These rules serve as proxies for the parents' genuine links to the country, not for the child's future residence. "Provisional ius soli membership for those born in the state, depending on continuing residence", as suggested by Honohan (p. 155), would instead undermine the idea that citizenship is a lifelong status and give to the state a power that liberal governments should only have in extreme and rare cases: the power to deprive citizens of their membership (Bauböck and Paskalev 2015). The same objection applies to "conditional ius sanguinis membership for those born to citizens abroad, retained only if residence in the state is subsequently established" (pp. 155–156). I assume Honohan would like to qualify this proposal with a condition that withdrawal is only possible if the person has acquired another citizenship. In the international state system, avoiding statelessness and securing a stable assignment of state responsibilities for individuals is an overriding imperative. States should therefore not be able to shed their responsibility for citizens based on a weakening of links for which residence serves as the proxy. Yet in combination with her advocacy of provisional ius soli, Honohan's proposal amounts to turning minor children born to either non-resident or non-citizen parents into citizens on probation who need to establish their links to one state or the other through continuous residence. Those who move too often or between too many countries will fall into the traps of residence-based citizenship. Imagine a child born in country A to parents who are native-born citizens of country B. If the family settles in country C before Honohan's continuous residence requirement has been met, the child could end up being stateless until she qualifies for naturalization in C.

From a stakeholder perspective, the links that citizenship status is meant to protect are primarily those that protect individuals' "right to have rights" in a world of independent states. This does not entail that rights of citizenship cannot be conditional upon residence. In fact, most rights are anyhow since states can only guarantee them within their territorial jurisdiction. As I will explain below, the core citizenship right of political participation in democratic elections should be attached to present or past residence. In other words, in contrast with membership in the citizenry, membership in the demos need not be awarded as an unconditional birthright. Instead of giving states the dangerous power to strip children born abroad of their citizenship status, I propose that such birthright citizens should not acquire membership in the demos at the age of majority unless they have connected to the state where they want to vote through a sufficient period of past or current residence. The same logic applies to the phasing out of birthright citizenship itself. If we are concerned about equality between citizens independently of how they have obtained their status and about the power of states to strip citizens of their membership, then it is much better if the third generation of emigrant origin no longer acquires citizenship by descent than if the second generation is put on provisional citizenship.

Stakeholder citizenship and liberal nationhood

David Miller engages most extensively with my search for a distinct normative principle that provides legitimacy to individual membership claims and to institutional membership rules in liberal democracy. Miller sees my account as a pluralistic one and urges me to consider combining several principles, which would open my approach also for a liberal version of the nationality principle that Miller defends. However, I am monistic in this respect. I propose that AAI, ASC and ACS each address a specific aspect of democratic inclusion, but that only ACS applies to membership issues. The price that I need to pay for this claim is that my statement of ACS remains necessarily quite general so that it can apply to the broad range of problems in which membership in a particular polity is at stake.

As Miller rightly points out, membership problems may either concern individual inclusion or territorial jurisdiction and collective self-government claims. Chapter 1 deals mostly with the former and only very briefly with the latter. Individual claims to citizenship generally presuppose uncontested territorial borders and collective identities as a stable background. When immigrants apply for acquisition of citizenship what needs to be considered is the democratic legitimacy of naturalization requirements and not that of jurisdictional boundaries. By contrast,

when a national minority demands stronger political autonomy or a
referendum on secession, what needs to be considered is the legitimacy
of existing federal or other arrangements for devolution and power-
sharing as well as how changes would affect individual memberships.
My claim is that ACS provides a general guideline for liberal responses
to both types of problems because it focuses on the relational nature
of membership. This relation is not just one between particular individuals
and polities, but is a triangular one between individuals, a particular
polity and other polities. When specifying rules for individual membership in a particular polity we need to keep the conditions in mind under
which that polity can be self-governing in its relations to other polities.
And when considering how jurisdictional conflicts between polities
should be sorted out we need to consider whether present or proposed
future arrangements provide adequate conditions for self-government
of all polities involved, as well as whether these arrangements satisfy
individual claims to membership.

Let me first address Miller's critique of ACS as a principle for
determining individual citizenship claims under conditions of stable
jurisdictional boundaries. Miller considers two interpretations of ACS:
a utilitarian one according to which individuals should be recognized
as members of those polities where their interests in autonomy and
well-being are best protected; and a psychological one according to
which individuals should be recognized as members of those polities
that figure most prominently in their personal identities (p. 136).[4]
I agree with Miller that both interpretations are problematic.

On a utilitarian interpretation, the strength of individuals' claims to
a particular membership depends on how well that polity would protect
their autonomy and promote their well-being. I suspect that if this view
prevailed, Swedish citizenship might become hugely oversubscribed,
which would lead to a collapse of Sweden's capacity for self-government.
What I have suggested instead is that citizenship ought to trace

---

[4]   I have deliberately rephrased Miller's statement of the two interpretations so that the
      question of contested jurisdiction is set aside.

individuals' genuine links to a particular polity. If my strongest links are to a polity that is currently not flourishing, then this will affect my well-being. Yet since my claim to membership in that polity is a relational one, it does not follow that I have now a stronger claim towards another polity that is currently doing better. What follows instead is that my polity needs to do better in order to make my own life go better. But it does not follow either that I am forever stuck with this particular membership. If the polity is a city inside a liberal democratic state, I can always move to another city where being a resident is sufficient to establish my claim to membership. And if the polity is an independent state, then it still has to guarantee free exit and ought to promote reciprocal free movement with other states. After some time of living in another country, my autonomy and well-being will no longer depend only on how my country of origin is doing, but will also be shaped by my country of residence. Rather than having a right to choose another citizenship that makes me better off, it is the changing circumstances of my life that give me a claim to a new citizenship. Whether I moved in order to improve my economic opportunities or did so for other reasons does not matter. What matters is whether the links that I establish with the polity match the conditions under which that polity can be self-governing. And these conditions differ for municipalities and independent states.

The psychological interpretation of stakeholdership is wrong for the same reason. Miller's Francophile (p. 137) does not have a claim to French citizenship because his subjective preferences are irrelevant for determining the membership boundaries of a self-governing territorial polity. This does not mean that it is not important that citizens share a sense of belonging. It is indeed important for the flourishing of a polity that citizens feel attached and attribute non-instrumental value to their membership. However, these psychological aspects are a consequence of experiences of collective self-government rather than a criterion for selecting members.

The secluded monk and the wealthy cosmopolitan who collects passports may not feel any particular psychological attachment of this kind. They are free riders on the benefits of collective self-government to which they do not contribute. This does not disqualify them from being members in those polities where they fulfil the criteria of residence, birthright or derivative citizenship, since these criteria refer to links that can be established independently of their subjective attitudes. The citizenship that they receive is objectively important for their autonomy and well-being – although they do not value it or value it only instrumentally – if it confers membership in a stable democratic polity. And in order to make the polity stable and democratic, the criteria for awarding citizenship must trace individuals' relevant objective links.

The general idea of triangular relational correspondence can be best illustrated by considering the different membership criteria for states, municipalities and sub- or supranational regional polities that I discuss in section 4 of chapter 1. It is perhaps easiest to understand for derivative citizenship. I am a citizen of the European Union because I am an Austrian citizen by birth and Austria is a member state of the EU. Member states are the constitutive polities of the EU as a union of democratic states. Such a union tries to combine the self-government of member states as independent countries in the international arena with supranational democracy at the union level. In order to do so, it links the citizenship between the two levels so that every citizen of a member state is also a citizen of the union. The fact that I have been living in Italy for several years activates some of my special rights as an EU citizen, but it does not affect my membership status. Instead, I have a stake in EU citizenship because I am a citizen of a state that has accepted the conditions under which the EU produces binding supranational legislation with supremacy over national law and direct effect on all EU citizens.

A similar story can be told about regional citizenship in federal states whose federal union and territorial integrity are conditional upon regional self-government. In order to govern themselves as autonomous provinces within a stable and self-governing federation, citizenship of the former must be linked with that of the latter. If the relevant relation between polities is, however, one between municipalities and the states within which they are embedded, then such a derivative link seems to me neither necessary nor justifiable and residence becomes instead the basis for claims to citizenship at the local level. Finally, if the relation is one between independent states in the international system, then it is imperative that citizenship be based on birthright and constructed as a lifelong status.

In a bilateral conception of the relation between individual and polities it might seem absurd to claim that individuals' stakes in citizenship can be fully and equally met by rules that attribute to them membership because they are already members in another polity, because they have been born to citizens or in a political territory, or because they are current residents in such a territory. These very different relations between individuals and polities seem to exemplify alternative conceptions of political community that cannot be reconciled with each other. It is the triangular relation between individuals and conditions for internal and external self-government that explains why these rules are appropriate interpretations of stakeholder citizenship that complement each other in a multilevel citizenship architecture.

The same triangular conception should also help to address the questions about national self-determination and secession that Miller raises. In section 3.3 of chapter 1 (pp. 42–43) I propose two criteria for establishing the legitimacy of self-government claims that contest the borders of current jurisdictions or the division of powers between regional and state governments: a criterion of compossibility of entangled self-government projects that considers how they impact on each other, and a criterion of representativeness of claims that considers the inclusiveness and internal support of the project.

The criterion of representativeness of claims relies on the bilateral version of the stakeholder principle. It requires that claims to enhanced self-government or secession must not only be internally supported by a relevant majority in a territory at a specific point in time (which would be sufficient for an associative secession theory) or be made on behalf of a culturally distinct historical community (which it would have to be under a nationalist conception of self-determination). I suggest instead that "the democratic people itself is constituted through representation of its claims to self-government" (p. 43).[5] This means that there is a lot of historical contingency in the construction of the people on behalf of whom self-government claims are raised, but these claims are normatively constrained by a requirement that they represent a political community that includes all citizenship stakeholders rather than a regionally dominant nationality.

The second criterion of compossibility should not be understood merely as a question about whether the polities involved could continue to exist as distinct from each other and with some degree of self-government, but also about whether their relations to each other can be regarded as free of domination. Algeria-in-France or Ireland-in-Britain could have become territories with some degree of home rule and a shared French or British citizenship for all inhabitants, but given the colonial nature of the relation, they would very likely have remained dominated in a way that undermined their self-government. Separation is not always necessary, however, in order to overcome a history of domination. In plurinational democracies, such as Belgium, Britain, Canada, India or Spain, the historical domination of minorities has been overcome to a significant extent, even if not fully, through federally nested self-government. In such arrangements, the territorial integrity and unity of

---

[5]   Perhaps I can illustrate this idea with the case I know best. An Austrian nation can hardly be said to have existed prior to 1945. The territory of the country consists of what was left over after the formation of nation-states out of the Habsburg Empire after World War I. In the interwar First Republic the political elite was convinced that Austria was not viable as an independent state and destined to join Germany. Only after the Nazis had followed up on this idea did Social Democrats and Conservatives agree that it was imperative for democracy to create a sense of national belonging. Approval rates to the statement that an Austrian nation exists soared to saturation levels only in the 1970s when Austria became a decent welfare state. Since the late 1980s, however, the rhetoric of Austrian nationalism has been gradually monopolized by the Freedom Party, which ironically had reassembled radical German nationalists and unreconstructed Nazis after World War II. In other words, during the interwar period the political elite failed to create a democratic people through representing its claim to self-government; after 1945 it succeeded in doing so, but the language of nationhood it used for this purpose paved the way for an antidemocratic and exclusionary populism. Of course this story cannot be generalized since every nation-building project has a unique context and history. But the mechanisms of elite construction of national identities and the current reactionary degeneration of nationalism are, in my view, general phenomena.

the encompassing state cannot be unconditional but must instead depend on constitutional guarantees for territorial autonomy of regions where minorities are concentrated and democratic practices of power-sharing that involve these regions in the government of the federation. Vice versa, where a plurinational democracy meets these conditions, national minorities are bound to respect its territorial integrity, since unilateral secession rights are incompatible with a right of self-government of the larger polity that encompasses the minority territory.

Miller finds it puzzling that I accept remedial secession in cases where primary rights to self-government have been persistently violated. Isn't this like saying "that I have no primary right to own property, but I do have a remedial right to take back stolen possessions" (p. 139, n. 9)? Not necessarily, if we distinguish between self-government as a right that can be exercised either as territorial autonomy within states or through independent statehood, on the one hand, and self-determination as a right to unilaterally decide between these options by changing the status or borders of a jurisdiction, on the other hand. This would be analogous to saying that my property rights do not include a right to use force against others who might be interested in my property, except if they actually attempt to steal it.

I fully agree with Miller that it is incoherent to attribute self-government rights to minorities while denying them to the larger citizenry of a state that includes these minorities. The compossibility test for self-government claims is not biased in this way but explains how territorially entangled projects can still be treated symmetrically: minority autonomy is the condition for territorial integrity of the larger polity and respecting the integrity of the larger polity is the condition for territorial autonomy of the minority.

Miller concludes by suggesting that "the nationality principle underlines the role of a shared identity in creating social and political trust, thereby facilitating the accommodations and compromises that are essential if democratic decisions are to be accepted as authoritative by all concerned" (p. 140). There is, however, a prior question as to whether the nationality principle is still able to create and sustain those jurisdictions within which democratic decisions need to be taken so that citizens can govern themselves in the contemporary world. I suspect that the once progressive role of the nationality principle in this respect has been largely exhausted since the times when it triggered decolonization and devolution in plurinational democracies. In the current highly interdependent world, democratic self-government can only survive if individuals can see themselves as citizens not only of nation-states, but also of local, regional and supranational polities that cannot be imagined as nations.

The test for this historical hypothesis is empirical rather than normative. In today's Europe the nationality principle is politically invoked mostly in order to deny immigrants access to citizenship, to reject solidarity between the member states of the EU and to break up democratic states or make their governments dysfunctional.

Miller is nevertheless right that there is a "tradeoff between thicker and more motivationally powerful forms of national identity and thinner and weaker, but more inclusive, forms" (p. 141). But this tradeoff should not be regarded as a static one. Growing interdependence between countries and growing mobility across their borders mean that national identities become not only ever more exclusionary but are also increasingly mobilized for the purpose of blocking emerging collective identities at local and supranational levels. The goal of liberal republicans should be instead to strengthen collective identities based on shared citizenship that can support social solidarity and democratic self-government across different levels and across borders of democratic polities.

Demos and citizenry

Nearly all theorists who have addressed the democratic boundary problem have considered inclusion in the demos as if it means the same thing as access to citizenship. Towards the end of my brief discussion of the citizenship stakeholder principle in section 3.3 of chapter 1 I suggest a distinction between the citizenry and the demos (pp. 44–47). The demos consists of adult citizens who can vote or be elected, while the citizenry is a broader category that includes minor children and others who are not capable of exercising the rights and duties of members of the demos. The comments by David Owen and by Sue Donaldson and Will Kymlicka challenge this distinction from two contrasting perspectives. While Owen wants to broaden the concept of the demos, Donaldson and Kymlicka question the distinction itself.

Owen identifies for each of the three inclusion principles a specific form of membership of the demos that provides democratic legitimacy for the corresponding process. The discursive demos provides legitimacy to political decisions through the input of affected interests; the editorial demos provides legitimacy to coercive subjection to government power through securing liberties and exposing this power to contestation; and the authorial demos provides authorization for democratic government and thereby enables the wider community of citizens to govern themselves collectively.

I find Owen's proposal congenial because it keeps the three inclusion principles apart and identifies for each a distinct set of persons whose inclusion fulfils specific legitimacy requirements. I still have some doubts about the terminology because the very concept of democracy refers etymologically to the rule of the demos. In my view neither the discursive nor the editorial demos is engaged in ruling in any meaningful way. Yet I do not want to put too much emphasis on terminology, not least because I do not have a better one to offer. So I will accept for the sake of this discussion that the citizenry (we might also call it the democratic people) is the political community that has a claim to self-government, whereas the demos is a functional entity that is constructed for specific purposes of democratic legitimation. The question I want to consider here is the relation between these different demoi and the citizenry.

The relation of the discursive demos to the citizenry is the most open-ended: the set of those who have a claim to be included changes all the time, depending on the decision on the agenda. It is a discursive relation in the sense of Habermas's discourse ethics (Habermas 1986). The discursive demos can be wider or smaller than the community of citizens. There is no specific requirement of congruity between the discursive demos and the citizenry, and thus also no implication whatsoever for membership in the latter.

The relation of the editorial demos to the citizenry is a much closer one: government power is legitimately exercised within territorial or personal jurisdictions. It is a relation of control by governments over subjects and contestation of governments by subjects. Being subjected to government power on a long-term basis gives rise to claims for membership in the citizenry. But, as I have argued, this is neither a strictly necessary nor a sufficient condition and governments must not themselves draw the boundaries of the citizenry through subjecting individuals to their power. They must instead enable a political community to be self-governing in its relation to other political communities. And this requires specifying membership and boundary principles for different types of polities and individuals' relations to these. The inclusion claims of immigrants and emigrants in a state that is embedded in the international state system are therefore different from those of residents in a municipality nested within a state.

Finally, the relation of the authorial demos to the citizenry is the closest one; it is a relation of representation. This may seem odd, since I am not talking about those who are elected but those who vote. Let me explain. One aspect of this representative relation is that the members of the demos represent those citizens who are not included in the former. In nineteenth-century democracy, when casting their votes, the male heads of households were assumed to represent their wives and children, who enjoyed merely "passive citizenship". In contemporary liberal democracies the adult members of the citizenry are also members of the demos, so the relation between demos and citizenry seems mostly one of identity rather than representation, apart from the remaining exclusion of minor children. (I will say more about this when discussing Donaldson's and Kymlicka's critique.) The second aspect is that citizens when they vote are, or ought to think of themselves as, representatives of the larger community of citizens of which they are also individually members. In other words, the members of the demos should think of themselves not merely as *electing* representatives but as *being* representatives. The reason for this is that elected representatives do not merely represent their voters' particular interests but have the power to shape an open political agenda for the community of all citizens. Only if voters see themselves as representing the common interests of this community will they elect representatives who carry out this mandate and hold these legislators accountable if they fail to do so. This is obviously a democratic aspiration rather than a condition for electoral participation; it does not rule out self-interested voting, but it constrains it normatively.

The representative relation between citizenry and authorial demos suggests furthermore that the demos must be a subset of the citizenry. Representatives elected by the demos must themselves be citizens, and so must those who are eligible to vote. If the authorial demos were composed of, or included to a significant extent, non-citizens this would undermine its functional task of representing the citizenry through authorizing and holding accountable their government. As I will argue in the next section, this leads me to resist Owen's suggestion that the principle of including all subjected to coercion might apply to determining a legislative demos that would then be composed also of non-citizen residents.

This interpretation of the role of the authorial demos makes it possible to resolve the problem of representation of citizens who are not included in the demos. In order to serve its functional purpose of authorizing a democratic government, this demos must consist of citizens who have certain cognitive capacities. The demos should therefore not be understood as if it were a distinct form of political community; instead its members ought to be regarded as the trustees of those citizens who are not included in the demos, such as minor children and mentally disabled resident citizens.

Donaldson's and Kymlicka's critique focuses on this point. They argue that my theory buys into a "linguistic capacity contract" that has historically served to support unjust exclusions and that is still invoked today when denying political rights to minor children or mentally handicapped persons and citizenship status to domesticated animals.

Donaldson and Kymlicka write: "On Bauböck's model ... our duty to support and enable the political participation of our fellow members of society depends on whether they fall above or below some stipulated threshold of cognitive or linguistic competence" (p. 175). This is not my view. We have duties to support the political participation of minor children and the mentally handicapped in proportion to their capacity and desire to participate (a point also emphasized by Honohan). A linguistic capacity threshold is only relevant for those who are members of the demos, that is, those who are called to participate in democratic elections and who qualify as candidates. Donaldson and Kymlicka also attribute to me the view that "we owe [minor children] participation not in virtue of what they are – not in virtue of their interests or membership *as children* – but in virtue of what they will become (adult citizens)" (p. 177, n. 23). Again, this is not what my distinction between citizenry and demos suggests. I have argued that "newborn babies are attributed citizenship not just because we regard them as *future* citizens" (p. 46), but because they belong to a transgenerational political community. Such a community would no longer be transgenerational if it did not include those recently born and those close to death regardless of their capacities and contributions. On my account, minor children are not, however, members of the demos.

Why? Donaldson and Kymlicka suggest that a principle of stakeholder citizenship should first identify those who have a claim to membership and then search how these could be enabled to participate as fully as possible in the governing of the polity. In this view, a lack of (full) linguistic and cognitive capacities does not justify exclusion but calls instead for enabling forms of inclusion. On this account, any hard boundary separating the demos from the citizenry looks suspicious. After all, children, cognitively impaired people and domesticated animals can and do communicate their needs. Even if these communications are addressed to their immediate care-givers, they can still be fed as input into political deliberations and decisions that apply to these individuals and regulate their lives.

Donaldson and Kymlicka have forcefully made this argument in their recent work (Donaldson and Kymlicka 2011, 2017) and I find this part of their theory convincing. I remain, however, unconvinced in two respects. First, I think that the distinction between demos and citizenry is essential for liberal democracy and, second, I do not think that the rights of domesticated animals are best expressed in the language of citizenship.

Let me start with what seems obvious. Linguistic and generic cognitive capacities are indispensable as a qualification for ruling a human polity. Candidates for public office who seek a mandate to represent citizens must have these capacities and this justifies age thresholds for candidacy rights. Citizens, including those of minor age, would not want to be ruled by individuals who lack this capacity.[6]

Maybe this is enough and we need to set thresholds only for candidacy rights and not for participation in elections? Yet if only rulers need to be linguistically capable, then citizens would be subjected to rule by an elite that they could not hold accountable. For Aristotle, democratic citizenship meant ruling and being ruled in turn, which implied that the same capacity requirements applied to citizens and those exercising public office. Yet Athenian office-holders were appointed through lotteries. For representative liberal democracy, this condition can be somewhat relaxed, but not altogether. Those citizens who vote do not have to be trained as professional politicians but must be capable of communicating with other citizens and understanding what candidates and parties stand for. They are also collectively responsible for their choices (Hobden 2015). Not to expect the members of the demos to have these capacities means accepting that they must be governed paternalistically by those who have them.

---

[6] William Golding's novel *Lord of the Flies* provides a sinister parable about what the rule of children over children might look like.

This does not entail that only those who have the relevant capacity can be citizens. First, as suggested by Donaldson and Kymlicka, capacities can be created by overcoming socially constructed and reinforced incapacity. Instead of presupposing that citizens are literate, economically independent and have enough leisure time to be politically informed and engaged, the democratic state has duties to develop these capacities and provide citizens with these resources. Second, individuals whose lack of these capacities cannot be overcome by such means can still be included in a wider self-governing political community as citizens. These citizens (minor children and the cognitively severely handicapped) will then indeed be governed paternalistically. Paternalistic government that is oriented towards the well-being and autonomy of individuals will not only protect them and provide them with resources but also promote their participation in accordance with their capacities, in the ways Donaldson and Kymlicka suggest. But this does not qualify them as full members of the demos who are responsible for their political choices and have to hold those who rule over the citizenry accountable.

Donaldson and Kymlicka may respond that my account fetishizes elections from which citizens without the necessary cognitive capacities are inevitably excluded over deliberations in which they can be included. Yet democracy is not just an ongoing deliberation about the common good; it is also the exercise of coercive power that is always in danger of being abused. Minor children (below the age of adolescence) have to trust that their parents have their well-being in mind, but rulers can never be trusted in this way. Even parents of minor children have to be checked by laws and political authorities that they do not abuse their paternalistic powers. Democratic elections and the division of power between branches of government are devices that have been designed to minimize such abuse of government power and build on the anti-paternalistic idea of democratic legitimacy through popular self-government.

Enabling minor children and cognitively impaired citizens to shape their own lives and have a say over the laws that regulate them is very important. But these inputs into the political process are, in my view, fully covered through the principles of including affected interests and those subjected to coercion. Under the latter, individuals who are not included in the demos enjoy not only equal protection under the law but also rights of contestation. Moreover, because of the transgenerational nature of political communities, minor children and cognitively disabled persons are also included in the citizenry. They are not, however, members of what Owen calls the authorial demos. Age thresholds for voting can and have been lowered, and cognitively impaired persons should retain voting rights by default. But none of this does away with the need for linguistic and cognitive capacity conditions for membership in the demos.

What we need to consider instead is vicarious representation in legislative institutions. Owen suggests a sophisticated model of indirect special representation for minor children based on second votes for enfranchised adult citizens (pp. 186–187). I find this an attractive proposal. A lot of details would have to be worked out. Should the representatives of citizens who are not members of the demos have veto power or rather the power of legislative proposal, or both? Would the powers of such special representatives be limited to certain policy areas that are specifically relevant for children? If we consider children's interests as continuous with those of future generations of citizens, then no policy area could be excluded.

Should all citizens without voting rights be represented indirectly in this way? This depends on the reasons why they are not enfranchised and their relation to the wider citizenry. Owen's proposal would hardly work for marginalized minorities, such as mentally handicapped citizens who should therefore be better generally enfranchised and additionally represented by specially appointed ombudspersons rather than by separately elected representatives.

Let me now address the second challenge raised by Donaldson and Kymlicka. If citizenship status does not depend on cognitive capacities why shouldn't domesticated animals be included as citizens? I propose three arguments why not. The first is that they are already sufficiently included under the affected interests and subjection to coercion principles.

I cannot see which kind of injustice is committed towards domesticated animals if they are considered members of the private households of their care-givers and as denizens of the polity that owes them protection under the law and has to take into account the needs that they articulate. Once this has been accepted, what would be gained by calling them citizens? My second objection refers back to the circumstances of democracy. These include not only internal diversity (which could very well cover a diversity of animal species) but also the condition of a pluralism of distinct and bounded polities. We may recognize that social animal species form distinct and bounded communities of their own and, as Donaldson and Kymlicka (2011) have suggested, we can then conceive of our relations to them, in analogy with those between states, as relations between sovereign and bounded communities of different species. Further progress in the study of animal behaviour might also lead to the discovery of norms and institutions in some animal societies that are functional equivalents of citizenship in human polities. But what Donaldson and Kymlicka propose is something quite different: cross-species citizenship through which humans and other animals share membership in political communities. Over the course of their history, humans have always formed political communities, membership in which has been determined through relations with other similarly organized human communities and through the imperative of maintaining transgenerational continuity of their particular community over time. These two features make it difficult to conceive of a cross-species citizenship that includes domesticated animals even if these have been bred to serve human needs and to live inside human societies in close relations with human beings.

A third objection builds on my interpretation of the stakeholder principle. We should see domesticated animals as stakeholders in the policies that affect and regulate their lives and also as having a stake in a government that protects them and enables them to articulate their needs. But, as I have argued, none of this is sufficient for citizenship as membership in a self-governing political community. Human beings have a stake in citizenship because their autonomy and well-being depend to a large extent on membership in a democratic polity. I am not convinced that domesticated animals have a similarly fundamental interest in recognition of their *political* membership and in the *democratic* constitution of the polity.

Transnational voting and multilevel citizenship

Unlike most contemporary political theorists, David Owen is not merely interested in defending general principles. He engages with comparative studies of democracy and offers a basket of concrete policy proposals. I share Owen's attitude. Normative theories become richer and more relevant when they address the puzzles and dilemmas that citizens and policy-makers face in real-world democracies. Comparing the variety of answers at different times and in different places cannot tell us what is the right solution. But it provides us with a broader view of options and constraints and focuses our minds on dilemmas that serve to test the robustness of our intuitions and principles.

My own thinking about the citizenship stakeholder principle did not start from the philosophical paradoxes of the democratic boundary problem. It was instead inspired by a puzzle about migrants' access to citizenship status and voting rights that I have studied comparatively for many years. Liberal theorists like Walzer, Carens and Kymlicka have provided us with rich accounts of immigrants' claims to membership and multicultural rights based on the idea that the rule of citizens over permanent strangers is a form of tyranny (Walzer 1983), that immigrants become over time members of society and democracies must be inclusive for all their members (Carens 1989), or that liberal democracies need to integrate immigrants into a shared societal culture that provides its citizens with a meaningful repertoire of options (Kymlicka 1995). These first generation theories ignored almost completely the well-known fact that international migrants retain their citizenship of origin. What has until recently been much less known is the strong global trend among source countries to let emigrants keep their membership and voting rights in home country elections even after becoming citizens of host countries.

Political theorists not only neglected the migrants' perspective, which requires combining an immigration with an emigration view, but their theories of political community and citizenship were also overwhelmingly statist. The second set of puzzles that emerged from my comparative research interests was about freedom of movement between the member states of the European Union, which seemed to challenge assumptions about immigration control as a requirement for state sovereignty, and about local voting rights that many of these countries grant not only to all EU citizens residing in the municipality but also to third country nationals.

My first discussions of the stakeholder principle saw it as an alternative to immigration-centric views of social membership: migrants are simultaneously stakeholders in a country of origin and settlement, which supports their claims to multiple citizenship and voting rights. However, this did not resolve the puzzle about local citizenship and voting rights, where the most progressive practices instead follow a principle of automatic inclusion of all residents and exclusion of non-residents. This latter democratic practice seemed to be much more in tune with ASC than with ACS. From a normative perspective it is obviously not possible to accept that one democratic inclusion principle applies to states and another to local polities, since these principles aim to spell out basic moral ideas about democracy and membership. The solution I found consisted of two moves.

The first was to restate the stakeholder principle as entailing a relational correspondence between individual inclusion and collective self-government claims. This made it possible to explain why the same stakeholder principle supports different rules for membership determination and voting rights depending on the nature of the polity and its relations to other polities as conditions under which it can be self-governing (see chapter 1, section 4). This explains why birthright citizenship is an appropriate interpretation of the stakeholder principle for independent states, while ius domicilii is for local municipalities. The second move was to consider AAI, ASC and ACS not as rival principles responding to the same question about membership in the demos and the citizenry, but as complementary ones that cover inclusion in the different domains and stages of the democratic process (see chapter 1, section 3).

I want to use this general approach now to explain why I am sceptical about Owen's further differentiation of the authorial demos into an executive, legislative and constitutional one, which aims to bring back ASC as the relevant principle for determining membership in the demos in specific contexts. Owen agrees broadly with my view that enfranchising first generation emigrant citizens in national elections is generally permissible but not required. As Owen correctly clarifies, I think that a stakeholder principle supports presumptive inclusion so that justification needs to be offered for denying non-resident citizens the franchise. Owen wants to go further by identifying instances in which emigrants have a justice-based claim to voting rights. I have myself argued that this is the case when emigrants have been unjustly driven out of the country. In section 3.2 of chapter 1 I claim that, insofar as the situation of exiled citizens is comprehensively marked by past subjection, a democratic successor state may have duties to provide them with ongoing protection of their rights according to the ASC principle – an argument that Miller finds mysterious (p. 133) because he misreads it as a claim to political participation rather than protection. The reason why coerced emigrants also have claims to membership in the demos is, however, a quite different one that does not rely on ASC: denying them voting rights would amount to democratically ratifying the results of political purges or ethnic cleansing (Bauböck 2007).

Owen proposes a second set of circumstances under which expatriates would have a justice-based claim to inclusion in a constitutional demos. It is not entirely clear to me for what kind of decisions a constitutional demos would have to be specified. Owen identifies a narrow class of constitutional decisions that "directly [concern] [non-residents'] very status as citizens" and that "specify the entitlements and obligations of citizens – such as, for example, laws on nationality and expatriate voting rights" (p. 193; see also Owen 2010). Yet most constitutional laws that "fundamentally concern the nature of the political association" (p. 192) are not of this kind. They often concern procedural aspects of democracy or entrench fundamental human rights. Should the demos for such constitutional changes be different from the legislative one? If not, is there really a need and justification for a special demos deciding on laws that concern the status and rights of citizens? Even decisions about nationality law are ambiguous in this respect. As Owen points out, the Irish ius soli referendum of 2004 was about changing a fundamental aspect of nationality law but its impact was on future generations rather than today's citizens. Assuming for the sake of argument that the current disenfranchisement of Irish non-resident citizens is permissible: was there a good reason to extend voting rights to them only in this particular referendum?

The strongest prima facie case for a specific constitutional franchise exists if the decision would change the citizenship status and rights of those who are not included in the current legislative demos. Consider first the case of the 2014 Scottish independence referendum. Would it have been required to enfranchise persons who might have become Scottish citizens in case of a yes vote? No, because this inclusion would have illegitimately pre-empted a possible future composition of an independent Scottish citizenry that was still to be decided depending on the outcome of the very same referendum. It was therefore right to stick to the current legislative demos for Scottish Parliament elections (Ziegler, Shaw and Bauböck 2014). Consider now as a contrasting case the Brexit referendum. Was it also right to use then the current Westminster franchise? No, because that franchise excludes British citizens who have resided for fifteen years outside the UK, which conflicts with their EU citizenship right to free movement. It is perverse to disenfranchise people in member state elections because they exercise their rights as citizens of a union formed by these states. The British Parliament should have exempted British citizens residing elsewhere in the EU from the fifteen years limit for retaining the franchise. This argument applies, however, to the legislative as much as to the constitutional demos. There is again no need to distinguish these two. Finally, consider a hypothetical case of a country that has the kind of franchise and citizenship law for non-residents that I advocate: native-born expats remain enfranchised but their children born abroad do not obtain the franchise at majority unless they have taken up residence at some point during their lives. Imagine there is a referendum on whether second generation emigrants that fail to meet this condition should also be allowed to cast ballots from abroad in national elections. Since this is an important constitutional change and since their rights and status might change, should they be included in the constitutional demos for that particular vote?

In my view, the relevant difference is not between legislative and constitutional decisions, but between two types of decisions that fundamentally change the composition of the demos: those that are permissible and those for which a specific outcome is normatively required. Holding an independence referendum in Scotland and a Brexit referendum in the UK may have been politically irresponsible, but it was democratically permissible to let a referendum determine the outcome. In such a case, the legitimacy of the decision is purely procedural. And if the legitimacy is procedural, then the demos for such a decision should be composed in the same way as the legislative demos for the polity whose future status is to be decided.

A second type of decision is where a specific outcome is normatively required. The inclusion of categories of citizens that were unjustly excluded in the past, such as women or African Americans, is of that type. Consider the plebiscite that was held in Switzerland in 1971 and that extended voting rights to women. Was the decision illegitimate because it was taken only by the then enfranchised male citizens? Would a negative outcome of a referendum on enfranchising women become legitimate if women had been enfranchised for that particular vote?[7] I suggest the answer to both questions is no. Including unjustly excluded

[7] This is not a purely hypothetical question. The last Swiss canton to introduce women's franchise was Appenzell-Innerrhoden in 1990, after a decision by the Federal Court. The decision had been delayed for a long time because in a consultative referendum on the topic in 1969 a majority of women had opposed their own enfranchisement.

categories in an ad hoc constitutional demos does not alter in any way the injustice of their exclusion from the legislative demos.

Consider now who should vote in a decision about extending voting rights to first generation emigrants. Imagine that Ireland, where they are currently disenfranchised, held a referendum on this question. There are many reasonable arguments on either side in this debate. But none of them strikes me as making a case that they must be excluded or must be included in the demos as a matter of justice. If their inclusion in the demos is permissible rather than required, then it can be legitimately decided by the current legislative demos, even if the decision concerns a fundamental democratic right. And if it were a matter of justice and for some reason must be decided by referendum rather than a constitutional court, then procedural legitimacy for the required change could still be better provided by the same legislative demos rather than an ad hoc constitutional demos whose composition pre-empts a desired outcome.

If it is generally permissible to decide democratically whether first generation emigrants should be enfranchised, then it follows that excluding foreign-born citizens by descent, whose ties to their parents' country of origin is weaker, from the legislative demos cannot be unjust. This holds not only for the legislative demos but also for a constitutional demos that decides on their status and rights. A stakeholder principle provides similar substantive reasons for other decisions about expatriates that could be taken by a constitutional demos. If the decision at stake were to abolish ius sanguinis for the first generation born abroad, I would consider this unjust, independently of whether those affected are enfranchised; if the decision were about enfranchising second and later generations born and residing permanently abroad, I would consider such a proposal over-inclusive and would therefore a fortiori resist the ad hoc inclusion of these categories in a plebiscite on that very question.

I am more sympathetic to Owen's proposal to include foreign-born adult citizens if they cast their votes in the territory of the home state. My preferred condition for including such second generations is their return. A single trip "back home" to cast a vote is not the same thing as taking up residence, which turns the foreign-born into resident citizens.

However, these are minor quibbles over practical criteria. Generally, I do not see why there would be any difference between returning for legislative elections or for a vote in a constitutional referendum.

Let me now consider Peter Spiro's objections to my proposal to phase out membership transmission with the first generation born abroad and not to enfranchise them automatically at the age of majority. There is a certain tension between Spiro's comments on external citizenship and his general diagnosis that citizenship is in decline because citizens are ever less interested in collective self-government. He sees diasporas as having a strong stake in their countries of origin.

There are some misunderstandings about what my proposal entails. Spiro quotes correctly my qualifier that source country citizenship should be phased out for third generations of immigrant origin "unless their parents have themselves renewed their links to this country through taking up residence there" (p. 69; p. 189). If second generations return to their parents' country of origin, they become first generation emigrants in relation to their own country of origin and their children born abroad should be dual citizens by birth and for life. So there is no assumption of "linear flows" in my account. I do, however, insist that holding a stake in collective self-government is not a matter of strength of subjective preferences for a certain citizenship because such preferences are quite naturally influenced by instrumental motives. Instead, objective facts such as prior periods of residence or dependency on citizen parents or partners who have previously resided in the country provide better proxies for a presumption of stakeholding.

What I find surprising about Spiro's account of diaspora is that he seems to think that being outside a state territory enhances one's interest in the flourishing of the political community whereas being inside diminishes it. Spiro says that "it is not clear that they [i.e. diasporas] have a self-governance interest in the community [of residence] defined in terms of the state, much less its 'flourishing'" (p. 208). At the same time, he sees diasporas as "the paradigm case in which individuals will feel exactly the sort of stake that Bauböck describes" (p. 217), citing the intense demand for multiple citizenship and voting rights.

This contradicts somewhat Spiro's later claim that "the average level of interest and participation will be lower in external communities, reflecting the aggregately lower, more highly variable self-governance interest" (p. 220). I find the latter statement plausible and it is supported by evidence about low turnout among external voters. As Brubaker has reminded us, we should not attribute diasporic identities to all individuals of emigrant origin (Brubaker 2005). Diaspora formation happens in specific contexts, mostly in response to violent conflict in the home country or segregation in the host country. In any case, even if communities mobilized as diasporas do not care much about citizenship in their country of residence and care a lot about politics in the country of origin, they should still be seen as having a stake in both.

Spiro advocates bespoke arrangements that reflect political pressure exercised by diasporas. But combined with domestic fears of excessive diaspora influence, these arrangements are likely to produce deviations from the ideal of equal individual citizenship. Extraterritorial electoral constituencies with reserved seats in parliament often under-represent external citizens numerically by weighting down their votes compared with domestic constituencies, while at the same time enhancing their substantive representation as a special interest group. Both features are problematic, although the former goal is possibly defensible where diasporas are very large compared with domestic populations (Bauböck 2007). From a stakeholder perspective, external citizens should have a vote only if and as long as they can be seen as sharing a common interest in the flourishing of the polity with those who reside in the territory. Their special interests do not warrant special representation in legislation any more than those of other special interest groups inside or outside the country who may be affected by its legislation. The MPs elected in extraterritorial constituencies in the Colombian, Croatian, Ecuadoran, French, Italian, Portuguese and Romanian parliaments do not merely vote on issues concerning expats; they participate fully in agenda-setting and decisions concerning all citizens.

Spiro is, however, right that setting and maintaining standards of equality among citizens become more difficult once we consider individuals' multiple ties to different polities across levels or international borders. This problem is exacerbated by transnational migration but it already exists within democratic states which are subdivided into self-governing territories. Most obviously, in democratic federations there is a tension between treating all citizens of the federation equally and treating the federal entities (provinces, cantons, regions, states) equally as constituent polities of the federation. This tension is institutionalized rather than resolved in bicameral legislatures. In the U.S. the votes of individual Californians and Rhode Islanders count equally for representation in the House, but unequally for the Senate, where each state has two delegates independently of its size. Unlike federal entities, external citizens do not form distinct constituent polities with a claim to collective representation – although they are sometimes labelled the $(n+1)^{th}$ province. Yet migration does create unequal stakeholdership between sedentary citizens with a singular affiliation to their state of residence, transnational migrants with a claim to dual citizenship and highly mobile persons who may not satisfy reasonable residence requirements for citizenship in any host country. Working out what equality entails in these contexts is a difficult task. However, it does not seem to me an impossible one as long as we keep the relational nature of stakeholder citizenship firmly in mind.

After discussing external citizenship and voting extensively, let me now consider more briefly voting rights for non-citizen immigrants, where it seems that Owen and I have a deeper disagreement over principle rather than policy. As we have seen above, with regard to emigrant citizens Owen wants to defend the stakeholder principle against my proposal to restrict voting rights for second generations who have not "touched base" with their country of citizenship. In his view, "ACS not only demarcates those entitled to citizenship, but it also simultaneously identifies those who are entitled to authorial membership of the constitutional demos" (p. 194). When discussing the claims of immigrants, however, he relies on Dahl's principle of full inclusion of non-transient residents with the necessary cognitive capacities and claims that ASC is the right norm for determining membership in the legislative demos. In policy terms, our disagreement seems a minor one: should immigrants who decline a fair naturalization offer still be entitled to vote in national legislative elections?

Let me first clarify again what may seem like an inconsistency: I have argued in chapter 1, section 4 that non-citizen residents should be included in the local demos. Does this mean that I apply ACS at the national level while accepting ASC at the local one, as Miller suggests in his comments? No, because foreign residents are non-citizens only in their relation with the national polity, whereas they should be regarded as full citizens at the local level where citizenship itself is derived from residence. At the national level, this is not the case and non-citizen residents are offered a choice to naturalize as a condition for acquiring voting rights. Owen defends instead that non-citizens who are not merely transients should be automatically enfranchised.

My objection is that this move would undermine the representative relation between citizenry and authorial demos that requires that the latter should be a subset of the former (as explained in the previous section). The members of the demos are those who exercise the core right of participation in collective self-rule of the political community. Only citizens should be able to rule over citizens and to authorize the rulers on behalf of all citizens.

Owen might point out that in some empirical cases non-citizens who meet certain residence requirements can vote (although not be elected) in national elections. I have endorsed the view that it is legitimate for democratic states to extend the vote to long-term residents who have not opted to become national citizens (Bauböck 2015).

In the empirical cases we find two reasons why national voting rights have been granted to non-citizens: one is where voting rights were not seen as an alternative to naturalization but as a pathway to it;[8] the second is where historical voting privileges for special nationalities were preserved or – in the unique case of New Zealand – extended to

---

[8]   This was the case in nineteenth-century U.S. States, many of which granted voting rights to "declarant aliens" who had declared their intention to naturalize (Raskin 1993; Hayduk 2005).

all long-term residents (Barker and McMillan 2014). None of these empirical cases lends itself to inductive generalization that liberal democracies endorse a national franchise for non-citizens who do not intend to become citizens.

Of course, a lack of empirical support is not sufficient to knock down a normative argument. Owen makes a pragmatic case that granting naturalization refusers voting rights "supports the conditions of genuine consent by weakening an instrumental reason for resident non-citizens to naturalize" (p. 202).

However, if immigrants who enjoy secure residence and all other rights desire to participate fully in the political life of the community by voting or running as candidates, then they have a *non-instrumental* motive for naturalization. They want to become members of the demos and it is not clear why they could reasonably reject to become also citizens in terms of their legal status.

Finally, there may be good reasons for democratic states not to enfranchise those who refuse to become citizens but still want to vote in national elections. Imagine a country (call it Luxembourg) where half the population consists of resident citizens and the other half of non-citizen residents who enjoy more or less the same rights apart from the right to vote in national elections.[9] Assume further that the non-citizen long-term residents could at any time decide to become citizens while keeping their citizenship of origin.[10] The reason why they do not want to naturalize is then presumably that they are not sure that they will stay in the country for much longer. Being aware that national citizenship is generally a lifetime status and lacking instrumental motives for acquiring it, they do not want to take such a step. This country faces a democratic dilemma. On the one hand, there is certainly a deficit of legitimacy if only 50 per cent of the resident population is eligible to

---

[9]   In Luxembourg this is a plausible assumption since most of its 46 per cent non-citizen residents are EU citizens and thus enjoy also nearly the same mobility and residence rights as national citizens.

[10]   The right to naturalization condition is not met by Luxembourg, which is why I model the case as a hypothetical one.

vote in national elections. On the other hand, is it really a requirement of justice on grounds of ASC to include them in the legislative demos? Wouldn't it rather undermine trust among the citizens if a large number of those who participate in elections do not commit themselves to be members of the political community for a long-term future? Couldn't the citizens point out that this amounts to being ruled by non-citizens who – by rejecting the naturalization offer – have demonstrated a lack of commitment towards the political community? Note that this second horn of the dilemma comes into sight only from a citizenship stakeholder perspective whereas it vanishes from sight if we cling to a principle of including as equal members all subjected to the same government.

I find it hard to resolve this dilemma either way, which is why I consider it permissible but not required to introduce non-citizen voting rights at the national level. Behind this dilemma lurks my deeper worry about the future of democratic citizenship in a hypermobile world where majorities of citizens are non-residents and majorities of residents are non-citizens.

In our present world, which is certainly not hypermobile, ius domicilii regimes at the local level are embedded within the territorial jurisdictions of states and their birthright citizenship regimes. Local citizenship helps democracies to "digest" hypermobility and superdiversity without endangering the transgenerational continuity of national citizenries. Contrary to Peter Spiro's reading of my view, I do not regard local citizenship as the "stepchild" of national citizenship. I see them as a symbiotic pair, so that the strengths of each compensate to some extent for the defects of the other. But this symbiosis might be threatened in a hypermobile world, which could be imagined as consisting only of provinces and municipalities under a world government without independent states. Ius domicilii would then remain as the only relevant rule for determining membership in the citizenry and the demos of territorial polities, while exclusionary birthright and naturalization regimes would probably proliferate within non-territorial associations and communities (Bauböck 2011). This is probably a fair description of the world towards which Peter Spiro thinks we are heading.

The future of citizenship

Peter Spiro's disagreement with me seems to emerge to a significant extent from arguing in a different register. While my theory is explicitly normative, his approach is more predictive. Spiro is convinced that citizenship is in decline or even already moribund. I am not convinced, but if he were right then I would be interested in how democracies should react to such a decline.

Spiro says he is "not proposing an alternative theory of citizenship" (p. 218). This is a pity, since I would be interested in knowing what follows normatively from his diagnosis of the demise of citizenship. A normative theory can best be refuted by a rival normative theory. Yet since "ought implies can", an applied normative theory, such as the one that I propose, can also be challenged on empirical grounds. If it were no longer possible to apply norms of inclusion and equality of citizenship to bounded and self-governing political communities, then my argument would be pointless. In fact, I acknowledged myself that what I called the "contexts of democracy" – territorial jurisdiction and relative sedentariness – are historically contingent. Elsewhere I reflected on the scenario of a hypermobile world in which these contexts would have vanished (Bauböck 2011). My conclusion then was that this is a dystopia in which not only citizenship but democracy itself would be much more difficult to realize. Spiro ends his comment by calling on theorists to "turn their sights towards carrying citizenship values forward to novel institutional arrangements" after the death of citizenship itself (p. 222). I would be keen to follow this call, but rather as an exercise in counterfactual reflection, since I am not at all convinced of Spiro's diagnosis of mortal illness.

In contrast with Spiro, I see the proliferation of citizenship statuses and rights across international borders and across levels of democratic polities not as a decline but as a liberation of citizenship from the straitjacket of state-centred nationalism – a liberation that creates new potentials for realizing democratic self-government. The new opportunities create also new challenges. Spiro correctly identifies the most fundamental of these: how to reconcile a transnational and multilevel conception of citizenship with the core value of equality.

 Before I address this problem, let me say that I am not naively optimistic about the prospects for citizenship, because I also see a serious trend towards decline. This is not the toleration of multiple citizenship or the emergence of sub- and supranational citizenship, all of which demonstrate the strength of the concept and its ongoing role in structuring the contemporary political world. It is instead the trend towards instrumental uses and abuses of citizenship both by states and by individuals. More precisely, it is the instrumental use of citizenship by states that creates new opportunities of instrumental abuse by individuals. Citizenship is not by nature a market commodity. States and other polities have the exclusive monopoly of producing it. If they start to sell their citizenship in a global market, then the value of this commodity depends entirely on the recognition of the status by other states. Investor citizenship thus epitomizes the over-inclusive side of this trend (Shachar and Bauböck 2014; Dzankic 2015; Parker 2017), but it also has an exclusionary side that is generally ignored by Spiro. One example is when governments restrict access to ius soli or to naturalization for refugees or family members of citizens in order to curb undesired migration inflows. Spiro himself mentions another instance where restrictions on citizenship create incentives for instrumental abuse by individuals: long-term residents who decide to naturalize shortly before returning to their country of origin in order to secure re-entry rights and – I would add – diplomatic protection in their country of origin. Isn't the problem here that the country of origin's non-toleration of dual citizenship and lack of protection of human rights (China is the best-known case) create perverse incentives to use U.S. or Canadian citizenship instrumentally? And would toleration of dual citizenship and respect for fundamental rights not remove this incentive?

 This broader point can be illustrated by low naturalization rates of EU citizens in other member states because of the absence of incentives for instrumental naturalization. Free movement rights, non-discrimination and respect for fundamental rights remove most instrumental reasons for changing citizenship between member states. Of course, they greatly enhance the instrumental value of EU citizenship for third country nationals, but for EU citizens they reduce the value of national membership to its intrinsic and identity components. My conclusion is that in a world with more freedom of movement between states and better protection of rights within them, citizenship would have little instrumental value but would not lose its intrinsic value as membership in a self-governing polity. Instrumental (ab)uses of citizenship result from a combination of enhanced interconnectedness and mobility between states and persistent disparities between them. From a normative perspective, we should try to reduce the disparities instead of abandoning citizenship.

Instrumental uses of citizenship diminish its intrinsic value as membership in a self-governing polity. They do not, however, change the background context within which this value makes normative sense and could be defended by the right kind of policies. Spiro's and my diagnosis of current threats to the value of citizenship differ in this regard and mine does not commit me to stop arguing for the therapy.[11]

The decline of citizenship is, in Spiro's view, just a symptom of a more fundamental change, which is the demise of the agent issuing citizenship certificates and passports: the state. The redistributive capacities of the state may be waning, the security imperative in relation to hostile competitor states has dissipated. "States increasingly serve as an administrative servant of the global system" (p. 212). The protection of individual autonomy is "now protected by substantive, exogenously imposed human rights more than procedural internally generated

---

[11] Our different attitudes show also where we agree on the diagnosis. As a reason for being sceptical of republican theories of citizenship, Spiro contrasts "today's appalling spectacle of national [American] politics with few entry points for responsible participation" with the late twentieth century's "period of contentious but genuinely engaged self-governance" (p. 207). I wonder what follows from this normatively. Doesn't such decline give us reasons to call for stronger citizen engagement and to think about institutional reforms that could bring it about?

self-governance" (p. 208) and even states' "own membership practices are increasingly set by exogenous agents" (p. 213).

Individuals still have an interest in public order but "it is not clear that they have a self-governance interest in the community defined in terms of the state, much less its 'flourishing.'" (p. 208) So individuals' interests in autonomy and protection are increasingly realized in other associations and communities than the state. Some of these (Spiro cites the Mormon Church) have greater capacities and enjoy better compliance of their members with associative duties. Under these circumstances, for most citizens "politics is a waste of associative energy" (p. 210).

Here are a few questions that I have about Spiro's account. First, who governs the global system of which states are now administrative servants? How are human rights maintained and secured except by states subscribing to them and committing to upholding them? Who are the exogenous agents that are independent of states? Consider the UN, the UNHCR and the Council of Europe, that is, those organizations that have tried – and to a degree successfully so – to constrain state practices in matters of nationality law through international legal norms. Aren't these still international organizations made up of states which agree on their mandate and which reserve for themselves the right to accept or reject the norms produced by these IOs?

Second, voluntary associations have often been regarded as schools of citizenship, but Spiro sees them instead (as did Rousseau) as its grave diggers. I remain agnostic on this point. My main objection is that polities are entirely different from voluntary associations and civil society communities and there is thus neither essential rivalry nor harmony between them. First, as I argue in chapter 1 section 4, none of the three basic membership rules in self-governing polities (birthright, residence, derivation) transforms polities into voluntary associations. Second, polities have coercive power over anybody within their jurisdiction to enforce laws emerging from an open legislative agenda. Self-government in voluntary associations may satisfy important psychological needs but it cannot substitute for the task of authorizing and taming government power through subjecting it to the votes of citizens.

Finally, I do not see any empirical evidence that citizens are merely interested in public order but no longer in self-government or the flourishing of their states. To the contrary, the rise of right- and left-wing populist parties in the U.S. and Europe seems to me – in a perverse way – proof that citizens expect much more from the state than maintenance of public order. We are witnessing a rather strong counter-movement against the thinning out of democracy that reclaims it in the name of popular self-government. Populists' appeal results from their promise to restore the power of the people against the elite, to purify the people by purging them from alien elements, and to restore the independence of the state from transnational corporations and supranational bodies like the EU. This is illiberal democracy running amok. But it is certainly not proof that citizens have lost their self-governance interest in the community defined in terms of the state.

Continuing the conversation

I am deeply grateful to my interlocutors, not only for their praise but especially for their frank critiques. They have made me acutely aware of the gaps in my argument. And my thoughts about democratic inclusion have already changed in some respects due to their feedback. I would love to know what they have to say about my self-revisions and rebuttals. Yet books do not only have their own fates (I wish I could say that about this one!), but they also have their own formats. Unlike the open-ended exchange of arguments in public spheres, a book is a container with limited space for ideas. The dialogue closes once the last page has been turned.

My hope is that the conversation about principles of democratic inclusion can be carried on in other forums and not just among theorists. I started my rejoinder by claiming that normative political theory ought to be informed by ideals that can guide reforms in the current world. If this is correct, then the most important test of the theory I have proposed is whether it can be accepted by reasonable and engaged citizens.

References

Barker, Fiona and Kate McMillan. 2014. "Constituting the Democratic Public: New Zealand's Extension of National Voting Rights to Non-citizens." *New Zealand Journal of Public and International Law* 12 (1): 61–80.

Bauböck, Rainer. 2007. "Stakeholder Citizenship and Transnational Political Participation: A Normative Evaluation of External Voting." *Fordham Law Review* 75 (5): 2393–2447.

Bauböck, Rainer. 2011. "Temporary Migrants, Partial Citizenship and Hyper-migration." *Critical Review of International Social and Political Philosophy* 14 (5): 665–693.

Bauböck, Rainer. 2015. "Morphing the Demos into the Right Shape: Normative Principles for Enfranchising Resident Aliens and Expatriate Citizens." *Democratization* 22 (5): 820–839.

Bauböck, Rainer and Vesco Paskalev. 2015. "Cutting Genuine Links: A Normative Analysis of Citizenship Deprivation." *Georgetown Journal of Immigration Law* 30 (1): 47–104.

Beckman, Ludvig. 2009. *The Frontiers of Democracy: The Right to Vote and Its Limits*. Houndmills, Basingstoke: Palgrave Macmillan.

Brubaker, Rogers W. 2005. "The Diaspora Diaspora." *Ethnic and Racial Studies* 28 (1): 1–19.

Carens, Joseph H. 1989. "Membership and Morality: Admission to Citizenship in Liberal Democratic States." In *Immigration and the Politics of Citizenship in Europe and North America*, edited by Rogers W. Brubaker. Lanham and London: University Press of America: 31–49.

Carens, Joseph H. 2013. *The Ethics of Immigration*. Oxford: Oxford University Press.

Dahl, Robert. 1989. *Democracy and Its Critics*. New Haven: Yale University Press.

de Schutter, Helder and Lea Ypi. 2015. "Mandatory Citizenship for Immigrants." *British Journal of Political Science* 45 (2): 235–251.

Donaldson, Sue and Will Kymlicka. 2011. *Zoopolis: A Political Theory of Animal Rights*. Oxford: Oxford University Press.

Donaldson, Sue and Will Kymlicka. 2017. "Inclusive Citizenship Beyond the Capacity Contract." In *The Oxford Handbook of Citizenship*, edited by A.

Shachar, R. Bauböck, I. Bloemraad and M. Vink. Oxford: Oxford University Press: 838–860.

Dzankic, Jelena. 2015. "Investment-Based Citizenship and Residence Programmes in the EU." *EUI Working Papers*. RSCAS 2015/18. San Domenico di Fiesole: European University Institute.

Frazer, Michael. 2016. "Utopophobia as a Vocation: The Professional Ethics of Ideal and Nonideal Political Theory." *Social Philosophy and Policy* 33 (1–2): 175–192.

Goodin, Robert. 2007. "Enfranchising All Affected Interests, and Its Alternatives." *Philosophy and Public Affairs* 35 (1): 40–68.

Goodin, Robert. 2013. "World Government is Here!" In *Varieties of Sovereignty and Citizenship*, edited by Sigal R. Ben-Porath and Rogers M. Smith. Philadelphia: University of Pennsylvania Press: 149–165.

Habermas, Jürgen. 1986. *Between Facts and Norms*. Cambridge: MIT Press.

Hayduk, Ron. 2005. *Democracy for All: Restoring Immigrant Voting in the United States*. New York: Routledge.

Hobden, Christine. 2015. "States, Citizens, and Global Justice: The Political Channels of Responsibility." PhD, Nuffield College, University of Oxford.

Honohan, Iseult. 2002. *Civic Republicanism*. London and New York: Routledge.

Kant, Immanuel. 1795/1991. "Perpetual Peace: A Philosophical Sketch." In *Kant: Political Writings*, edited by H.S. Reiss. Cambridge: Cambridge University Press: 93–130.

Kymlicka, Will. 1995. *Multicultural Citizenship: A Liberal Theory of Minority Rights*. Oxford: Oxford University Press.

Macdonald, Terry. 2008. *Global Stakeholder Democracy: Power and Representation Beyond Liberal States*. Oxford: Oxford University Press.

Oberman, Kieran. 2016. "Immigration as a Human Right." In *Migration in Political Theory*, edited by Sarah Fine and Lea Ypi. Oxford: Oxford University Press: 32–56.

Owen, David. 2010. "Resident Aliens, Non-resident Citizens and Voting Rights." In *Citizenship Acquisition and National Belonging*, edited by Gideon Calder, Philip Cole and Jonathan Seglow. London: Palgrave: 52–73.

Parker, Owen. 2017. "Commercializing Citizenship in Crisis EU: The Case of Immigrant Investor Programmes." *Journal of Common Market Studies* 55 (2): 332–348.

Raskin, Jamie. 1993. "Legal Aliens, Local Citizens: The Historical, Constitutional and Theoretical Meanings of Alien Suffrage." *University of Pennsylvania Law Review* 141 (April): 1391–1470.

Shachar, Ayelet and Rainer Bauböck, eds. 2014. "Should Citizenship be for Sale?" *EUI Working Papers*. RSCAS 2004/01. Florence: European University Institute.

Walzer, Michael. 1983. *Spheres of Justice : A Defense of Pluralism and Equality.* New York: Basic Books.

Weil, Patrick. 2002. *Qu'est-ce qu'un Français: histoire de la nationalité française depuis la Révolution.* Paris: Grasset.

Ziegler, Ruvi, Jo Shaw and Rainer Bauböck. 2014. "Independence Referendums: Who Should Vote and Who Should be Offered Citizenship?" *EUI Working Papers*. RSCAS 2014/90. Florence: European University Institute.

Index

Note: index pages in bold refer to the main discussion of the term. When 'n.' appears after a page reference, this indicates the number of a note on that page.

EU authorised representative for GPSR:
Easy Access System Europe, Mustamäe tee 50,
10621 Tallinn, Estonia
gpsr.requests@easproject.com

www.ingramcontent.com/pod-product-compliance
Lightning Source LLC
Chambersburg PA
CBHW051953270326
41929CB00015B/2635